Birding

Western Massachusetts

A Habitat Guide to 26 Great Birding Sites

written and illustrated by Robert Tougias

New England Cartographics
2003

Cover design by Valerie Vaughan, Bruce Scofield and Mike Scofield
Cover illustration (Pine Grosbeak) by Robert Tougias

Library of Congress Number 2003-103682

Text, illustrations and maps by Robert Tougias
Text editing and typesetting by Valerie Vaughan
Photos by Robert Tougias and Bruce Scofield

Publisher's Cataloging in Publication

Tougias, Robert
    Birding western Massachusetts: a habitat guide to 26 great birding sites /
by Robert Tougias.
    256 p. Includes maps and illustrations by the author.
    ISBN 1-889787-08-6
    1. Birds -- Massachusetts
    2. Massachusetts -- Description and travel -- Guidebooks.
    3. Bird watching -- Guidebooks
  598.297   03-103682

Printed in the United States of America
10 9 8 7 6 5 4 3 2 1   09 08 07 06 05 04 03

Attention! Birders:

* Some trails listed in this book may cross through portions of private
  land and may not always be open to the public. Please respect the
  rights of owners and heed "No Trespassing" signs.
* The conditions of trails are constantly changing. While every attempt
  has been made to provide current information in this book, the use
  of such information is at the sole risk of the user.

Sharp-shinned Hawk

Acknowledgments

I would like to thank Dr. Peter Vickery (author of *Birder's Guide to Maine*) for his encouraging words, advice, and recommendations during the early stages of preparation for this guide. Tony Gola of the Massachusetts Department of Fish and Wildlife provided detailed information on birding in the Berkshires and shared many interesting anecdotes. Thanks also to Andrea Jones and Rene Lebach from the Massachusetts Audubon Society for their knowledge of the birds at the Audubon Sanctuaries. Generous help was provided by John Hutchison (president) and Dr. Nancy Eaton (former president) of the Allen Bird Club. Claudia Becker was particularly helpful with the first draft, offering corrections and improvements. Thanks to Mary Ann Shultzki for her support when I first began talking with publishers and researching birding sites ten years ago. Finally, thanks to my wife Laurie for her patience while I took on this extra project.

About the Author

Robert Tougias syndicates nature articles in newspapers throughout New England and writes two columns on birding for newspapers in Connecticut. His articles on wildlife have appeared in many magazines, including *Appalachian Trailways* and *Fur-Fish-Game*. Robert began birding at the age of seven and was presenting his artwork in juried shows by age eleven. A native of western Massachusetts, he has been birding the sites in this guide for many years. His favorite bird is the Wood Thrush.

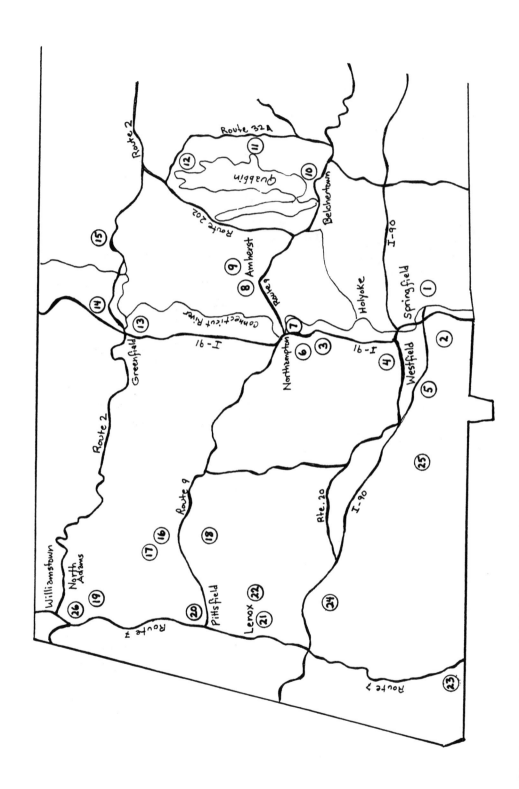

Contents

Introduction

This book features over 26 great birding locations in Western Massachusetts, and each site is unique. Some have rolling meadows and fields of grass, others are densely forested hills, and many are near lakes or reservoirs. Every site will offer the birder an outdoor setting of natural beauty and peace. Each has been chosen either for diversity and volume of bird life or for its unique and rare birds. All are easily accessible and are open year-round. Whether you are an avid birder looking for specific birds, or a casual nature enthusiast with an interest in seeing different kinds of birds, this guide will provide you with information on the locations and the skills necessary to do so.

Western Massachusetts is one of the most exciting places to be a birder. Nowhere else in the United States, except perhaps Michigan, are there as many people interested in birds. Although a densely populated state, Massachusetts has a long heritage of environmental concern. An interest in wildlife has allowed for intelligent planning and conservation priorities which provide and protect numerous birding sites of remarkable integrity.

Readers who are unfamiliar with New England and are expecting a provincial experience will be surprised at the wilderness quality of places such as the Quabbin or Mount Greylock. The former was intentionally devised as a virtual man-made wilderness, and the latter was chosen to be preserved for its obvious scenic and natural resource value. In between these geographic points is a mix of urban cultural areas, suburbs, and small family farms nestled within acres of forestland. In the region surrounding the Quabbin, where the State created a reservoir by damming the Swift River and flooding the surrounding valley, birders can find several wooded preserves and forgotten acres.

To the west of the Quabbin is the town of Amherst, where a semi-rural atmosphere persists, even with a major university and two colleges in its midst. Near Amherst are the towns of Northampton and South Hadley, which are invigorated by two additional centers of higher education. Together, the "five-college" area contains over 50,000 enthusiastic students that add vitality to the region. Originally, these educational institutions were founded by the wealthy industrialists who harnessed the region's rivers with numerous mills, many of which are still standing. Today, the area offers a cultural Mecca.

To the south, the city of Springfield rises from the banks of the Connecticut River and prospers economically as the largest and most significant city in Western Massachusetts. As a gateway to the Pioneer Valley, Springfield is home to many entertainment establishments and fine dining experiences.

Radiating outward from the high rise towers of the downtown Springfield are a collection of well-planned and groomed suburbs that eventually yield to the rising slopes of the hill towns. Heading west along the Massachusetts Turnpike or Routes 57 and 20 is a hilly region of inspiring tranquility called the Berkshires, which has been the destination of many of our nation's best writers and artists. These hills attract many tourists who represent a long tradition initiated one hundred years ago by wealthy New Yorkers travelling by train to build impressive summer homes and cottages.

During pre-colonial and early colonial times, the Berkshires were sparsely populated. White European settlers arrived late to these rugged hills; they were kept at bay by the determination of Native Americans defending their homeland. Indian attacks on the early white settlements in Northfield and Deerfield made life in the Pioneer Valley a courageous venture and prevented occupation of the Berkshires until Native Americans were driven further west. Eventually, farming began in the region, but was soon abandoned when more fertile soils and warmer climates became available elsewhere. Thus, the land was laid to rest and reclaimed by the forest. Wildlife returned, and then later, as attitudes changed, additional species were re-introduced. Presently, there are coyote, bobcat, fisher and moose living in these forest-cloaked hills. Black bears roam the woods, and they are currently expanding their numbers at a rate of 10% each year.

Largely forgotten through much of the year, the Berkshire hills come alive ever so briefly during the fall foliage season of mid-October when hoards of "leafer-peepers" travel to Western Massachusetts, especially the Berkshires, to witness what is one of the best foliage shows in the world. Small farms and country roadside stands open up for the tourists and bus loads looking for cider, fresh produce, candied apples, or souvenirs.

Refreshed by the clear air and the sharp blue skies, visitors enjoy their rambles through places like Mount Greylock Reservation, where a view of five states is possible and there are over 12,000 acres of unspoiled forest. Hidden on the back roads are the State forests and wildlife management areas. October Mountain contains over 16,000 acres, Pittsfield State Forest has 10,000 acres, and many more State parks create corridors connecting to lands of the Appalachian Trail and the non-profit concerns such as Massachusetts Audubon, Trustees of Reservations, and New England Forestry Foundation. All of this protected land contributes to making Western Massachusetts an excellent birding experience.

Birders in search of a wild environment need not always travel this far west, however. Every fall, dozens of birders flock to Easthampton and Holyoke to witness the migration of hawks from atop Mount Tom. These birds convey the awesome power of wilderness and majesty.

In winter, the place to be is Quabbin Reservoir at the Enfield lookout, where each February as many as 45 eagles can be seen in one visit. Our nation's symbol is back from the brink of extinction, thanks in part to places like the Quabbin where the concern for these birds was brought to the attention of the policy makers and implemented as a wildlife re-introduction program. Western Massachusetts is home to several nesting pairs, many of whom are found along the Connecticut River.

The Connecticut River is the largest river in the state. It flows south from the Canadian border and reaches its widest point along the shores of the Stebbins Refuge in the Massachusetts town of Longmeadow. Three rivers of significance to the region flow into the Connecticut River -- the Westfield, Deerfield, and Chicopee Rivers. In the Berkshires, the swift-flowing Housatonic River defines the landscape. With mountains, rivers and reservoirs, a wide variety of habitats exist to create a rewarding birding experience in this part of Massachusetts. Everything from sub-alpine conditions to pitch pine scrubland can be appreciated. Within each habitat, a unique set of birds can be found.

There are over 100 different birds nesting in the region, and as many as 300 different birds are recorded annually through the seasons. Few people realize the ideal situation of such a large variety of birds, together with a large number of easily accessible places in which to see them. It is a winning combination for every birder at every level to enjoy. This guide allows you to seize this opportunity in an easy, user-friendly way. With clear directions, some of the most productive birding sites west of the Quabbin are readily available.

With years of experience in birding these sites, the author takes the birder into their depths. With descriptive writing, the guide offers precise locations and seasons where rare and abundant species may be found. By carefully selecting the sites, the birder is given the chance to see everything from songbirds to rare owls. And although no ocean shoreline is found in Western Massachusetts, there are places where, at certain times, shorebirds and waterfowl may be viewed conveniently. Also revealed are the sites where you can encounter southern and northern species that many people assume are out of reach for their local hikes.

Unlike other bird finding guides, this book is written in a readable style that goes beyond mere directions and hiking distances. It motivates the reader and helps ensure a productive birding day afield. Instilled with the many facts contained in this guide, birders can also learn to better appreciate the visitors to their backyard feeders. With this guide, birders will no longer be limited to the sightings of common birds.

Imagine discovering a Great Blue Heron rookery, viewing the majestic Bald Eagle, watching thousands of birds of prey during one afternoon, or being surrounded by dozens of intricately colored Wood Warblers on an early spring morning. Readers can go beyond sighting the familiar Blue Jay to observing brightly colored Indigo Buntings, or replace views of Northern Cardinals with the more brilliant, fire-red Scarlet Tanager.

This guide not only brings the reader to the rare birds, it also addresses the problems that birders may encounter. The challenge of finding and identifying birds is made easier with the chapters on *How to Use Habitat to Find Birds* and *Bird Identification Helper*. A unique and highly useful feature of this guide is the *Quick Locator Reference*, enabling a birder to quickly locate the best sites for any bird.

With illustrations (by the author), trail maps, and advice on birding techniques, this guide will soon make better birders out of each reader. The author hopes that, with this new knowledge and eye-opening appreciation, readers will be inspired to help protect these and other great natural places before they are forever lost to the bulldozer and blacktop.

Pine Warbler

How To Use This Guide

This guide was designed to be user-friendly and to indicate where to bird and where to find certain birds in Western Massachusetts. Everything within the guide is self-explanatory. It is recommended that, before going afield, readers first study the sections on *Birding Techniques, How to Use Habitat to Find Birds*, and *Bird Identification Helper*. The information in these sections will prove most helpful as you begin to bird the sites.

The main body of this text is the *Guide to 26 Birding Sites*. The sites were chosen primarily for their birds. Each site description includes a brief overview of the terrain, acreage, ownership, and history. The number of species present at each site is given when known. In most cases, there is information on the relative abundance or scarcity of a bird and the best time of year to see it. At the beginning of each site description there is a list of birds of special interest. The list usually consists of birds that are uncommon but are available to see at that particular location. Occasionally, a common species may be listed if it is especially abundant at that site. Sometimes the exact location of a bird is provided, such as: "on the Red Trail near the bridge" or "along the shore of Bigelow Pond beneath the large white pine."

At the beginning of each site description, there is information on *Seasonal Abundance, Advice/Rules, Best Months, Bird Specialties, the Closest Town* where the site is located, directions for *Getting There*, and a trail map. The *Best Months* tells you the most exciting or productive time to bird at that site. *Bird Specialties* lists some of the significant birds that can be seen at each site. Some of these birds are rare and can be best found at the site mentioned. Others are uncommonly seen in Massachusetts but are locally common at one site. If you cannot identify a bird, any one of the popular field guides can be helpful, especially when used with this guide's *Bird Identification Helper*.

Before you arrive at a chosen site, you should read the entire site description and examine the site's trail map. Then take the guide with you; it will fit neatly into any daypack. If the guide is with you, it can be reviewed so that you will not overlook trails or sections that might reveal rare species.

Throughout the guide, the names of birds are capitalized, as recommended by the American Birding Association. Thus, the proper name of a bird (such as American Goldfinch or Lesser Black-backed Gull) is capitalized, while the generic name (such as goldfinch or gull) is not.

One of the best ways to learn about birds and become a better birder is to join one of the many local birding clubs. These are listed in the *Resources* section, along with other useful information on birding magazines, organizations, websites, sources for audiotapes, and phone numbers of the birding sites.

A unique feature of this guide is the *Quick Locator Reference* (found at the end of the book). It provides a complete list of all birds that are possible to see in the Western Massachusetts region. It can also be used as a general checklist of birds for the whole area of New England. It is designed so that the reader can look up any birds and find their locations among the 26 birding sites listed in this guide. The species noted are birds that have some kind of status at their locations. The *Quick Locator Reference* can also be used as a life list.

Scarlet Tanager

Birding Techniques and Advice Afield

Finding birds involves much more than just arriving at the location of the bird or birds that you wish to observe. From the moment you leave your car, birds are keen to your presence and will begin to flee and head for cover. The birders with the most success are those that know when to arrive at a site and what to do or where to go once they get there.

The Best Time of Day

The best time to arrive at a birding site is *very* early in the morning. This is especially true in the spring when the birds are migrating and singing. For those who love birds and the outdoors, there is nothing more thrilling than an early spring morning when the trees and shrubs are alive with an endless variety of birds. On those mornings, the level of birdsong is often so intense that the individual songs are indistinguishable.

The exceptions to this rule apply toward those birds that are nocturnal or that become more active at the end of the day rather than in the dim light of dawn. Owls, for instance, are nocturnal and become active at dusk and remain vocal throughout the night as they hunt and defend territories. The American Woodcock and the Nighthawk are two species that are best encountered during the dusk. Hawks are best looked for in the mid-morning or early afternoon, as this period produces the thermals which they use for migration. There are other exceptions that result from variable weather conditions.

The Best Time Of Year

There really is no best time of year for birding; however, the most activity or greatest concentration of birds can be found in the spring and summer. Certain times of the year offer better opportunities for viewing different birds. As a general rule, the places of lower altitude along the Pioneer Valley and the Housatonic River Valley will experience good birding in the spring and winter. In contrast, the hills and mountains are often hot spots during the nesting season.

Birding seasons do not match traditional calendar seasons. For example, the so-called "fall migration" is well underway in the summer and will have actually declined by the fall equinox (Sep. 23). *Fall migration* simply refers to the southward return of nesting species that pushed through in the spring migration. Fall migration begins as early as July, while the "spring migration" actually begins in February.

Spring

Red-winged Blackbirds return to the cattail marshes in late February. This is the first obvious sign of the spring migration.

In early March, the lakes and ponds begin to pick up a few local migrants from the coastal regions to our immediate south.

By mid-March, several kinds of water birds begin to appear while on their way north to breed. This is soon followed by terrestrial species that show up annually along the river valleys.

In April the first big wave of migrants pushes through, and birds of all kinds can be found in the early mornings or evenings resting and feeding before finishing their migration routes.

A second wave, usually more concentrated, comes in mid-May. This is often the best time for birding species such as wood warblers and common songbirds.

Later, about the first of June, the early mornings gain new strength with a third wave of migrants -- the return of tanagers, orioles and thrushes. Every local nesting species is usually in place before the second week of June.

Summer

The birds around your yard have already started incubating their eggs. Shorebirds to the north are feeding their young before mid-July. Listen to the morning chorus, and you will notice it getting quieter even before this.

Be sure to schedule several birding trips before the July 4th weekend, as the breeding season passes quickly. Locate nest boxes of favorite birds, and watch for behavior. With all species present and accounted for, the summer offers great opportunity for adding new birds to life lists. Visit the mountains for nesting northerners and many wood warblers.

By August, birds from the tundra are migrating south. Check sandbars along river real estate and Quabbin Reservoir for shorebirds.

Fall

Migrants that you missed in the spring may be hoped for again, but now many birds are in less obvious plumage. The fall migration is generally less noticeable, and most birds are unobtrusive this time through. Fall is the time for the last waves of shorebirds, large groups of hawks, sparrows, and ducks.

Visit reservoirs and rivers from late October through early December.

November is best for diving and dabbling ducks. Loons and grebes are seen in late October and November. Birds are now becoming more numerous at the feeders. The woods are quiet, and all territorial singing has ceased.

Winter

Contrary to common belief, birding does not stop in the winter. In fact, the wintertime offers opportunities that cannot be had at any other time of year. This is when Bald Eagles congregate at the Quabbin, and to a lesser degree, along the Connecticut River.

Winter finches may make sudden appearances and form large flocks among the conifer plantations. Northern species are often driven south in search of food. This provides a chance to see birds normally dwelling far to the north and even as far away as the Arctic. Snowy Owls visit airports and grasslands. Short-eared Owls frequent similar habitats.

Late winter is when local year-round resident owls begin to become vocal and exhibit breeding behaviors. Winter is also the time for feeding birds at your window, but also to visit others' feeders, such as those at nature centers.

Weather Conditions

Birds are generally effected by the weather in much the same way we are. They seek shelter on cold, windy, and snowy days, and they move about freely on warm, sunny days. As you become more experienced, you will know the days or kinds of weather that seem to activate birds. Overcast days afford a longer activity period for singing and feeding. In the cooler months, birds often feed more diligently when there is some light precipitation. Storms can bring in rare vagrants or accidentals. Feeder birds seem to reflect this exceptional pattern. Snowy, cold days bring birds into the feeders by the dozens. This is best seen in the increase of ground feeders, like Dark-eyed Juncos and White-throated Sparrows. They have a difficult time finding seeds beneath the new snow accumulations. Nesting birds usually become inactive during cold, wet spells.

Techniques Afield

Aside from traveling through each site along the prescribed trail or network of trails, there are various other methods that can be employed as you make your way through. Most important of all is to remember to take the time at some strategic location to sit still and **listen and wait** for birds or other wild animals. The second and most basic thing in bird watching is to **remain silent** and, if in a group, avoid constant talking or loud noises. If you proceed through the site talking loudly, the odds are that you will finish the walk feeling disappointed and will probably conclude the worst about the area or the activity itself. Enter the trail quietly. Birding can be a time of spiritual renewal and relaxation. Listen to the woods for the songs of different birds and the insects. Notice the other wildlife, and be sure to stay alert for possible sightings of such thrilling creatures as moose or bobcat.

Several basic approaches can be worked into your visit. The first employs entering a site and finding an active area in which to hide and wait patiently and quietly for birds to reveal themselves. This is often a choice taken at the end of the walk, when the site has been explored and your feet are tired. Good places to wait and watch are along streams where there is some sound of water, such as near a small riffle or waterfall. Another good place is near the edge of a field or pond. You can see plenty of birds right from your car. Try parking along a road near cornfields or at a boat launch. Many of the methods used in hunting are effective for birding, since birding is somewhat like hunting. You may want to construct a bird blind, similar to a hunter's blind, near one of these active sites.

Bird Blinds conceal observers from birds and allow freedom of movement without scaring the birds away. They are not an especially effective technique for birding, as success is limited to the birds in the immediate location of the blind. They are effective for studying nesting birds or for photography. Try setting one up a few feet away from an active bird feeder. Small, light-weight, pop-up blinds are available commercially. Sometimes blinds can be constructed of natural material found near the site, such as a few branches placed around the birder.

Using **Bird Calls** is another method; it is especially useful where there are tall weeds and dense shrubbery in which birds may be hiding. Bird calls are created with your hands by blowing hard against the skin and making a "kissing" sound. Birders also have luck making a "pisssh" sound through the teeth. Commercial bird calls are effective, too. They consist of a pewter knob fitted into a small block of hardwood; turning the knob creates a variety of bird notes.

The use of playback **audiotapes** is especially useful for finding birds in the wetlands. Biologists use them to inventory specific wetlands for the existence of rare species and birds that live in heavy vegetation. Primarily, playback tapes are used to locate species of birds that are endangered. Birders can use call-back methods to locate the general area of a bird, and then home in on it until it is sighted. This is usually conducted for a group in a bird club, when members employ the guidance of an experienced biologist. However, it should be remembered that birds can become stressed by the over-use of call-back tapes.

Observing signs of bird activity is another method. This may be a set of tracks along a muddy shoreline or an owl pellet beneath a pine tree. Birds are stealthy, but they are not ghosts. You can find signs of their previous activity, and then you can return later or wait at these places. A tree full of ripe crabapples is a sure bet for bird sightings. Return and observe the tree in the early morning. Large drill holes in mature trees are a sign that there are Pileated Woodpeckers in the vicinity. The next time you are afield, be observant and take note of nature's hidden messages.

Binoculars

Every birder should have a pair of binoculars, although good birding is possible without them. Birders have different requirements, depending on whether they wear eye-glasses or have other personal considerations. Generally, the best binoculars for birders are either 7 X 35 or 8 X 40.

Without going into great technical detail, all binoculars and spotting scopes are standardized and can be understood the same way. The first number indicates the power of magnification; binoculars with 7X magnification will make the object appear seven times closer than it would be with the naked eye.

The second number is the diameter of the lens opening at the farthest end from the viewer. The larger the opening, the more light that comes in, and the wider the field of view. Thus, binoculars with 7 X 35 has a lens opening of 35 millimeters.

What to Bring

Every birder should have a special pack in which to put basic birding supplies. A small but durable waterproof pack is best. You will want it set up so that your hands are free to use a binocular or camera. In this pack, there should be two items that are essential to your enjoyment: The first is some form of mosquito control. The second is your identification guide. The guide is most useful if placed in a side pocket where it can be easily retrieved. The quicker you can access it, the better your odds are at definitively identifying your sighting.

Some people carry their binoculars in the pack, but many leave them around their necks where they can be had in an instant. But there might be a time when you will want all your gear in the pack, and there should be ample room for them or a larger pair in case you someday purchase a different model. While bug spray, field guide, and binoculars are essentials to any day afield, you will undoubtedly want to take along a few other basic items. For most outdoor explorers, these include things such as a water bottle, snack, hat, sunglasses and sunblock. Experienced birders may also bring along a notepad. You might want to take notes on the color patterns of a bird you cannot immediately identify. You will also want to note the place where it was seen and the behavior of the bird. This information can be referred to later when you are able to study a few field guides.

Most other items to consider have much to do with the season or location of your birding excursion. For winter birding, always bring an extra pair of gloves and socks. A thermos filled with something warm and delicious is appreciated after an hour or two in the woods. In the spring, a bug net or head net is a practical precaution for blackflies. On hot, humid summer days, an extra bottle of water is a smart choice. If you have room, take along a pair of rubber totes or slip-on boots during rainy periods.

Cattle Egret

For birding trips in remote areas, a topographical map is useful, as is bringing along extra food of high energy value. You can also bring a knife, rope, and waterproof-packed matches. In general, for the majority of sites mentioned in this guide, you will need only your appreciation and common sense.

Final Word

While all this advice will add to your comfort level and increase your birding success, it cannot guarantee that you will find what you are looking for each time you go afield. Even the best birders do not see dozens of different species at any particular site. Rather, they may encounter a few of the birds mentioned in this guide and only occasionally spot a new one that they have never seen before.

There is a reason your own personal list of bird sightings is called a life list. It is because birds are seen through repeated visits over time. The more you go birding, or visit a site, the greater your odds are of success. The more closely you obey the laws of nature and follow the habits of birds, the better each visit will turn out. Those who continually bird at noon time or who make noise while on the trail are destined to see only the usual and the assured.

The real winners at this activity are the ones who are not overly concerned about checking off names from a list, but rather those who remember the experience of each sighting. The moods of the land and the sounds of the forest are always as important an element to those who love the outdoors, as the birds themselves. In that sense, any excursion can be victorious and always will be.

Birding Ethics

* Keep your birding experience safe. Use caution on trails and while crossing streams, roads or railroad tracks. Always keep an eye out for sudden changes in weather, and be sure to dress appropriately. Bring along a day-pack with some basic first aid materials, sun-glasses or gloves, depending on seasonal needs. Before leaving on a birding trip, tell a friend or family member your intended route. Use the "buddy system," and avoid hiking alone in out-of-the-way places.

* Get involved in the rescue and support of important birding habitats. Find out if your favorite birding site can be expanded to better protect it. Join a conservation group or find out about local land trusts.

* Respect private property, and seek permission before trespassing. Many great private sites are open and welcome to birders, while remaining closed to other forms of recreation. Do your part to ensure continued cooperation from land owners -- always be polite, and keep group size to a minimum.

* Be sure to read posted signs, and follow the posted rules at reservoirs and sanctuaries. Never leave litter. Always park to the side of entrance gates. Obstructed gates can hinder the access of emergency vehicles into the site.

* Many casual birders go on to become advanced and may join special clubs where they may one day lead a group. Be sure to keep group activities open to all interested parties, as to promote the welfare of birds and enjoy the rewards of teaching and common courtesy. Remember to keep the groups to a small number, except when you are sure that larger groups cannot impact the environment in a negative way.

* Report violations of wildlife laws to the Massachusetts Environmental Police. Such violations may include the removal of plants and the harassment of wildlife. Poaching should be reported immediately.

* Keep a reasonable distance from nesting birds. Do not stress them with repeated visits or prolonged observation. Approaching any kind of wildlife is cause for caution. Allow the wild animal an escape route, and observe from an appropriate distance. If you continue to sneak up, eventually the animal will flee or retaliate in defense.

* Leave orphaned wildlife alone. Fledgling birds are never far from their mothers. Attempts to rescue offspring usually results in the death of the bird.

* Keep birdfeeders clean and the water in bird-baths fresh. Feeding birds irresponsibly can lead to the spread of disease. If you are feeding birds in the winter, you must continue to do so throughout the season -- except during unseasonably warm weather or snow-free conditions. Suddenly stopping your feeding routine will leave birds vulnerable when weather becomes severe.

How to Use Habitat to Find Birds

This guide helps you find birds in Western Massachusetts, and it helps you locate specific species, sometimes giving the exact location at a given site. Throughout the guide, reference is given to those specific locations in terms of the habitat found there. Anyone using the guide cannot avoid gaining some insight into the relationship between the habitats and the types of birds frequenting them.

A very important element in birding is knowing the connection between birds and habitats. This chapter will empower you further, beyond the site visit, enabling you to develop as a birder -- improving your own ability in hunting down certain birds. As you use this guide, you will notice that there are certain plant communities or micro-habitats that you should search and which you will pass through or hike near, but which are not mentioned in this guide. Since habitats change as plant communities grow and as other factors effect them, it is not always practical to mention the pinpointed location of each bird at each site. Space would not permit that in this guide. What is more practical and of use to the birder is acquiring a knowledge of the *habitat approach* to birding.

The following pages will provide just that, and thereby allow birders to develop and enjoy some of their own strategies. In doing so, this guide does more than tell birders where and when to bird. It helps them become more effective birders -- the kind who are eager to explore or who are motivated to quickly find new species by going to the appropriate habitat.

Anyone with a basic knowledge of birds knows that Blue Jays prefer woodlands and that herons like the water. However, there are factors that may make a woodland attractive to jays or a pond to a heron. Many of these factors have been mentioned already in this guide. These factors determined whether a site was chosen for listing here, or has been referred to or left out completely. Sites listed in this guide have the features that set them apart from the other similar habitats which are less productive.

This chapter contains two parts. **Habitats--with Associated Birds** will describe the habitats (and micro-habitats) found in Western Massachusetts, along with the qualities that can make such a habitat more productive for certain birds. A "Sample of Birds Present" will list the birds associated with each habitat.

In the section following this, **Birds--with Associated Habitat**, the birds are listed by family, along with the habitat associated with each group.

Habitats -- with Associated Birds

Forest Land

Hardwoods

This is the most extensive kind of forest in the eastern United States, and it covers most of the western part of Massachusetts. There are over 100 species directly associated with hardwood forest. In the spring, about half that many will nest within the different micro-habitats that it offers. The hardwoods consist of the broad-leafed trees that shed their leaves in the fall. These include trees such as oaks, hickories, and cherries.

The presence of cleared parcels with enough sunlight to support an understory can greatly enhance this habitat, as can an unbroken extensive tract of hardwood forest. In either case, the variety of hardwoods is an essential factor for bird species. Also, the presence of older trees in combination with younger ones can make a positive difference. A productive hardwood forest has plenty of dead standing trees and the presence of blow-downs or snags to add value by providing cover and protection for small rodents that birds of prey require. A wetland component is ideal for many species, including the thrush family.

Sample of Birds Present in Hardwoods

Black-capped Chickadee, Brown Creepers, Tufted Titmouse, Common Crow, Blue Jay, White-breasted Nuthatches.
Flycatchers: Acadian, Great Crested, Eastern Wood-Pewee.
Blue-gray Gnatcatcher, Rose-breasted Grosbeak, Ruffed Grouse.
Hawks: Broad-winged, Red-shouldered
Owls: Barred, Great Horned.

Mixed Hardwoods

This forest is characterized by the presence of an evergreen or conifer component. Typically found at higher elevations, it can be also called the Northern Hardwood forest. It is the most common forest in the Berkshires, where it is recognized by the presence of eastern hemlock, white pine, spruce, yellow and white birch. The maples and the beech are also prevalent. This type of forest has more birds than the hardwood forest without the white pine, hemlock, or spruce.

Many of the factors that make this forest productive are the same as those for the hardwoods, but generally other habitats that join with this one can increase its value. This would include streams, where the hemlocks may flourish, or farmlands, where predatory birds may journey to at night from under the cover of the conifers. Such forests that have groves of evergreens banding on north slopes or on hilltops provide the variety needed by many species. Because this forest is often less disturbed by people's activities, the size of the forest is important. Fragmented mixed hardwoods are less valuable unless interfaced by hayfields and lakes that may enhance the habitat. Many of its species require extensively large unbroken forests.

Sample of Birds Present in Mixed Hardwoods

Hairy Woodpecker, Yellow-bellied Sapsucker, Great Crested Flycatcher, Red-eyed Vireo, Black-throated Green Warbler, Barred Owl, Northern Goshawk, Broad-winged Hawk, Evening Grosbeak

Conifers

These forests do exist naturally, but only in a few places and within a limited amount of space. You will find them on the higher peaks along the Berkshire plateau and along some streams in shaded ravines. There are many artificially-planted groves as well, but they are usually the least productive for birding among forested types. However, they harbor a few birds that specifically seek them out and are unlikely to be found elsewhere.

Most conifer forests are comprised of the spruces -- red and white or sometimes black in the bogs. Along streams they may be made of hemlocks. White pine groves occur naturally; but are less likely to extend for long distances and are sometimes artificially produced, like the red pine plantations which are common on state parkland.

Smaller conifers provide good habitat for Short-eared Owls and Northern Saw-whet Owls. If the white pines are thinned and sunlight is allowed to hit the lower canopy, then herbaceous plants will grow successive to shrubs and hardwoods and will add a positive value to the grove. Likewise, if hemlocks are adjacent to herbaceous lower canopy growth, they become an attractive site for a greater variety of birds. This may occur naturally along wide, gravelly streambeds or near blow downs on hillsides. Conifers are, nevertheless, essential to any forest or field nearby, as they provide cover above and below for a wide variety of creatures.

Sample of Birds Present in Conifers

Brown Creeper
Flycatchers: Olive-sided, Yellow-bellied.
Red Crossbill, Purple Finch, Evening Grosbeak, Dark-eyed Junco, Pine Siskin, White-throated Sparrow
Grouse: Ruffed, Spruce (Vermont and Maine).
Goshawk, Golden-crowned Kinglet
Nuthatches: Red-breasted, White-breasted.
Owls: Barred, Great Horned, Long-eared.
Thrushes: Hermit, Swainson's.
Blue-headed Vireo
Warblers: Bay-breasted, Blackburnian, Blackpoll, Black-throated Blue, Black-throated Green, Canada, Magnolia, Myrtle, Nashville, Palm, Pine, Northern Parula
Woodpeckers: Northern Three-toed (rare visitor), Black-backed (rare visitor).
Winter Wren

Pitch Pine / Oak Scrubland Woods

The pitch pine forest is associated with sandy soil and has a modest variety of birds that choose it for the cover it provides. A patch of blueberries will enhance its value, as will a variety of oaks.

Sample of Birds Present in Pitch Pine / Oak Scrubland Woods

Blue Jay, Northern Mockingbird, Eastern Towhee, Common Grackle, Mourning Dove, Black-billed Cuckoo (sometimes)

Flood Plain Forest

This is a highly productive habitat with a wide variety of birds both nesting and migratory. Trees found in the flood-plain include silver maple, red maple, cottonwood, green ash, sycamore, and the pin oak. There are over 200 birds regularly found in this forest, which is characterized by its proximity to a river or oxbow. The rich soils found in these forests, along with the abundance of water and the warmer climate of the bottomland, make the river edge a rich place for wildlife when managed properly. An abundance of sumac or fox grape can add value. Dogwoods and elderberry are often good for cover, as is Joe-Pye weed and sensitive fern. All these fruit-bearing plants attract birds.

Sample of Birds Present in Flood Plain Forest

Wood Duck, Mallard, Barred Owl, Red-bellied Woodpecker, Red-shouldered Hawk, Fish Crow, Green Heron, Veery, Wood Thrush, Tufted Titmouse, Eastern Phoebe.

Transition Zone

Abandoned Farmland

Abandoned farmland is excellent birding country. However, the age since the abandonment will make a difference for the kinds of birds found. A weedy field left untilled only a year or more brings in birds such as American Goldfinch or Bobolink, but a farm left alone for a decade will have species such as Yellow Warblers. Much of the land in Western Massachusetts is abandoned farmland. Some 150 years ago, about 75% of Massachusetts was open farmland. Today the forest is still growing back, and the land now 75% forested. Because much has been logged again since the great clearing, the forests are still young. But some regions are now maturing so that birds such as Wild Turkey are finding the increase of mast (acorns and nuts) to their benefit.

There is an ongoing struggle among plants that are trying to establish themselves in this changing habitat. In the beginning, every plant seems to have a fair chance in direct sunlight; but eventually, the diversity is narrowed as the faster growing species begin the shade the less competitive ones. Birches and shrubs dominate at first, but are soon defeated by the oaks and maples that will prevail to reclaim the area back to the forest.

Sample of Birds Present in Abandoned Farmland

Cuckoos: Black-billed, Common, Yellow-billed.
Mourning Dove, Eastern Kingbird, Indigo Bunting, Northern Cardinal, American Goldfinch
Sparrows: Field, Song, Savannah.
Eastern Towhee, Grey Catbird
Warblers: Blue-winged, Chestnut-sided, Prairie, Yellow.
Hawks: American Kestrel (falcon), Red-tailed, Sharp-shinned.
Eastern Screech Owl, Eastern Bluebird, Northern Flicker
Wrens: Carolina and House.

Brushy Borders

This is another highly productive habitat for birds and birders. Such areas of dense vegetation offer a wide variety of sapling trees and shrubs mixed with herbaceous growth. Places that contain this kind of habitat are also known as hedgerows or "edges." The hedgerow is often a band or divider traveling a land boundary or planted as a windbreak. The most productive ones are wide enough to shield nesting birds from predators coming in from the open sides. Another value is the thickness of the hedgerow or how dense it is. If the plants are so thick that it is impenetrable, then it can be a highly desirable place to bird.

Look for a diversity and the presence of conifers or fruiting plants that will really attract the highest number of birds possible. Plant communities are key to the birding. Find areas with barberry, multiflora rose, choke-cherry, autumn olive, honeysuckle, Virginia creeper, poison ivy, bittersweet, silky and gray dogwood, crabapple, and wild apple

While a hedgerow is considered to be an "edge," true "edges" are more typically places where two habitats collide. This may be where a field returns to woods or a road meets a forest. A very important "edge" is a swamp that is filling in and transforming to a meadow. Power line right-of-ways and un-mowed hayfields are often called "edge" habitats. Any of these sites that are thought to be in the early stages of succession are considered good to very good habitats for birds. There are usually between 120 and 270 different kinds of birds frequenting this habitat.

The presence of a small stream or a pond will determine how good such a habitat is for birds. Those with water and some agriculture, such as cornfields, are more attractive to birds. If a site has all of these components and a band of evergreens winding throughout the area, it should be outstanding birding.

Sample of Birds Present in Brushy Borders

Black-billed Cuckoo, Mourning Dove, Eastern Kingbird, Indigo Bunting, Northern Cardinal, American Goldfinch
Sparrows: Field, Song, White-throated.
Northern Mockingbird, Brown Thrasher
Warblers: Yellow, Blue-winged, Yellow-breasted Chat, Chestnut-sided, Prairie.
Eastern Screech Owl, Eastern Bluebird

Wetlands

Bogs

A bog is characterized by the presence of sphagnum mosses and herbaceous plants growing out of the water. These are places of poor soil and drainage. If found in higher or northern locations within this part of the state, they have white cedar or black spruce. The diversity of plants is not great, but there are many members of the heath family. These are good places for northern species. A few good examples of spruce bogs are located in the northern end of Berkshire County.

Sample of Birds Present in Bogs

American Bittern, Common Moorhen
Rails: Virginia, Clapper, Sora.
Warblers: Northern Waterthrush, Yellow, Nashville, Prothonotary.
Flycatchers: Least, Olive-sided, Alder, Willow.

Ponds

Based on the technical definition of the term pond, there are far fewer in existence than widely believed. A pond must support the capability of plant growth across its entire surface. It is generally not more than six feet deep or 100 acres in size.

Ponds are rich in wildlife, including birds. Birds will utilize ponds for their abundance of insects and diversity of plant life along the shoreline. Ponds are usually better for birds than lakes are, as they are less developed. Some are even undeveloped or little known.

The type of cover along the shore has much to do with the kinds of birds found. Shores that are open, grassy, or muddy may attract shorebirds; but those with tall weeds and bushes often have flycatchers and redwings. Tall trees and dead standing timber may mean Wood Ducks or aerial feeders hawking for insects above the water. If the pond has a hidden, grassy shoreline and a wooded shoreline with older, dead, and hollow trees nearby, it can be thought of as ideal.

Obviously, dabbling ducks and wading birds are the main attraction to a pond. But flycatchers and aerial birds are also of importance at this habitat.

Sample of Birds Present in Ponds

American Bittern, Great Blue Heron
Rails: Virginia, Sora.
Common Moorhen
Warblers: Northern Waterthrush, Yellow, Nashville, Prothonotary.
Flycatchers: Least, Olive-sided, Alder, Willow.
Kingfisher, Tree Swallows

Vernal Pools

These are bodies of water that dry out before the end of the summer and fill up again in the spring. Dabbling ducks, shorebirds, and wading species are seen along their edges. When they are located along a flyway or near a bigger body of water, they are better for birding.

Sample of Birds Present in Vernal Pools

Herons: Great Blue, Green, Northern Waterthrush
Eastern Phoebe

Bufflehead

Common Merganser

Black Duck

Green-winged Teal

Wood Duck

Northern Pintail

Lakes, Rivers and Streams

Lakes

A lake is defined as being over 100 acres or as having a depth beyond which aquatic plants could survive on the surface. Lakes are natural bodies of water as compared to reservoirs, which are man-made impoundments. Lakes typically do not have a great abundance of insect life above them and are generally not without development or human disturbance. A few reservoirs in the region have undeveloped shorelines. The extent of the development and the kind of shore-line vegetation can play an important part in the ability of the water body to sustain birdlife. Clear water is more valuable for diving ducks and loons, while shallow coves are attractive to dabbling ducks. Lakes with wooded shorelines and shallow cattail coves are of greater value than those lined with cottages or bordering grassy lawns and roads.

Sample of Birds Present in Lakes

Bufflehead
Ducks: Northern Pintail, Northern Shoveler, Redhead, Black, Ring-necked, Ruddy, Wood, American Wigeon, Common Golden Eye, Mallard.
Mergansers: Common, Hooded.
Teals: Blue-winged, Green-winged.
Swallows: Tree, Barn, Bank, Cliff.

Rivers

A river is generally defined as a permanent flowing water source greater than 20 feet across. Rivers have the most insect life in the air above them -- even more than streams, ponds or lakes. A river with a gravel bottom produces more flies that insectivores feed on from aerial flights or local perches. A muddy shoreline or an island with rocks also increases the bird numbers by providing feeding areas and protective perches or hunting sites. The presence of dead trees and utility wires will increase the likelihood of flycatchers and cavity nesting birds in general. It is believed that 200 species of birds utilize a river for one reason or another. The river is especially good birding in the early to late spring. In the winter, birding is good if the river water is open while other water bodies are frozen. Birds that eat fish will concentrate on the rivers that have sheltered coves, shallow pockets or deep pools.

Sample of Birds Present in Rivers

Mergansers: Hooded, Common.
Common Loon, Bald Eagle, Osprey
Swallows: Tree, Barn, Bank, Cliff.

Streams

Streams are small and may even disappear in the summer. They are often found at higher elevations. Streams enhance adjacent habitats by providing food, water, and bathing sites. In woods with streams, other wildlife than birds may increase, and this may often in turn increase birdlife. A deep slow-moving stream is always more productive than a fast, shallow stream. The Winter Wren and the waterthrushes are found in this habitat.

Open Land

Grasslands

A grassland is loosely defined as an area of extensive openness, void of consistent tree cover. The herbaceous plants are mostly grass and are allowed to grow unmolested throughout all or most of the growing season. While this definition includes hayfields planted with exotic grasses and mowed each spring, such fields are not true grasslands. Grassy areas are productive when mowing is delayed into mid-summer, as this allows breeding birds to remain undisturbed. Short grassy lawns are excellent birding sites when there are flooded areas and weedy borders nearby. They often attract shorebirds. Grassy or grassy-to-shrubby areas located along a river valley or small flyway are productive and great for birding. Pastures with manure piles are also good for certain species such as Horned Lark, Snow Bunting, Pipit, and sparrows.

Sample of Birds Present in Grasslands

Sparrows: Field, Vesper, Song, Grasshopper, Tree, Savannah.
Bobolink, Eastern Meadowlark, Eastern Bluebird
Hawks: Northern Harrier, Kestrel.
Owls: Short-eared, Snowy.

Airports and Athletic Fields

Airfields are unique habitats for the open-land-loving-birds. The airfield is characterized by extensive short grasses (less than six inches high), which is a rare habitat in western Massachusetts. Athletic fields can attract many aerial feeding birds, especially in late summer and fall. Some athletic complexes offer a value similar to the grasslands and may even attract gulls or shorebirds when wet. The athletic fields at the University of Massachusetts are an example of a large complex that attracts such species.

Sample of Birds Present in Airports and Athletic Fields

Owls: Snowy, Short-eared (winter).
Common Nighthawk, Tree Swallows, Purple Martin.

Black-billed Cuckoo

Mourning Dove

Downy Woodpecker

White-breasted Nuthatch

Barred Owl

Red-shouldered Hawk

Ruffed Grouse

Ring-necked Pheasant

Birds -- with Associated Habitat

Different kinds of birds usually appear far from one another, but those of the same taxonomic family or with great similarities usually appear in groups together. The following is a breakdown of these bird groups and the habitats they are associated with. An annotated list sometimes appears with or within each group. The species mentioned here are often those that are not discussed or seldom mentioned in the 26 site chapters.

Loons, Grebes and Cormorants

These birds may be found on large bodies of water, usually during spring or fall. They may appear in large groups but sometimes they are seen alone. Loons are restricted to large lakes and prefer clear water with good visibility for finding and chasing fish underwater. The loon is not built for quick take-offs and thus needs space. The grebes are suited for less space but when nesting, usually require extensive wetlands. Try the Meadows off Pondside Road and Shagnassey Swamp on Route 57 (before North Road) in Granville. The Berkshire Lakes and Ashley Reservoir are good places in November or April for grebes and loons. Other good places not mentioned earlier are Richmond Pond, Congamong Lakes, and Cobble Mountain Reservoir. Visit the Quabbin for a chance at seeing the Red-throated Loon and Red-necked Grebe. The Red-necked Grebe is usually found in small groups, and the Horned Grebe is found in larger groups.

Herons

The herons frequent marshes, swamps, and pond edges. Most are limited to the warmer months, but the Great Blue Heron can live through a cold New England winter. This family of birds consists of the bitterns, Green Heron, Black-crowned Night Heron, Great Egret, Snowy, and Little Blue Heron. In the spring there may be a few Glossy Ibis or Cattle Egret. A Wood Stork was seen in "The Meadows" (Site #1) a few years back. A huge rookery, or group nesting site, made up of 60 Great Blue Heron nests can be seen off of Route 2 in Acton. Arcadia, The Meadows, and Canoe Meadows are good for the smaller herons. There are numerous small rookeries in the region, some at the Quabbin, others tucked away in the beaver ponds throughout Western Massachusetts.

Ducks, Geese and Swans

These birds are a diverse group, which can be found along streams or rivers, but usually ponds and lakes. Most prefer to breed farther north but are seen during migration. The exotics are often seen at the Quabbin, but many domesticated varieties can fool beginners at Forest Park. Birders of all levels can look for those rare species during the fall in larger groups of Canada Goose. Such species to look for are the rare Tundra Swan, Eurasian Wigeon, Brant, Greater White-fronted Goose, Ross's Goose, and Barrow's Goldeneye.

Vultures, Hawks, Eagles, and Falcons

This group of birds are more efficiently observed during the fall migration. However, when they are encountered at close range in the field or forest, they are equally impressive. This is one group of birds that can be readily observed from the car on country roads and highways. Wachusett Mountain and the Petersburg Pass are two good fall hawk-watching sites.

The osprey is most often seen during migration in the spring, hovering over lakes and ponds. The Northern Goshawk and Sharp-shinned Hawk are woodland birds, while the Broad-winged is a secretive forest-dwelling species. Look for the Peregrine Falcon in Springfield, where it has nested on the Monarch Towers and below the Memorial Bridge.

Grouse, Turkey, Pheasant

The Ruffed Grouse is reasonably common in the Berkshire Hills. They are hard to find in the suburban sprawl of the Pioneer Valley. The Dorothy Frances Rice Sanctuary is a good spot, and also Pleasant Valley. Otherwise, look for them in the State forests along the edges of forests and adjacent to some conifers. The Wild Turkey, on the other hand, is increasing everywhere, and it can be found even in the Connecticut River Valley. The Quabbin Reservoir has always been a good site for these large birds. Without the political pressure of sportsmen and sportswomen, we would not have these birds returning in the numbers they are found today. Ring-necked Pheasant are rare and may turn up anywhere that they have been released for a hunt. Generally, the Moran Wildlife Management Area can produce a sighting. Ring-necked Pheasant prefer large open fields and cornfields in the fall.

Woodcock, Snipe

Both birds prefer a shrubby "edge" near a large wet meadow. They are most often observed in the spring when their courtship flights allow birders to locate them. The Meadows and the fields near Arcadia are good places to find them.

Rails, Sandpipers, and other wetland shorebirds

With the exception of the rails, these birds can be found in the late summer along rivers and lakes where there is some exposure of mud or shoreline. Look for the rails and moorhens in large swamps within the grass or along the shore. Phaloropes are extremely rare, but try the Dana Flats at the Quabbin off of Gate 40. You will find the sandpipers and plovers along this mudflat, too. The Meadows and Arcadia have been very good for these birds from mid-August into early September. Check similar habitat along the Housatonic River, especially at Bartholomew's Cobble. Large grassy fields and sod farms are worth checking as well.

Gulls and Terns

The gulls can be seen on the larger reservoirs. They will flock along the Connecticut River and at waste-fill sites. To enjoy the rare species, look for them during the winter or in the early spring. The Berkshire Lakes and the Ashley Reservoir are productive. Many interesting species are found on the river near the south-end bridge in Agawam and at East Meadow in Northampton. Usually a Bonaparte's or a Lesser Black-backed Gull can be found. Many gulls are observed overhead flying high after a storm -- keep looking up -- especially after March winds.

There is no suitable habitat for the terns in Western Massachusetts, but they do turn up after storms or during migration at the same places you will encounter a gull.

Cuckoos

The cuckoos enjoy a meadow or slightly open setting to slightly wooded or brushy habitat. Birders, however, look for infestations of tent caterpillars where they know the cuckoo can be found feeding on its favorite food, the hairy tent caterpillar. Cuckoos are common in some years and uncommon in others, depending on the varying outbreaks of the caterpillars.

Owls

There is diversity among the subspecies, but the owls you are likely to find birding in Western Massachusetts are the Barred, Great Horned, Northern Saw-whet, and Eastern Screech. Many naturalists consider the Barred and the Red-shouldered Hawk as partners -- always sharing similar habitat within the wet woodlands. For years the Barred Owl has been type-cast as a swamp dweller, but they are common in larger woodlands adjacent to water or expansive forests without major wetlands. Great Horned and Eastern Screech may be more closely associated with each other, as they prefer the broken woodland with some farms or orchards available. Screech Owls can be found in parks and suburban areas. Great Horned Owls sometimes surprise people with their tolerance to human disturbances. Northern Saw-whet Owls are found on Greylock and at the Quabbin. In fact, the Quabbin once had the largest concentration of these birds in the northeast.

The Snowy Owl may visit during winter, always preferring habitat similar to its homeland on the tundra. Thus, you will want to look for them in open fields, grasslands, or airports. The Short-eared and Long-eared Owls can also be found but are uncommon. Short-eared Owls are seen in the winter where there are open fields with small trees. The Barn Owl is very rare in Western Massachusetts. It has been known to nest within the Pioneer Valley at lower elevations. The Springfield area defines its range at the northern limit. Barn Owls can easily be seen on Nantucket at the Felix Neck Wildlife Sanctuary.

Nighthawks, Whippoorwill

The Common Nighthawk's call on an August evening as dusk settles in is the first confirmation that the summer is nearing its end. These birds can be seen in large numbers flying high above cities or suburban yards. Their distinct buzzing call will verify their identification. The Whip-poor-will is often heard at dusk, but then becomes quiet as the night advances. These birds prefer orchards and open park-like settings. Although their habitat is common, the bird is not. Both are members of a family of birds called Goatsuckers.

Hummingbirds

The Ruby-throated Hummingbird is the only nesting species in the East. Hummingbirds feed on the nectar of flowers and also on tiny insects. They are attracted to gardens with large red tubular flowers that harbor nectar. Hummingbirds are not limited to domestic gardens, but are common in the forests where they feed on the drilled sap running holes of the Yellow-bellied Sapsucker and on small flowers within clearings or along streams.

Woodpeckers

The woodpeckers are woodland birds that never stray far from the trees. The Northern Flicker is probably the most adventurous in this sense, as they enjoy feeding on lawns and in open fields adjacent to the woods. The Downy and Hairy Woodpeckers sometimes share habitats in the woodland. However, Downy Woodpeckers are more common in the suburbs and at feeders, while the Hairy is more often seen in the larger woods and forests. The Red-bellied Woodpecker is expanding its range, but is still uncommon in the upland forests. Red-bellies prefer the river valleys and oak-dominated woods in the bottomlands.

Flycatchers

The majority of flycatchers are birds of the wetlands, often found along the shorelines of ponds and marshlands. Others, like the Eastern Phoebe, nest in the woodlands not far from some source of water. The Eastern Wood-Pewee is independent of the wetland and is a high-canopy dweller in forests or extensive woods. Phoebes are often found nesting under bridges above small rivers. They can be found in the yards of suburbia, where they will nest under decks or in tree crevices. Great Crested Flycatchers are easy to identify by song, and they prefer mixed deciduous forests where they frequent the upper canopy. They are not likely in fragmented woodlots in suburbia. The Quabbin has a healthy population of them along Gate 40. Several flycatchers will migrate through the region. The Alder and Willow are impossible to identify after they stop singing. The Least and the Yellow-bellied are also a challenge. The Olive-sided has a northern affinity, but can be found at Pleasant Valley and at Greylock.

Swallows

The swallows are skilled aerialists that can be seen in several different habitats, but the edges of ponds and lakes are among the most common. Cliff and Bank swallows will also select such a nesting habitat (banks or rocky cliffs) near open fields or water. The Purple Martin is sporadic after July, but will prefer an open field to nest in. They are often sharing perching wires with the Tree Swallow.

Purple Martins are cavity-nesters and they stay in colonies. Barn Swallows search for abandoned homes or barns -- frequently settling for the undersides of overhanging roofs.

Jays and Crows

Among the most intelligent birds in the Western Massachusetts area, jays and crows frequent a variety of habitats. While jays prefer woodlands or open park-like environs, the crows are seen almost everywhere. They are always taking advantage of available food supplies. However, the crow will require a nest site in the woods or among a cluster of evergreens, where they build their nests high up in these trees. The Fish Crow is moving north and can be found at Stanley Park.

Titmice

Chickadees and Tufted Titmice are a part of this family. The Tufted Titmouse is more specific in its habitat choice, liking the bottomlands. Chickadees are found throughout Massachusetts wherever there are a few acres of woods or yards with an abundance of good trees. Chickadees have winter and summer territories.

Wrens

The Carolina and House Wren are often found near one another. These two prefer woodlands with open lawns or orchards. The Winter Wren can be seen in a different setting, often more remote, within ravines shielded by hemlocks along streams or near waterfalls. Thick secondary growth found after logging cuts are performed are good habitats when located near some conifers and water.

The Marsh Wren is a difficult bird to find but has been known to nest along the rail tracks near Richmond Pond. They frequent the cattail marshes. A Sedge Wren has been observed at Moran.

Thrushes

Wood Thrush are woodland birds preferring the lower canopy. Hermit Thrush are found at higher elevations in the mixed hardwoods where there are hemlock and a few spruce. Swainson's are uncommon in the valley, but can be found at Monroe State Forest. The Gray-cheeked and Bicknell's Thrush do not nest in Massachusetts any longer. They may return and would be likely found on Mount Greylock or at other higher elevations. Veery are found in moist woodlands near bogs or seeps; they also prefer the ground. All of these species prefer the dark woods and shy away from open, sunlit areas. The Eastern Bluebird is on the comeback, but is still relatively uncommon. Look for them within open fields and in orchards.

Pipits and Larks

The Horned Lark frequents open agricultural fields (Northampton/Hadley) with stubble growths of grass and weeds. The American Pipit is a rare migrant found often at airfields. Try Turners Falls Airport or East Meadow in Northampton for possible sightings.

Waxwings

The Cedar Waxwing is fond of water during the summer. They feed like flycatchers until the winter, when they frequent fruit trees and bushes. They can be found almost anywhere and can take advantage of a large variety of habitat. Be alert for the rare Bohemian Waxwing mixed in with the Cedar Waxwing in winter.

Shrikes

The Northern Shrike is an inhabitant of open land. You will find them at Moran in the winter. They may be common in other local spots during the winter, but usually this is not the case. The Loggerhead Shrike is now absent from the state, but does appear on extremely rare occasions as a vagrant.

Vireos

The Red-eyed Vireo is one of the most common nesting woodland birds in Western Massachusetts. The Blue-headed Vireo prefers open woods with some field habitat close at hand. The Philadelphia nests to our north; there are some reports of these in the spring. White-eyed is found to the immediate south. On rare occasion, one may be spotted in its preferred habitat of brambles and thickets. Both Warbling and Yellow-throated nest in the region; the latter preferring poplar trees and shady deciduous groves.

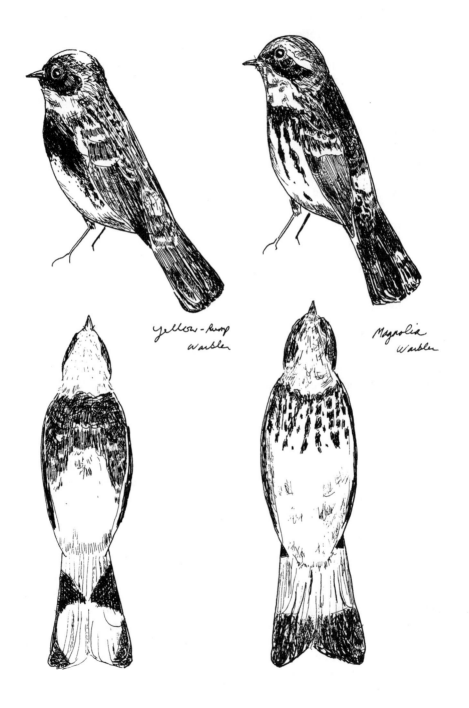

Yellow-Rump
Warbler

Magnolia
Warbler

Wood Warblers

In this family, there is a wide variety of subspecies -- all with an equally diverse set of habitats and nesting requirements. Spring migration is the best time to find these birds, sometimes outside of their preferred habitat, but often this is more conspicuous for the birder. The Yellow-rumped, Chestnut-sided, and Common Yellowthroat are some of the more common ones. The following is a list of those least often mentioned in this guide:

Blue-winged -- Look for these warblers along powerline right-of-ways and shrubby clearings with weeds. This warbler likes sunny orchards and abandoned farmlands in succession.

Golden-winged -- This warbler prefers abandoned pastures and power-line cuts or utility right-of -ways. It may be found along streams with shrubby sides or along shrubby waysides.

Brewster's -- This is a hybrid found in the same habitats of either parents, the Blue-winged and Golden-winged Warblers.

Yellow-breasted Chat -- This chat frequents dense thorny tangles of multifold rose or other prickly brambles. Sometimes found near the edge of a large deciduous woodlot or in disturbed areas after digging or filling. The Meadows may reveal one some year, but otherwise a rare and threatened species.

Northern Parula -- The parula is usually associated with the moist hemlock or spruce forests near slow moving water. The presence of lichens is usually essential.

Prothonotary -- Found in wooded swamps and flood plains with cavity-producing trees.

Bay-breasted -- It prefers conifer forests with bogs.

Tennessee -- The Tennessee likes to nest in black spruce bogs where it can find moss for nesting. A boreal species that can tolerate deciduous groves with understory, it prefers a young forest.

Orange-crowned -- This bird likes a variety of habitats that have brushy components.

Grosbeaks, Sparrows, Finches

This group of birds are some of the most familiar to us because of their diet of seeds. However, many species of sparrows, for example, are virtually unknown to most casual birders. Sparrows are some of the most difficult birds to identify. Birding these species by habitat can assist in meeting the challenge.

Fox Sparrow -- During migration this large reddish brown sparrow can be found at feeders scratching the ground for seeds. Check woods with understory, too. It spends the breeding season in the far north in brushy locations.

Grasshopper Sparrow -- A grassland species found in a few specific places such as Arcadia off of Old Springfield Road.

Vesper Sparrow -- This is a sparrow of farmland and extensive hayfields or meadows. It is usually difficult to find, but when located, can be approached.

Henslow's Sparrow -- This small grassland and meadow-loving bird no longer nests in Massachusetts. They may return unexpectedly to the Moran Sanctuary.

Lapland Longspur -- This longspur is a visitor from the tundra and can sometimes be found in large fields in winter.

Snow Bunting -- This bird is actually more common than many believe. It nests in the circumpolar region on tundra, but periodically wanders into our region in search of food. It is found in large fields, airports, and grasslands.

Dickcissel -- A locally very rare grassland species that has been found at the Moran Sanctuary.

Evening Grosbeak -- From the grosbeak family, the Evening Grosbeak is the most likely to be encountered. They prefer higher altitudes and cooler temperatures. There are a few cases of Evening Grosbeaks staying through the summer, but winter is when they ought to arrive. This is a woodland bird that is common in Vermont.

Pine Grosbeak -- This large finch needs a habitat that consists of fir and spruce with some hardwoods. Pines feed on seeds and love fruit trees during the winter. It does not usually appear in the region, but can be expected to visit Greylock or Moran in the winter.

Common Redpoll -- A true northern species frequenting boreal habitats that include birch. A redpoll may turn up in similar habitat in Western Massachusetts during the winter. It sometimes shows up at feeders in impressive numbers. Check the heart-shaped leafed birch and spruce stands of Greylock.

26
Great Birding Sites
in
Western
Massachusetts

White-throated Sparrow

Chipping Sparrow

Fox Sparrow

Swamp Sparrow

Field Sparrow

American Tree Sparrow

Song Sparrow

Sparrow
R Taylor

1   The Meadows

Closest Town: Longmeadow

Best Time To Visit: Late Winter, Spring, Summer, mid-Fall.

Method Of Birding: Trail Walking, Car, Bicycle.

Birds Of Special Interest: Shorebirds (August-September), Wood Ducks (April-Nov), Blue-winged Teal (September-November) Pied-billed Grebe (August-September), Green Heron, Black-crowned Night Heron (spring to summer), Bald Eagle (spring), American Woodcock (April), Red-bellied Woodpecker (year-long), Flycatchers (spring), Warblers (May).

Advice/Rules: The Meadows is a breeding ground for mosquitoes. You will not last long without bug repellent. Bring boots during wet periods. This is a good place for the Audubon Bird Call. Dogs must be leashed.

The Fannie Stebbins Memorial Wildlife Refuge and surrounding conservation areas are on the eastern banks of the Connecticut River in Longmeadow, Massachusetts. Known locally as *The Meadows*, this wildlife-rich acreage has been noted for its excellent birding for decades. Positioned along the river and having dense vegetative covering mixed with vernal pools, the refuge offers a convenient stop-over site for neotropical migrants and waterfowl using the eastern flyway. Here they rest, feed, and take shelter before moving on again.

Understandably, the spring and fall are the best times to go. Because the Meadows is primarily a wetland habitat, late summer is also a fruitful time to visit. During August and September, shorebirds that are through with breeding and raising young move down the river. Herons and egrets turn up in good numbers, too. However, even when migration is not taking place, the Meadows teems with birdlife, and the birding remains exciting.

Summer can provide opportunities to find nesting warblers and less evident species that enjoy the deep thickets, such as Brown Thrasher, Wood Thrush, American Woodcock, Eastern Towhee, Yellow Warblers, and Black-billed Cuckoo. In winter, the open fields attract a variety of sparrows, such as Savannah Sparrows and other seed-eaters. In the spring, a walk on an early May morning will be filled with a deafening chorus of songbirds, which will last into June before running out of breath.

The Meadows

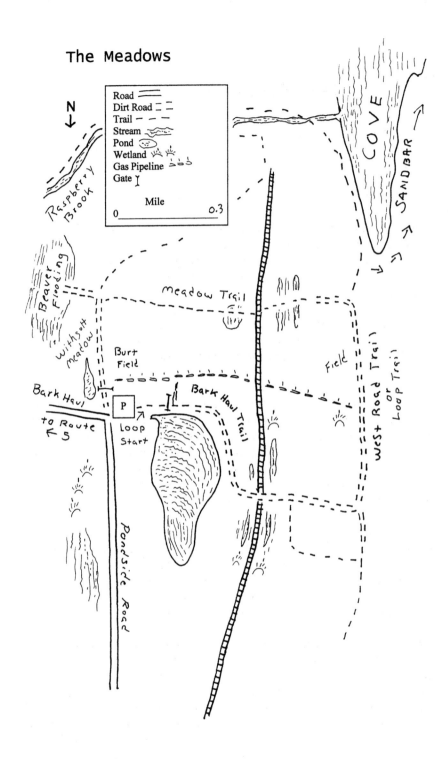

Road
Dirt Road
Trail
Stream
Pond
Wetland
Gas Pipeline
Gate

Mile

0   0.3

N

Raspberry Brook

COVE

SANDBAR

Beaver Flooding

meadow Trail

Withsoft meadow

Burt Field

Field

West Road Trail

or Loop Trail

Bark Haul

Bark Haul Trail

P

to Route 5

Loop Start

Pondside Road

44

In 1993, the Nature Conservancy allocated funds to help purchase a large part of open acreage within the site. The entire site has value not only for birders but for historians as well. Set aside for its unique river ecosystem, this tract of nearly 1,000 acres is the product of town conservation efforts, the Allen Bird Club, and the Fannie Stebbins Memorial Wildlife Refuge, Inc. Except for the Allen Bird Club, each of these entities owns separate pieces which together comprise the area known as the Meadows. The refuge is maintained by the Stebbins Refuge Trustees, elected from the membership of the Allen Bird Club. Registered as a national landmark for its diverse and plentiful plant and bird life, the sanctuary has received much support, both locally and from nonprofit environmental groups.

Getting There

From I-91 South, take the Forest Park/Longmeadow Exit 1, and go 2.7 miles, passing the town green and the big white church, until you come to a set of lights and begin to look for Bark Haul Road on the right. Now travel about 0.5 miles over the highway to a posted map where the road turns and there is parking either on the side or off the shoulder.

From I-91 North, take the Longmeadow Exit right, go through four sets of stoplights, and down a small hill. Immediately after a circular pull-off on the left; turn left into Bark Haul Road. The Refuge and Conservation properties can also be accessed from Emerson Road across from the light at Saint Mary's Church on Longmeadow Street (Route 5).

Birding the Meadows

The Loop Trail (Bark Haul to West Road)

The Loop Trail begins and ends at the bottom of Bark Haul Road. It is often referred to as the Bark Haul Trail. Look for the gate to your immediate right. The birding starts here. In fact, if you traveled no farther, your trip would probably be worthwhile, as the entrance path and the nearby pond are home to several species. Mallards and Canada Geese may be seen in the foreground, but the real surprises are found through careful and patient observation at the back of the pond. Look for Green-winged Teal, Wood Duck, and sometimes Northern Pintail. Perched on the dead, waterlogged trees that stand like poles near the pond's edge are Willow Flycatchers. Tree Swallows are a common sight; their cheerful notes and dauntless flights are an added bonus to any hike near this pond.

In early to mid-spring, this area has been consistently productive for those interested in warblers. Immediately to the left of the gate there are alder bushes, cattails, and other shrubs that may harbor more than one species. Frequently, several Yellow-rumped, Yellow, Black-throated Blue Warblers, and American Redstarts can be encountered here. If your timing is right, you may find the Black-throated Green Warbler moving about the higher tree branches above the bushes. Because water is often rushing out of the overflowing pond through a small pipe beneath the road, a concentration of warblers here is not unusual. Birds love the sound of moving water.

In early spring, the Palm Warbler and Yellow-rumped Warblers are seen with Black-and-white Warblers, but later (about the first week of May), you can find the Magnolia, and on occasion the Blackburnian Warbler. Chestnut-sided Warblers are usually seen, too. Moving along the Loop Trail and after turning to the right and then to the left, you will become shaded beneath some very impressive oaks and maples. Sometimes Wild Turkey are seen here in late summer and in the winter. Continue walking until you come to the Conrail tracks. Use caution when crossing these active railroad lines. At a safe distance from the tracks, observe with binoculars the many ponds on either side. Rigorously check for the Wood Ducks that are usually feeding in the cover.

On the other side of the tracks, the setting changes. As you walk down from the railbed, you see what appears in spring or summer to be a long green tunnel. The surrounding vegetation is thick and impenetrable. Go slowly here and search for the neotropical migrants that love heavy cover. This region is very much like a jungle without the parrots. Giant grapevines make one think of "tropical birding."

Some possibilities in this area are the Blue-gray Gnatcatcher, Common Yellowthroat, and Yellow Warblers. More likely, you will find Gray Catbirds, Wood Thrush, Northern Cardinals, and American Robins. Up in the canopy, scan for Rose-breasted Grosbeak and Baltimore Oriole. Scarlet Tanagers are not well represented nesters, but are sometimes seen during migration, as are Ruby-crowned Kinglets. In winter, the refuge yields Yellow-crowned Kinglets and Common Redpolls.

Longmeadow Brook to West Road

There is an interesting side trail that branches off from the right of the Loop Trail and goes along the Longmeadow Brook, which is a feeder stream into the Connecticut River. Look for Northern Waterthrush. At a bridge about a 0.1 mile in, stay to the left to West Road. This section is blocked to motor vehicles and is narrow until it joins with the Loop Trail. This little diversion can be rather messy as there are many large, muddy puddles.

The intersection of West Road to the Loop Trail signifies its end (many may call this dirt section West Road Trail). The joining of these paths creates a small opening in what is otherwise a densely shaded section of the Fannie Stebbins Refuge. Here a profusion of red clover carpets the ground, on which white-tailed deer are often spotted feeding in early summer. Coyotes frequent this part of the refuge; in the summer they often raid the corn fields off West Road. Coyotes are an adaptable, intelligent species, and they utilize roads or eat vegetables as needed.

Northern Flickers are often seen here in the summer and in many other sections of the refuge. They are found occasionally in winter, along with woodpeckers -- Downy, Hairy, Pileated, and Red-bellied Woodpecker (*illustration* next page). Yellow-bellied Sapsuckers are found seasonally, but are less common.

The Fannie Stebbins Refuge is a great place to find the brave wintering species such as American Robin and Eastern Bluebird. They are a rather cherished species during the cold months. Robins, as well as many others, find low-lying river bottoms and wetlands an attractive place to survive the winter. The temperatures are often warmer, and snowfall is usually less. Muddy places and seeps do not retain snow as well, and insect life is easier to find in softer, exposed soils. Wild Turkey, an increasingly common bird in the greater Springfield area, sometimes shares these seeps during the winter.

Sherwood Section and Natti Trail

As you walk east on the Loop Trail, there are trails to the right that slip into the enchanting Sherwood Section. Perhaps the best is the Natti Trail. These woods are unique because there is little groundcover or shrubbery. Great-horned Owls have been reported here. Pileated Woodpeckers may be found searching for food or drumming loudly among the mature stand of red maple. In the early 1990s, a pair nested here. This is also a good area for vireos. Up in the canopy, focus on Red-eyed, Warbling, Yellow-throated, and on rare occasion during migration, the Philadelphia Vireo.

Within the smaller network of trails that criss-cross the Sherwood Section is an interesting colony of evergreens. Boy Scouts planted these conifers thirty-five years ago. Now the spruce provide much needed shelter in this open park-like part of the sanctuary. If you approach them with stealth, you may see a Ruffed Grouse. This well-camouflaged bird has been officially recorded in the refuge only a few times, but they *are* here. In the 1970s and early 1980s, they were found consistently under the spruce grove during snowstorms. During the winter, you will enjoy seeing chickadees and titmice.

Red-bellied Woodpecker

Back at the intersection of trails, the Loop Trail continues left, cuts through a mature forest, and then opens into a meadow. In the evening, the light captures this meadow, and it resembles an Impressionist's work, sometimes complete with hay-bales reminiscent of a Monet painting. Thoroughly scope the area, including the higher tree line along the meadowed edges. During the fall, Connecticut Warblers have been seen infrequently.

Later in the season, the grasses and weeds reach maturity for a second time after the spring haying. In September, these meadows are in full bloom. Beautiful Joe Pye-weed and goldenrods sprinkle the fields with color. They attract dozens of migrating monarch butterflies and sometimes Ruby-throated Hummingbirds.

Perimeter Trail

At the end of the meadow, where the Loop Trail turns sharply to the left, there are two small paths (referred to as Meadow Trail on some maps). One is on the immediate right, and the other branches off and heads more to the left into the woods (Cutback Trail). Follow these to the outer limits of the refuge land. This is the Elliot Section, and you are now on the Elliot Trail (both paths are in Elliot Section). Pass by an inlet from the Connecticut River on your right and cross Raspberry Brook to join up with the Knoll Trail. This takes you to the edge of the Refuge and becomes a new trail. Appropriately, it is named the Perimeter Trail.

A longer way of joining up with the Loop Trail, the Perimeter Trail turns quickly to the left and back toward Bark Haul Road beside the Colleen Withgott Meadow, in order to complete its loop. The Perimeter Trail offers another opportunity to view migrating warblers, including on rare occasions Hooded Warblers. If you are lucky, the trail may reveal beautiful Canada, Nashville, and Wilson's Warblers. This section of the trail is full of wetlands. Green Heron and Black-crowned Night Heron are present but unobtrusive. Likewise, sighting the American and Least Bittern is possible, but they are very rare now.

Colleen Withgott Meadow

Over the years, the Colleen Withgott Memorial Meadow has produced some very exciting finds. Today, Eastern Bluebirds back from the brink of extinction are nesting here with Tree Swallows, Savannah, and Song Sparrows. The typical meadow-loving species such as Goldfinch and Red-tailed Hawk are constants. Goldfinches nest in late summer when other birds are on their way out. Notice the males' territorial flights that encircle the open field. Less conspicuous and living here seemingly undetected are the much less common American Woodcock. Woodcock can be seen in the first few weeks of spring; after that they stay rather concealed.

The arrival of Woodcock to the Meadows each spring is a moving experience. Just about the time when the ground thaws and spring peepers begin to become vocal, listen for the famed *peent* call of the Woodcock at the start of dusk. Sounding similar to the call of the Night Hawk, the buzzing *peent* of Woodcock heralds spring's arrival at the Meadows. If you tune into the call, you will notice it quickly changes into a more musical twittering when the male Woodcock has reached the apex of its courtship flight somewhere high above the soggy grasses below. Suddenly the night air falls silent. At that point, the Woodcock has finished with its acrobatic spiraling and is tumbling in a free-fall back to the exact spot where it will rise again after a series of peenting calls. When you recognize its call and begin to hear it repeat, watch the horizon for its abrupt ascent; at such times it can be spotted and observed readily spiraling high above the meadow. This is the courtship "sky-dance" that has inspired many a birder.

This section of the Loop Trail where the Woodcock performs its courtship flight is just a few hundred yards from Bark Haul Road where you parked your car. This makes it a convenient place to observe Woodcock that become active at dusk, the time we humans have difficulty seeing and tend to avoid the woods.

The Connecticut River Sand Bar

Although making your way to the sandbar can be a bit of a struggle, the actual sand spit is very accommodating. A few weedy brambles exist, but much of the sandbar is open with hard-packed sand to walk on. The sand extends out into the river, where driftwood logs make nice places to sit and enjoy the birds. Sunsets are inspirational, and it is exceptionally peaceful. The sandbar reminds you of a scene from Mark Twain's Mississippi.

Late summer shorebirds are the main attraction out here. Watch for Black-bellied Plovers and Ruddy Turnstones. In 1992, a Black Tern showed up on the sandbar. Sandpipers are sure bets. The following have been observed at one time or another -- Baird's, Buff-breasted, Pectoral, Semipalmated, Stilt, and White-rumped. You should see Spotted and Solitary Sandpipers. These two species are more common here than other sandpipers. The Least Sandpiper is seen here each year, and Greater and Lesser Yellowlegs can be expected, too.

Often, other birds associated with water may be seen here. Double-crested Cormorants and Osprey are not unheard of. Fish Crows have also been documented. Egrets are occasionally flushed as you approach through the tangle and snarls of jewel weed, nettle, and cinnamon fern. Some of the region's more serious birders have been known to spend entire days out here and thus have had impressive rare sightings. Birds occasionally reported on the bar include Whimbrel, Little Blue Heron, and Bonaparte's Gull. There was even a Northern Wheatear recorded. The more time you spend on the sandbar, the better your odds of seeing that rare one fly-in. Make this a timeless visit.

Pondside Road (Big Loop)

At the end of Bark Haul Road, where the Loop Trail begins and a car can be parked, there is an opportunity to enjoy a larger hiking circuit, or loop. Walk the complete 1.5-mile length of Pondside Road, the road that Bark Haul Road empties into on the right. At the end of Pondside Road, turn left over the tracks and continue until the road twists left and passes a few residential homes. This is West Road, and it will soon arrive at a large agricultural field. Follow this dirt road all the way to where it runs to the left, and you can see a smaller trail continuing straight. Follow the straight trail into the woods for about two-tenths of a mile, at which point it brings you across the Longmeadow Brook and eventually to the intersection of the Loop Trail. This route, along with what has been more thoroughly covered as the Loop Trail, provides a grand tour of The Meadows. If included with the Perimeter Trail, it results in a fairly long hike of about 3.5 hours.

For the first half-mile, most of the action is found on the right-hand side as you walk down Pondside Road heading north. This area is characterized by a series of ponds of various depths. Cattails battle the ever-intrusive invasion of purple loosestrife. This exotic, flowering European weed has done untold damage to wetland quality all across the continent by competing with native plants and creating habitat loss.

The Red-winged Blackbird, being common, is conspicuous here. Their pleasant- sounding calls are always welcome after several weeks of winter but are then lost within the chorus of other summer birds. Marsh Wrens do not occur here, but Soras and Virginia Rails have frequented the site on rare occasions.

Evidence of beaver can be seen where the Longmeadow Brook crosses beneath Pondside Road. Be sure to stop at this point and look for water birds. Great Blue Heron are common, often accompanied by Great Egret in the late summer. During migration, several Great Blue Herons will appear at once. In 1990, 35 Great Blue Heron and half a dozen Great Egret were observed. Great Blues are sometimes seen in the winter!

The open waters at about the one-mile mark offer some of the best birding along the Connecticut River Valley. Enjoy small groups of Pied-billed Grebe that are seen frequently in late summer. Wood Ducks, Great Blue Heron, Swamp Sparrows, Mallards, and Red-winged Blackbirds are well represented. Shy water birds are found, including an occasional group of American Coots and rarely, the Common Moorhen. Other birds that can be seen are Blue and Green-winged Teal, Northern Pintail, and American Wigeon. Less common are Gadwall, Hooded Merganser, Ring-necked Duck, and Redhead.

The walk or drive down Pondside will almost always reveal White-throated Sparrows and Tree Sparrows. Song Sparrows are also common. Pondside is an excellent place to find hawks at all times of the year. Watch the Broad-winged Hawks, Cooper's, and Sharp-shinned soar effortlessly. The Red-shouldered may rarely turn up in warmer seasons. Bald Eagles nest across the river in Suffield, Connecticut. They have been seen hunting over the ponds along Pondside. In spring, all northern species of swallow except Purple Martin are enjoyed. House, Winter, and Carolina Wrens can be heard singing from this road.

West Road

In the fields along West Road, check with binoculars for fall sparrows, which find these fields attractive and show up from mid-September through early October. Most of the species seen are of the common varieties, but be alert for White-crowned and Lincoln's. Walking the road is preferred to driving because a car might scare the birds far out in the fields. Sometimes in the winter, the fields hold Horned Larks and Snow Buntings. Purple Finches are regular during fall migration, and are not limited to West Road.

On the other hand, Pondside is a great place for those who prefer to bird by car, and there are plenty of viewing areas where you can aim scopes on the ponds. Remember to check the wooded side for woodland species following the river as a flyway. Each year, dozens of Yellow-rumped Warblers rest and feed along this side. And no winter visit to this sanctuary would be complete without seeing the Red-bellied Woodpecker or even the Belted Kingfisher.

2   Robinson State Park

Closest Town: Agawam

Best Time To Visit: Winter, Spring, late Summer

Method Of Birding: Trail Walking, Car, Bicycle

Birds Of Special Interest: Common Merganser (winter - March and April), Wood Duck (spring to summer), Pileated Woodpecker (year-long), Warblers (May).

Advice/Rules: Do not underestimate this site. There is no camping nor open camp fires allowed.

Robinson State Park, an urban park, offers shelter for both wildlife and humans in the midst of busy Greater Springfield. Unknown to many, this hideaway is often overlooked by casual visitors and birders alike. Yet birding is quite good here because of the age of the forest and the extensive undeveloped river frontage. The park was created in 1934 through the wishes of a local farmer who donated the land we now know by his name.

Situated along the twisting Westfield River, Robinson State Park has 150 different species to excite birders of all levels. Most of the 811-acre park consists of mature hardwoods. These woods are hilly but gentle for hiking; they contain cool hemlock groves, large sycamores, some maples, birch, and many majestic oaks. The remaining parts consist of open lawns, a few ponds, wetlands covered in brushy tangles, wet meadows, and power line cuts. The trails are short, with the exception of one at the western boundary, and usually offer a loop hike. For birders, this reforested farmland offers good birding by car and a convenient approach to both waterfowl and woodland passerines.

Getting There

From Springfield, take the Memorial Bridge into West Springfield and follow Route 147 through the city past the Big E fairground and over the bridge into Agawam. Turning right with Route 147, travel until you see the sign for Robinson State Park. Turn here on North Street to find the main entrance at 1.0 miles further on the right.

From Interstate 91, take Exit 7 for the Memorial Bridge, and then follow the directions given above.

Robinson State Park

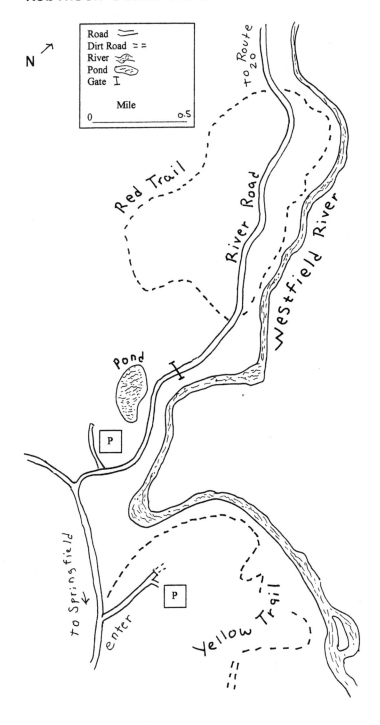

Road
Dirt Road ==
River
Pond
Gate I

N

Mile

0 _____ 0.5

Red Trail

to Route 20

River Road

Westfield River

Pond

I

P

to Springfield

enter

P

Yellow Trail

Birding Robinson State Park

After passing through the main gate and taking a left toward the heart of the park, you can begin birding. Immediately, you will notice the many white birch trees and the scores of large oaks and white pines. You may choose to continue birding by car or park your car along the shoulder and walk a few yards in order to look more carefully. In summer there will be Red-eyed Vireo, Scarlet Tanager, and plenty of Eastern Wood-Pewee. At 0.5 mile, there are hemlocks of all sizes, and then a power line cut. This area is worth checking for breeding warblers. After 0.9 mile, you will arrive at a sharp turn in the road where a gated drive stretches off to the left leading to North Street.

There is also a utility cut (aqueduct) here that offers grassy and shrubby habitat usually good for White-throated Sparrows in the late fall and winter. Here again, there is plenty of shoulder to park on, should you decide to investigate this hilly trail. Otherwise, continue heading down the road where you soon notice some parking areas and open lawns. In early spring, these lawns are brown and soggy, but usually covered with dozens of American Robins.

The first road on the left leads up to the Trestle Pavilion. This is a nice place to unfold a blanket and picnic after a morning of birding. Below is Robinson Pond, where a sandy beach allows for still greater relaxation. Robinson Pond may be a bit active for any serious birding, but it makes for a good, cool swimming hole. Occasionally there may be a pair of Mallards or a few Tree Swallows swooping across this shallow impoundment.

On the opposite side of the road from the pond you can see the Westfield River. Parking places conveniently allow for good viewing of the river from your car, but from this point on, vehicular traffic is not allowed -- an inconvenience for some, but a blessing for others in search of a quiet walk. Closing the road to traffic has probably increased birding success.

You will notice the closed traffic gate a few feet past the pond. Walk around it and head into the woods with the Westfield River on your right. At any point along this quiet road, you can walk down toward the river and check for the park's resident population of Common Mergansers. While these birds are more common here in the winter, they do nest and can be seen all year long. Their nests are farther up-river. Sometimes there will even be a few Hooded Mergansers. As expected, Mallards and Black Ducks will cause birders to raise binoculars and disappoint those in search of more unusual species. But late March and early April will bring down uncommon passing migrants. American Wigeon and Blue-winged Teal are just a few of the exciting possibilities. Be sure to scan the water closely with binoculars for those semi-rarities such as Ring-necked Duck and Northern Pintail.

Red Trail

About 0.3 mile past the gated entrance, you will see the Red Trail on the left, after a white guard post. This trail loops through the woods up a steep hill and turns back north toward the road. It follows a stream on the left, climbs a hill across a powerline cut, turns right, and descends, turning right to follow another stream back to the road (at a stone bridge). Along this part of the trail, listen for Louisiana Waterthrush from April into July. The loud ringing song of this waterthrush is usually heard before the bird is seen, flitting down the edge of the stream. The Red Trail can be picked up again directly across the road where it follows this same stream for a short while before turning west and traveling parallel with the river. As you get closer to the riverbank, there is denser underbrush, and the trail heads back toward the road. At this point you can continue back toward the pond and your parked car, or turn right and head northeast to explore more of the park.

On this trail and in the woodland throughout the park, there are 15 different warbler species that pass through each spring. The Canada Warbler nests where there are mountain laurel or young hemlock. Look for the shy Black-throated Green Warbler high up in older hemlocks. A Black-throated Blue Warbler may reveal itself beneath the understory or lower canopy on the less traveled paths. There are also reports of Cerulean Warblers at Robinson. Non-nesting warblers can also show up along "edges," either near the streams or along the lawns. Migrating warblers are abundant from the last week of April to mid-May. Warblers typically encountered include Yellow-rumped, Chestnut-sided, Pine, Blackburnian, and American Redstart. Black-and-white Warbler and Pine Warbler are early migrants, arriving in April.

Impassable thickets grow on either side of the road for 0.5 mile, providing a chance to see Common Yellowthroat, Grey Catbird, and other secretive birds associated with wet, densely foliated areas. Song and Swamp Sparrow can be found here in spring or fall. Expect Northern Cardinal to frequent the thickets, and Common Grackle working the ground in flocks during migration.

The entire length of this wetland offers good habitat for Veery, which sing with passion through the month of June. Other typical woodland breeding birds are Ruffed Grouse, Pileated Woodpecker (*illustration*), Wood Thrush, and Rose-breasted Grosbeak. The Pileated Woodpeckers are well represented here. They enjoy drumming the giant sycamore trees, and are supported by the size of what can be considered mature trees in a deeply wooded park. Little wonder there are at least three pairs of these giant woodpeckers residing in the park all year. Other woodpeckers to look for include the Downy, Hairy, Northern Flicker and Red-bellied Woodpecker. There are many Red-bellied Woodpeckers here, making this one of the best places to add this bird to your list. White-breasted Nuthatch and Brown Creeper (uncommon) can also be seen. Sometimes the Yellow-bellied Sapsucker shows up during spring migration in mid-April.

From the stone bridge down to the opposite gate on Route 20, the woods open up a little and provide more views of the river. These woods harbor a fairly good variety of interesting songbirds. Some of the species present in May and June include: Great Crested Flycatcher, Baltimore Oriole, Yellow Warbler, Black-and-white Warbler, Yellow-throated Vireo, Warbling Vireo, and more Red-eyed Vireo. From atop the taller trees, the Eastern Wood-Pewee continues to sing well into July.

On rare occasion, migrating Bald Eagles are seen circling above the large bend in the river. Likewise, wayward Ospreys may travel through the region. Check the shoreline for more ducks, and in late August or early September, there may be a few sandpipers or other shorebirds. Listen for the cheerful rattle-like call of the Belted Kingfisher.

The shoreline will also reveal a few Cedar Waxwings (late summer), Eastern Kingbirds, and more Eastern Phoebes. While flycatchers are apt to be along the river, check the pond on the right immediately past the stone bridge as you are walking back to the car. This is a good place to see the Least and sometimes the Willow Flycatcher. There are nesting Wood Ducks at the back of the pond during most breeding seasons. Wood Ducks are also common on the river where the current is slow. Sometimes they paddle up-stream on the brooks feeding into the coves.

The Yellow Trail

At the start of the driveway for the Ranger Station, there is a long trail called the Yellow Trail. The Yellow Trail winds its way along a small ridge above the Westfield River. At 1.0 mile, it meanders away from the river into the wood-land before turning back again toward the water. It then runs close to the water for another few hundred feet before abruptly turning west and paralleling a dirt track. This is the James Street entrance gate road. Heading toward the entrance gate from the river, there is a side loop on the left. This is a much quieter part of the park, where few visitors have the ambition to hike.

On late winter evenings, listen for hooting Great Horned Owls and maybe a lingering, wintering Barred Owl. There are other large birds of prey in this neck of the woods, including Red-tailed, Broad-winged and Cooper's Hawk. From the banks of the river, Bald Eagles can sometimes be seen in the late spring. These eagles are from an active nest in West Springfield. Winter birding can be slow at times; but even when there are few birds, you can enjoy the walk, the character of the plant life, and the scenic river. Robinson State Park is a hidden treasure within the urban landscape.

3   Mount Tom State Reservation

Closest Town: Easthampton/Holyoke

Best Time To Visit: Spring, early Summer, September and October.

Method Of Birding: Trail Walking, Car, Bicycle.

Birds Of Special Interest: Hawks (September-October),
Northern Raven (year-long);
Warblers -- Worm-eating Warbler (May-June), Scarlet Tanager (August)

Advice/Rules: Use safety on the trails. Be sure to pack a day-pack for hikes.
Some hawk-watching may be conducted from your car. No camping.
   Note: It is imperative for any visitor to this reservation to realize that the
eastern timber rattlesnake and copperhead live here (both are endangered). No
one searching skyward for birds should forget to *first* look to the ground.

Mount Tom is known throughout western Massachusetts, if not the nation, as
an excellent place to see hawks during their fall migration. The reservation is
also a great place for viewing summer song birds and woodland species that
prefer mature trees. Since its inception in 1903, the reservation has been jointly
operated by the two adjacent counties, Hamden and Hampshire. Now the State
has taken it over. Since its beginning, Mt. Tom has been a popular place for the
region's urban dwellers who come to admire the view, breathe the fresh air, or
hike the various trails.

At 1,115 feet, the peak of Mt. Tom barely qualifies for status as a "mountain,"
but when viewed from the flat Connecticut River Valley from which it ascends,
the summit appears much grander. Its expanse of forest, totaling 1,683 acres,
also stands in contrast to the agricultural river valley that surrounds it. History
tells of the naming of this mountain by two explorers paddling up river, one
choosing Mount Tom for his namesake; the other, Mount Holyoke on the other
side of the valley, for his.

Getting There

From the Springfield area, take exit 17B off of I-91 for Easthampton and follow
the signs for Route 140 over the mountain. Directly across from the Harvest
Valley Restaurant, the entrance on Christopher Cark Road will appear on the
right (turn here before descending). From Northampton, travel south on Route
10 to Easthampton, and turn left onto Route 140 in the village of Easthampton.
Travel in the direction of the summit heading south toward Holyoke and in full
view of the Mountain.

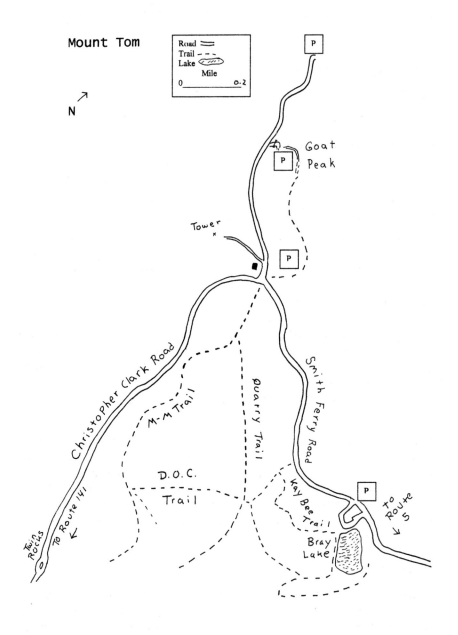

Mount Tom

Road ═══
Trail - - -
Lake ◯
Mile
0 _____ 0.2

N

P

Goat
Peak

P

Tower
x

P

Christopher Clark Road

M-M Trail

Quarry Trail

Smith Ferry Road

D.O.C.
Trail

Kay Bee Trail

P

to
Route
5

Bray
Lake

Twins
Rocks

To Route 141

Birding Mount Tom

Hawk watching is not always easy. Sometimes the hawks are far overhead, and identifying their plumage is affected by the sunlight. However, at Mount Tom, the hawks are frequently at eye level, and a simple pair of binoculars brings them in for easy identification. In the case of more distant viewing, there are alternative methods discussed in various guides.

Even if some birds escape your keen eye, you can still enjoy the experience. Bright clear autumn days allow for great moments spent on Mount Tom. It's not always the number of birds seen or the variety of sightings, but rather the acquaintances, the spectacular views, and the invigorating outdoor experience that makes fall hawk watching so attractive.

The Lookouts

The best spot for hawk watching is the Goat Peak Tower located on the right side of the Christopher Clark Road just before reaching the summit or turn-around at Nonatuck Lookout. Look for the gravelly turn-off, and walk in over some flat rocks to the ledge of Goat Peak. From the tower, there is a wonderful 360-degree view.

The Nonatuck Lookout is another excellent hawk watching site. You can park your car and get out, or stay in to keep warm until hawks come into view. Since the lookout is adjacent to the parking area, it is very convenient to spend an entire morning or afternoon. The people who see huge numbers of hawks do so by "camping out" and waiting for them to come in, and the reward is well worth the wait. Others can realistically expect to see a few dozen, but sightings are variable. Reports of several hundred hawks are not uncommon; some birders have seen thousands in just one afternoon.

Review your field guides, as the species will be mixed within their groups. The hawks of the buteos group will be seen most often. In southern New England, this means the Broad-winged Hawk, Red-tailed Hawk, and Red-shouldered Hawk. The Sharp-shinned and Cooper's (both accipiters), Osprey, Bald Eagle, and Kestrel, while less likely, can be seen by paying attention to their specific migration timings. For example, American Kestrels and Peregrine Falcons are early migrants, appearing first in early September. Mid-September is famous for the Broad-winged Hawk and other members of the buteos such as Red-tailed and Red-shouldered Hawks. During October, you might speed identification of Cooper's Hawk with a quick glance in your field guide where this bird is featured, as they are the common migrant for that month.

While late October can still produce great numbers of hawks, this is the time to catch the Bald Eagle and Turkey Vulture migration. The Broad-winged Hawk is the most frequently observed during fall hawk watches. Making sure you know this hawk well will prevent mis-identification, and your experience will be much more enjoyable.

The spring and fall hawk migration is an excellent opportunity to add a new species to your life list. Fall is magnificent because of the huge numbers that can be sighted; but the spring, while lacking in such volume, sometimes offers a larger *variety* of species in a shorter period of time. Some hawks even nest here. In the past, the Peregrine Falcon made its home here. Its aerie was located on the western cliffs. Birders hope to someday hear the awe-inspiring cry of this, the world's fastest bird, return to the mountain. Try the Bray Tower for spring hawk viewing to the south.

The lookout at the top of the Christopher Clark Road can be a busy place during ideal fall migration weather patterns. In Massachusetts, these weather conditions typically appear about the second week of September, but many more great days may occur much later. Every year there are certain variables in cold fronts or low pressures that can alter the exact timing, but in general, you should look for the day when a high pressure cold front settles in from the north. Ideally, this front will arrive as a back-door cold front pushing down from the St. Lawrence and driving the birds in a southwesterly direction.

As these fronts push in, the cool autumn air warms up about mid-morning, rising and creating a lift. These thermals occur for miles along mountain ridges and escarpments. They are the vehicles upon which the hawks ride. Such large groups of hawks riding on the thermals are referred to as kettles.

Bray Lake and Surrounding Woods

Bray Lake offers some variety in this mainly wooded reservation. Here, some open grassy areas mix with shoreline and dense shrubby sections to increase the number of species that can be sighted. Waterfowl and other water-dependent birds frequent this area, but they are mostly limited to Mallards. Occasionally, other dabbling ducks are recorded -- Black Duck or Wood Ducks in migration.

Flying about the lawns that slope into the east side of the lake are Tree Swallows. Beyond the lake, within the brushy areas, you will find Red-winged Blackbirds and Song Sparrows. The back side of the lake is a known site for Louisiana Waterthrush. Belted Kingfishers take full advantage of the area as well. Listen for their vivacious rattle-like call.

New trails have recently been upgraded to allow near perfect access to the shoreline along the lake's circumference. These barrier-free trails do not spoil this park-like lake setting; but rather, allow for quiet approaches and many good birding moments.

Bray Lake

Surrounding the low-lying area of Bray Lake are more natural paths that lead to older tree growths. These larger trees in and along the streams and wet areas provide excellent habitat for Barred Owls that live here. The higher branches of larger conifers may contain some year-round residents who are especially vocal in mid-winter. Unfortunately, many of these trees are old hemlock and are now succumbing to the hemlock blight, so you might look for a Black-backed Woodpecker (very rare) in winter. These birds love to feed on large, dead hemlocks.

During the spring, watch for warblers, such as Chestnut-sided, Black-throated Blue, and possibly Tennessee. Rose-breasted Grosbeaks can also be added to the spring and summer birdlife adjacent to Bray Lake. Later in the spring, Scarlet Tanagers are visible feeding on the higher leaves of oak trees. Great Crested Flycatchers are common, but they are more commonly heard than seen. High in the canopy, scan carefully for Yellow-throated and Red-eyed Vireo, as they are reasonably common in summer.

Keystone Trail and Beyond

A few yards along the Bray Loop Trail is the Keystone Trail on your right. Follow this trail, which is steep and difficult in places, up the western slope of Mount Tom. Eventually you will come to the Keystone Junction. If you turn right, you will descend back down to Smith Ferry Road, but if you continue onto the Keystone Extension Trail, you will make your way deeper into reservation forest. And from this point, a number of options will lay ahead of you at the intersection of the Quarry Trail and the D.O.C. Trail.

The D.O.C. Trail will bring you into the Metacomet-Monadnock Trail -- also known as the M & M Trail. This well-established trail winds its way along the wooded edge of Mount Tom's western ledge. Beneath the steep ledges are tangles of mountain laurel that conceal the beautiful Black-throated Blue Warbler. In the spring their sweet notes echo off the rocks.

Taking a left here would put you on the southern branch of the Quarry Trail. Instead, turn right, and walk 0.7 mile to the junction of the two D.O.C. trails. Things get more invigorating here with some semi-views of the western horizon and steep rocks to climb up, over and in-between. Notice the sheered-off rock outcroppings that remain as evidence of the tremendous forces of glacial ice, which scraped off whole rock segments of the western slope during the last Ice Age. These ledges now make a perfect home for a nesting pair of giant Common Raven.

Larger than the crows, ravens give this peak a northern affinity. Here, they are at the southern limit of their New England range. At a time when so many birds are extending their ranges northward, the raven is pushing their range south. Ravens are intelligent birds, as are many members of the crow and jay family. In scientific experiments involving tests of memory, they have scored on equal terms with humans.

At a point where there is little else but ledge or rock, huge slabs of basalt make for easy footing. Stiff aster and blue stem grass grow in the crevices. Birch trees can be seen growing just off the trail, and reindeer moss covers some parts of the forest beneath them. During their fall forays or local migrations, the White-throated Sparrows are especially common, as are Dark-eyed Juncos. Certainly, a few Juncos remain to nest here each year.

A variety of communication antennae are visible here and will likely detract from the beauty and inspiration of your mountain hike; perhaps you can dismiss them as necessary evils of our convenient lives in this modern day. Before re-entering the woods, remain here and listen for American Robins, Hermit Thrush, and Eastern Bluebirds (a member of the thrush family) feeding off of the mountain ash scattered about near the summit. Fall is indeed a good time to visit the peak, as many migrants are seen resting or feeding on the peak. The Swainson's Thrush is possible and even Grey-cheeked Thrush could be sighted, but neither of these will be found nesting. The Hermit Thrush is an assumed nester, but are few in number. Woodthrush and Veery are well documented. Blackburnian Warblers are occasional during the spring migration; they are fond of larger hemlocks.

Likewise, Black-throated Green Warblers (*illustration*) can now be considered uncommon at this site. What will happen to their populations if the hemlock blight spreads northward is a frightening thought.

Black-throated Green Warbler

Re-enter the woodland, and seek the Red-breasted Nuthatch in autumn and the Eastern Wood-Pewee in summer. Varieties of larger oaks create a haven for the Northern Flicker. Mixed in throughout the steep mountainside are red, white, and black oak. The red oak appears to be most successful. The louder-sounding flickers that you hear may actually be Pileated Woodpeckers. These giant woodpeckers resemble the Ivory-billed Woodpeckers which once lived in the southern swamps before logging robbed them of their habitat of mature forest. The Pileated also prefers a mature forest.

The M & M Trail continues past the antenna farm and heads over to a series of ski slopes. Rather than following this trail, turn around and find a secluded view upon the many rocky clearings found all along the M & M Trail. Wild columbine grow liberally in this vicinity. It is hoped that eventually, the State will acquire the ski area, which was shut down. This will open up a new region and preserve a shrubby habitat known to be frequented by Prairie Warblers.

Worm-eating Warbler

This is another good spot for fall hawk watching. Great views can be enjoyed all year long, and time should be spent here if you are interested in Turkey Vultures. You might catch a glimpse of a Turkey Vulture pushing off from the ledges below. You could see this year-round if you are here in the early morning when the vultures awaken and depart for the day. Resident Red-tailed Hawks are seen here regularly; their wings often capture the sun and glisten, making them visible across the Connecticut Valley.

Return back the same way you came, or be adventurous and detour along the Quarry, Keystone or Kay Bee Trails to Smith Ferry Road and then back to the Bray Lake area. An alternative is to park at the ranger station and cross the road over to the M & M Trail where it crosses Smith Ferry Road. Either way gives an opportunity to see woodland species and the hawks, vultures and ravens riding the thermals along the western escarpment of basalt glacier-sheered rock.

Whatever path you choose at this point to follow -- either more trail or birdsong -- there is one last treasure at this mountain site which cannot be missed. Drive slowly down the Christopher Clark Road toward Route 141. Where the road splits through giant boulders, find a place to pull over and stop. Yes, this is a place for Winter Wrens, or additional sightings of Great Crested Flycatcher and Pileated Woodpecker. Eastern Wood-Pewee are concentrated here -- more so than at the summit, and very vocal in late spring into mid-summer. These are canopy-dwelling birds. Continue your walk from the car for a few dozen yards past the split rock and listen and search the understory. The reward, heralded by a series of high-pitched notes (sounding like the Dark-eyed Junco), can be a sighting of Mount Tom's specialty -- the Worm-eating Warbler (*illustration*).

4   Ashley Ponds

Closest Town: Holyoke

Best Time To Visit: April, November.

Methods Of Birding: Walking Trails.

Birds Of Special Interest: Horned Grebe (fall),
Diving and Dabbling Ducks (spring, fall).

Advice/Rules: Bring Binoculars. No swimming or picnicking.

Ashley Reservoir provides water for the city of Holyoke, as well as habitat for a wide variety of waterfowl during the spring and fall migration. Birders arrive each November and April to walk along the reservoir's four miles of shoreline and search for exciting varieties of dabblers, divers and geese. The reservoir contains 550 million gallons and offers direct access to the shore. Long jetties extending across the water allow for good visuals and sightings close enough to leave little doubt for beginners. An added bonus are white pines that nearly engulf the shoreline; they attract interesting warblers and wintering species of many kinds.

Getting There

From I-91, take Exit 15 (Holyoke Mall/Ingleside). Turn left (from northbound lanes). Continue heading west, passing some industrial offices, and take your first right onto Homestead Avenue. Follow this road until it intersects with Route 202/Westfield Street at 0.9 mile, and turn left. Bear left off of Westfield Street for the large metal gate, and park away from the gated entrance. The entrance of the Ashley Reservoir is immediately after Sunset Road. Parking space is sometimes limited.

Birding Ashley Reservoir

To begin birding, walk around the large metal and stone gate; this is the main entrance. With the gate behind you, immediately check the large pines on your left for early-arriving grackles and late-lingering woodpeckers. Chickadees and Downy Woodpeckers are found here dependably in winter or early spring. A closer examination of the lower branches and underbrush may reveal an Eastern Phoebe in late March.

Ashley Ponds

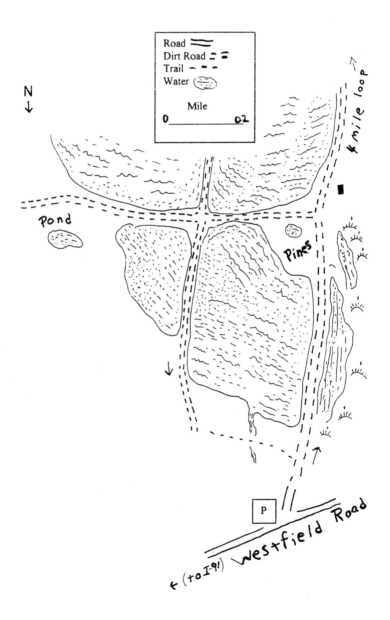

Road
Dirt Road
Trail
Water

Mile

0   02

N

4 mile loop

Pond

Pines

P

← (to I-91) Westfield Road

Phoebes land here because of the presence of water, which is often the first place that seasonal insect life appears. Phoebes will feed on flies first and then change to a more varied diet as other insects emerge with the season. The call of the Phoebe is often mistaken by some as that of the chickadee's familiar call. Generally, the bird is rather conspicuous, it is the most familiar of the flycatchers. They are easy to identify with their dark heads and habitual tail bobbing. Phoebes are the first flycatchers to arrive in the spring, often getting here before spring.

Just beyond these pines, you can see the crystal-clear waters of what locals call the Ashley Ponds. Walk out onto a narrow strip of land surrounded on each side by water. The main reservoir will be on the left, and to the right is a smaller pond . In spring, there are often a few flycatchers perched on the overhanging branches and dead snags along the back shoreline. Sometimes a Great Blue Heron may attempt to feed here.

Immediately begin looking for waterfowl, using your binoculars. Be sure to scan the far sides of the shoreline. There are usually a few Mallards in the vicinity. At 0.5 mile, the red brick pumping station houses can be seen. Turn left here to enjoy a short but productive walk around the first pond or continue straight for an extended 4-mile walk around the entire reservoir. Either way, the pines on the left ought to be explored for Pine Warblers and early migrating Yellow-rumped Warblers. Also, there is a small pond a few yards in on the left where Wood Duck are sometimes seen.

After passing the pines, views of both sides of the reservoir can be had. This is a good spot to seriously scan the water for both predictable and uncommon waterfowl. Many Canada Geese gather here, with fewer numbers of Mallard and Black Duck. At the southern end of the reservoir, in the shallow waters to the left, look for American Coot, especially in November. Also scan further out for Common Loon, Red-necked and Horned Grebes. In the open water of the main reservoir, birders usually find a few Ruddy Duck, Old Squaw, Black Scoter, and White-winged Scoter. While these four species are rare in the spring, they are frequently seen from October to late November. Also at this time there may be a few Hooded Mergansers. At Ashley Reservoir, there is usually a small group of Common Merganser well past November.

Common Loons are known to land on the reservoir during the fall migration. They migrate by day and land in the evening. Loons will migrate along the coast or inland, where they stop over on larger lakes and reservoirs. Fall migration begins in September and may last into November. Loons are often seen in small groups when flying south, but sometimes they may group into larger flocks. A good time to check the reservoir is after a violent storm or during bad weather.

Wood Duck

Bad weather often forces dozens of loons onto bodies of water such as Ashley Reservoir. After the weather clears, the loons move on. Some will winter within sheltered bays and coves along the Atlantic Coast, while others spend the season in the Gulf of Mexico. Hundreds of loons can be found gathering in the evening along the coast in the winter. While such numbers are possible at Ashley reservoir, usually birders are lucky to find more than three.

If you are able to walk slowly and quietly, proceed out to the strip of land on your right. This is where you will want to look for Goldeneye, Greater Scaup, and perhaps even a Bufflehead. Upon returning, take a right and head over to the point where a lone ornamental weeping willow tree grows. Just around the corner from here, a sheltered cove usually harbors a Wood Duck (*illustration*) or American Black Duck. From July through September, these are about all one can expect. But during migration, there might be a flock of Ring-necked Ducks. They have a preference for smaller ponds and sheltered shallow coves.

Continue up the little hill, and you'll notice another good place for flycatchers. Carefully check this hidden little pond for more woodies. In October, the bright yellow foliage of the birch trees encircling this pond makes for appealing photographs. Fall warblers found here include Pine, Yellow-rumped, Chestnut-sided, and Yellow.

Backtracking to the larger reservoir, turn right across the narrow road surrounded by water on either side. Turn back briefly and enjoy another view of the sheltered cove, checking one last time for extreme rarities such as Redhead, Gadwall, or Barrow's Golden-eye. There are often reports of at least one rare species per year -- you could be the next lucky birder. Continue across to the other shore from whence you came, and follow the trail back to the gate and your car.

5 More Great Birding Sites near Springfield

Stanley Park

Habitat

Lawns: grassy manicured lawns, open athletic fields.
Woodland: maturing woodland, some succession growth.
Streams: woodland and park streams.
Parkland: planted shrubs, large trees.

Seasons/Birds

Fall: migrating warblers, thrushes, songbirds, some sparrows.
Winter: woodland species (jays, chickadees), owls.
Spring: migrating warblers, thrushes, songbirds, vireos, owls.
Summer: few warblers, fish crows, some ducks. Songbirds.

Description:

This is an urban park with large, open athletic fields. There are streams and trails in a nice park-like setting. The bonus is a wildlife sanctuary tucked in the westernmost entrance. This sanctuary offers well-marked nature trails.

Getting There

From I-91, take Exit 9 for Route 20 west; follow signs to downtown Westfield. From Westfield Center, stay on Route 20 west and travel half-way around a rotary bearing onto Court Street (passing a United Savings Bank). After turning onto Court Street, proceed for 0.6 mile until Court street turns into Western Avenue. Follow Western Avenue for 1.0 mile. The park is on the left.

Birding Specifics:

This is an excellent site for year-round, accessible and easy birding. It is great for beginners and pros alike. The specialty here is nesting Fish Crows. This is the number one site for these birds in western Massachusetts. Look for them near the big pines next to the Rose Garden.

The other big attraction at Stanley Park is a high population of nesting Pine Warblers. The spring is very productive with a premier warbler migration. Species of interest include Black-throated Blue and Green warblers, Yellow-rumped, and Yellow warblers, Great Crested Flycatcher, Least Flycatcher, Eastern Wood-Pewee, and Scarlet Tanagers. This is an excellent place to find both Blue-headed and Yellow-throated Vireo; it is also the closest place to Springfield for Hermit Thrush.

Forest Park

Habitat:

Lawns: wide open grassy hills
Woodland: older oak and pine woods, some diseased hemlock groves.
Streams/Ponds/Lakes: woodland streams, smaller brooks,
         small stagnant ponds, small lake.
Parkland: variety of large and ornamental trees.

Seasons/Birds:

Fall: migrating songbirds, wood warblers in migration, waterfowl,
         maybe some shorebirds.
Winter: few owls, woodland birds, sometimes lingering waterfowl.
Spring: migrating neotropical birds, warblers, backyard species,
         sometimes northern thrush.
Summer: few nesting warblers, common ducks, thrush.

Description:

Forest Park is primarily an excellent place for migrating warblers and other neotropical migrants. There are a few nesting warblers such as Pine Warbler, Black-and-white (beyond Porter Lake in brush), and some Chestnut-sided Warblers. The Yellow Warbler can be expected everywhere. Each year, up to about 25 migrating warbler species can appear. Swainson's Thrush may be seen in the spring under cover in the woods. The lake may have some Northern Pintails, Wood Ducks, or American Wigeon during November and April. Summer offers mostly Canada Geese and Mallards.

Getting There

From I-91, take Exit 1 (Longmeadow/ Forest Park) and travel on the ramp over the highway toward Longmeadow. The Entrance is on the left. An alternative is the Sumner Avenue entrance off Exit 2, following signs for Route 83.

Laughing Brook Wildlife Sanctuary

Habitat:

Woodland: maturing forest with some variety of species.
Pond/Stream: large stream and very small pond.
Garden: sometimes flowers for hummingbirds.

Seasons/ Birds

Fall: Migrating thrush and songbirds
Winter: owls and woodland birds, feeder birds.
Spring: few migrating warblers, songbirds, few hawks.
Summer: owls, neotropical nesting songbirds

Description:

This is a Massachusetts Audubon Center with an educational pond. Most of the land is cloaked in forest of the oak/hickory type. The Education Center offers a bookshop and many programs for children and adults. There are interesting trails that work upward from the Laughing Brook and beyond a glacial erratic boulder. The woodland has a nice loop hike in a quiet, peaceful setting.

Getting There

From I-91, take Exit 2 onto Route 83, and follow it into East Longmeadow. Travel 1.5 miles past the center of town, and turn left at the sign for Hamden and Hamden Road. Continue to follow Hamden Road until its end, and turn right onto Somers Road for 0.5 mile. Turn left at 0.5 mile onto Main Street and proceed for 2.5 miles. Look for Massachusetts Audubon sign. The Sanctuary is on the left.

Birding Specifics:

There are not many rare species frequenting the site, but it is convenient to the bedroom communities of Springfield. Look for the typical songbirds such as Red-eyed Vireo, Wood Thrush, Rose-breasted Grosbeak (*illustration* next page), and Scarlet Tanager on occasion. Sometimes Louisiana Waterthrush are heard singing along the brook. The Ovenbird lives in the woods, where you also might find a Great Horned Owl. A Belted Kingfisher or heron may show up at the pond.

Rose-breasted Grosbeak

6   Arcadia Wildlife Sanctuary

Closest Town: Easthampton/Northampton

Best Time To Visit: Spring, Fall, Winter

Method Of Birding: Trail Walking, Canoe, Car.

Birds Of Special Interest: Shorebirds (late summer), Upland and Spotted Sandpiper, Green Heron, Black and Yellow-crowned Night Heron (spring to summer), American Wigeon, Wood Duck (spring-summer), other Dabbling Ducks (breeding season-November), American Woodcock (April), Warblers (May), Song Birds (spring-summer), Screech Owl (spring), Feeder Birds (winter), Bobolink (June, July), Eastern Meadowlark (summer), Savannah Sparrow (summer to fall).

Advice/Rules: Visit the Center and talk with the staff. Watch the feeder for unexpected winter finch. Be sure to visit the grassland areas. No dogs allowed.

Situated along the Mill River and an old oxbow from the nearby Connecticut River, Arcadia Wildlife Sanctuary is a well-known birding site, wherein five miles of trails lead through a variety of habitats. Waterfowl have been the main attraction here, but now recently-protected farmland along the oxbow has been reclaimed into grassland, providing the expansion of such appropriate species as Savannah Sparrow and Bobolink. This sanctuary has grown well beyond the original 200 acres of marsh, field, and woodland that were acquired in 1944. The land was given by Professor Zachariah Chafee and Mrs. Bess Searle Chafee, as a memorial to honor their son Robert.

Today the sanctuary consists of 755 acres and supports a full staff. Sanctuary personnel offer a summer day-camp, guided tours, lectures, and after-school programs. The newly renovated conservation center enhances the educational experience of Arcadia. A large auditorium is the setting for many fascinating programs offered by local naturalists, scholars, and the friendly staff.

In the back of the Center there are thistle, sunflower, and suet feeders. Brightly colored American Goldfinch flash their brilliant gold and black feathers, and bold little chickadees swoop in and out with their close cousins, the Tufted Titmouse. The Black-capped Chickadees are rather approachable and can be coaxed onto your hand to steal a seed and fly away. You may want to give it a try before getting down to the serious business of bird finding.

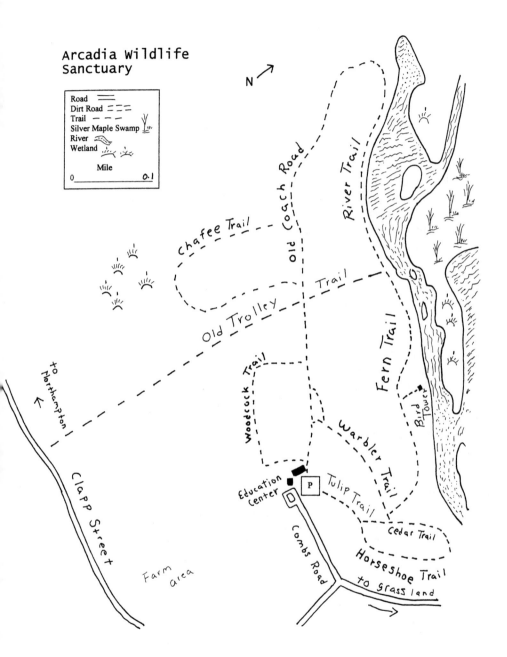

Arcadia Wildlife Sanctuary

Road
Dirt Road
Trail
Silver Maple Swamp
River
Wetland

Mile

0   0.1

N

Chafee Trail

Old (Coach) Road

River Trail

Old Trolley Trail

Fern Trail

to Northampton

Woodcock Trail

Warbler Trail

Bird Tower

Clapp Street

Education Center

P

Tulip Trail

Cedar Trail

Combs Road

Horseshoe Trail
to grassland

Farm area

Getting There

Take Exit 18 off I-91, and drive south on Route 5 for 1.3 miles. Turn right onto East Street and follow for 1.2 miles to Fort Hill Road. Turn right again for the sanctuary at 0.7 mile off this road. From the south, take Exit 17B and travel toward Easthampton over Mount Tom. Once over the mountain, take your first right onto East Street and follow this until the signs for Audubon Sanctuary.

Birding Arcadia Wildlife Sanctuary

In winter, look for uncommon species that frequently make at least a few appearances. These may include flocks of Hoary Redpolls (very rare), which were frequently seen in the winter of 2000. Others that may visit are Common Redpoll, Evening Grosbeak, and Pine Siskin. Red-breasted Nuthatches also show up from time to time. During Visitor Center hours you can view the feeder from inside, and one of the staff should be able to tell you what birds have been appearing lately.

Although walking the trails near the center is usually possible in winter, early spring is a better time to enjoy this part of the site. Climb the deck just past the feeder and walk along the new boardwalk. The boardwalk will bring you through a vernal pool, a temporary body of water created by the spring rains and melting snows.

There is much activity in a vernal pool that goes largely unnoticed. Beneath the melting ice, the vernal pool is teeming with life and continues to be that way well into the summer. Marbled salamanders, dragonflies, and ferry shrimp abound, along with tiger beetles, fingernail clams, and flatworms. Vernal pools also provide a breeding site for amphibians. The chorus of frogs is an experience not soon forgotten. Vernal pools are crucial recharge areas for future human water needs, as they filter and fill the aquifers underground.

The boardwalk is actually a part of the Woodcock Trail. This trail is short but worth the time because it takes you under a beautiful growth of mature white pines and over a carpet of needles. In early spring this quick walk can yield the sighting of a Brown Creeper. Brown Creepers are not particularly common and are often overlooked. Few people realize that this tiny bird can produce a song. Great Horned Owls have been said to frequent these pines, and they have been observed with young in spring. Sometimes Screech Owls are seen here. They are often found perched near a tree cavity or inside one. In the early hours, the Pileated Woodpecker can be spotted.

Warblers may turn up along the left side of the trail, where there is a ridge that drops down into a more foliated, deciduous grove. In just 0.5 mile, the trail joins the Old Coach Trail and returns back to the Center. Always check the skies above the Center's front yard for wayward Turkey Vultures, Bald Eagles, and common hawks. During migration times, be especially alert to this, as nearby Mount Tom and the expanse of open farmland in the area often create thermals. In the late summer dusk, expect to see migrating Night Hawks.

Some of the best birding Arcadia has to offer is found in the immediate vicinity of the Nature Center. Take the wood-chip-covered trail to the right of the Visitor Center (on the left if you are returning), until you see the sign for the Tulip Tree Trail. Follow this trail to the Horseshoe Trail. At that intersection is a network of short but wide accommodating paths. They are all good and will allow for sighting those birds who favor cover or edge woodland. Specifically, the Northern Cardinal is quite abundant here. Also seen here are Gray Catbirds, Common Yellowthroat, and Indigo Bunting.

In the fall and winter, White-throated Sparrows are common, as are Dark-eyed Juncos. In spring, migrant warblers include Yellow-rumped, Pine Warblers, and Yellow Warblers. Look for these also in other thickets and along the edges of open fields or near the Arcadia Marsh. Follow The Horseshoe Trail over to the old orchard for further inspection. Approaching quietly on a carpet of needles beneath the towering grove of white pines allows for more sightings of cover-loving species in this old orchard. Because there are apple-laden trees and thick brambles, several different kinds of these birds may possibly be seen. Under the apple trees, you can expect sometimes to encounter a Ruffed Grouse and a number of Cedar Waxwings. In winter, the old orchard is often filled with waxwings, an intricately colored bird that feeds on the fallen fruit.

To return, try looping back and going straight into The Cedar Trail. As its name implies, this trail has many cedar trees. To the right are woods and to the left beyond the cedars is a clearing with a new growth of sumac and other brushy vegetation. This trail will come out at the Tulip Tree Trail to bring you back to the Center. Along the way, Cedar Trail crosses The Warbler Trail, which heads up a small hill and follows a ridge along the Arcadia Marsh. There is a bench where you can sit and enjoy the view (in winter) across the marsh. Further on, the trail enters a pine woodland and leads into The Old Coach Trail.

The Old Coach Trail

The Old Coach Road Trail begins in front of the Nature Center and curves to the right, slipping behind the Center and up a small hill. You will soon enter an area dominated by white pine. These trees, like the ones on the Horseshoe Trail, are mature. But here they cover a larger piece of land and shelter a thick carpet of soft needles.

To the left is the Woodcock Trail and to the right a ridge and a drop down to the Fern Trail. In winter you can appreciate a view of Arcadia Marsh. At this point, the Warbler Trail climbs up from the thickets and away from the Cedar Trail and Old Orchard.

The Old Coach Road banks down beneath the pines and under a growth of hemlock to cross the Trolley Trail. A right here quickly connects you to the Fern Trail. This can be enjoyed as a loop circuit. A left on the Trolley Trail will bring you out to Clapp Street.

The Old Coach Road continues straight and enters deciduous woods. The trail extends far out into sanctuary land, eventually connecting to the River Trail before disintegrating. It crosses three streams and then exits Arcadia. Exploring two of these streams, Hitchcock Brook and its tributary, would be worthwhile.

Fern Trail

The Fern Trail starts in the western part of the sanctuary near the old orchard. Find the trailhead by walking along the Cedar Trail away from the Center and taking your second left. The Arcadia Marsh will be on the right, and an undulating ridge made up of several slopes will snake along the entire way on your left.

At the edge of the marsh, scan carefully for shorebirds, wading birds, and ducks. This marsh is unique in the Pioneer Valley for its tall grasses. Silver maple and buttonbush are also thriving, as they are typical in bottomlands. The water quality is good, and numerous mammals associated with wetlands go about their secret lives all along the way. Although bears are by no means common in this populated part of the state, they have been sighted here. Coyotes, on the other hand, are well-established and flourishing in this region. They enjoy the mix of agricultural land, wetland, and woods. Coyotes are transient; they move into a woodlot, take excess prey, and then move on to find better hunting. With the diversity of habitat at and near Arcadia, their presence is rather permanent.

Birding is good all along the trail, so keep alert from the very start. Common species are Red-bellied Woodpecker, White-breasted Nuthatch, Tufted Titmice, and Black-capped Chickadees. Out in the marsh, Mallards, Black Ducks, and Wood Ducks are common. Less common birds such as Mute Swans, Snow Geese, and Great Egret make Arcadia popular among the general nature enthusiasts. These birds are conspicuous to even the most untrained eye.

For the hidden treasures, try the observation tower on the right. In winter there may be a few Belted Kingfisher, and perhaps a brave Great Blue Heron (many fly south). In late February the marsh comes to life with the return of Red-winged Blackbirds, followed by Common Grackles.

Wintering Robins are seen here; they help to cheer the soul by their association with summer. By March they are numerous along the marsh. In the days to follow, birding becomes very exciting here, and the reclusive species begin to reveal themselves to the astute observer.

Frequenting the marsh in spring are Green-backed Herons, Black-crowned, and Yellow-crowned Night Herons, Northern Pintail, Blue-winged Teal, American Wigeon, Hooded Mergansers, Greater and Lesser Yellowlegs, and Osprey. Continue walking along the marsh under the canopy of shagbark hickory, black birch, and maple. During mid-April and all of May, hundreds of neotropical migrants are working their way along the river. The expansive marsh and oxbow flood plain lure these migrants down into Arcadia.

Throughout the breeding season, look for Rose-breasted Grosbeaks, Eastern Phoebes, and Red-eyed Vireos moving about the upper canopy. The Eastern Phoebe is a favorite bird among visitors; it is commonly seen along this trail. About 0.2 mile from the observation tower, there is a bench beside a hemlock. A variety of ferns grow here, and a few baneberry show their poisonous white fruit. At the intersection of the Trolley Line Trail, there is a gully, and across the marsh an old cement foundation where the trolley once crossed the water. This is a nice spot to slow down and enjoy the sun while checking the muddy banks of the Mill River for mammal tracks. Mink, weasel, and otter have been observed slipping in and out of the cover that lines the shoreline. The Mill River runs through and supplies the marsh before flowing into the Oxbow.

The Fern Trail ends after crossing the Trolley Line Trail. It now becomes the River Trail. Five hundred feet along this trail, there is a small stream. Cross the stream on the little footbridge and note the blue blaze on the big oak tree to the left. This blue-blazed trail enters a part of the sanctuary land that is all deciduous. In the fall, look for Wild Turkey feeding on red oak acorns. Sometimes the layer of acorns becomes so deep it makes for tricky walking.

Wild Turkey love woodlands that have a variety of habitat, and they find Arcadia's wetlands particularly attractive in the late winter. In 1991, there was one individual turkey that was fond of the children at the nursery school. This particular bird chased children across the Center's front yard, so it had to be relocated.

Five hundred feet further on, the trail splits; taking a left will lead back to the Old Coach Trail. Go further for just a few feet and look for Northern and Louisiana Waterthrush (in migration) at another stream. Return by way of the Old Coach Road or backtrack and increase the odds of seeing more water birds. This point is approximately 1.3 miles from the Nature Center.

Old Springfield Road And Grasslands

Grassland habitat was once common in New England, but has rapidly declined, resulting in the disappearance of many grassland-dependent species. The Vesper Sparrow and the Upland Sandpiper have been most affected. Other species of plants and insects associated with the grasslands have also declined. The regal firtillary (a butterfly) is one example. Needless to say, the grasslands at Arcadia are a birder's dream. The Massachusetts Audubon Society is restoring about 300 acres of former cropland here. Native grass species planted here include broom sedge, wild rye, switch grass, deer tongue, and purple top. They require late season mowing, in contrast to many of the region's fields containing European grasses that grow early.

Old Springfield Road can be found by taking a left out of Combs Road while leaving the sanctuary. Cross over the Mill River on the metal bridge and begin birding.

In summer there will be a decent number of Bobolink. The song of this grassland species makes a walk along Old Springfield Road a special delight. The success rate of nesting Bobolinks was doubled by postponing the cutting of grasses until after July 15. Bobolinks are probably the more conspicuous nesters here. Eastern Meadowlarks may be easy to spot, too. Meadowlarks are not presently nesting here, but have in years past.

Presenting a more serious challenge to find will be Savannah and Grasshopper Sparrows, which at a distance seem similar. Only the Savannah Sparrow nests. They are numerous throughout the open spaces along the oxbow flood plain. In the fall, there can be hundreds of these birds hiding in the grasses and weeds. Many at the sanctuary consider this bird to be their own specialty; although Savannah Sparrows are found elsewhere, Arcadia is probably the best place to find them, due to their sheer numbers and easy proximity to a road. Upland Sandpipers are unique, but may be confused with Common Snipe. Look for the Upland Sandpiper during fall migration. Spotted Sandpipers are found nesting most years.

This road stretches 1.0 mile, paralleling the oxbow which is about 300 feet to the right. At 0.3 mile on the left, access to other fields is possible along a dirt road hedged with thickets and grapevine tangles. Grassland species can also be plentiful here; Bobolink, Eastern Meadowlark, Savannah, and even Vesper Sparrows can be expected. The Lincoln's Sparrow is usually reported sometime in the fall. Also check for Sharp-tailed Sparrow in the weedy patches. There are no reports of Henslow's Sparrow, which has become extremely rare. The last Henslow's Sparrow nesting in the state occurred in 1995.

The open fields and shrubby thickets attract many birds that are not considered grassland species. These include Indigo Buntings, Brown Thrasher (rarely), Field, Chipping, and Song Sparrows. In the middle of this composite of fields and shrub, there is a slight chance of seeing Arcadia's prized Glossy Ibis. Look in the wet depression known fondly as the Ibis Pool.

Warblers associated with the open fields and brushy cover are well represented here during their peak migration time from late April to late May. The Prairie Warbler is a nice find and surprisingly, rather reliable. It is seen here in the fall as well. Blue-winged and Golden-winged Warblers have been recorded, and in the shrubs along the edges, there are Yellow-rumped Warblers and the American Redstart. The Common Yellowthroat can be seen, too. Eastern Kingbirds are to be expected, as are a few Kestrels, which probably breed here. The Black-billed Cuckoo is eagerly sought, a challenge even for the most ambitious birder.

Larger birds that are a part of this habitat include Northern Harrier and American Woodcock (*illustration* previous page). Both are seen regularly. The Northern Harriers are exciting to observe. They are under-appreciated hunters, with a variety of skills at their disposal. They can take small passerines in flight or hover-hunt and ambush. The Woodcock arrives early in April and can be heard performing its courtship display or "sky dance" throughout the early spring at dusk. Look at the far side of the field -- on the left as you drive away from the Nature Center.

Short-eared Owls are a possibility in winter. They are a pleasant sight during the dark, cold days of January and February. In 1999 and 2000, two Short-eared Owls wintered in this vicinity. The Horned Lark is another occasional visitor in winter. Horned Larks love snow-covered weedy fields with windswept, exposed patches where the tops of stubble grass poke up in the snow. The Snow Bunting is much sought after, with a reputation for frequenting the Arcadia grasslands and hay fields. Observers in some winters have witnessed sizable flocks. Look for Dark-eyed Junco, White-throated Sparrows, White-crowned Sparrow, and American Tree Sparrows in open areas free of snow near snags (branches-blowdowns). The White-crowned Sparrow is considerably less likely to be seen than the other common wintering birds.

At this site, the future looks bright for the acquisition of more open land that can be converted into native grasslands. Massachusetts Audubon will continue to convert land and expand the sanctuary as long as it receives support. Perhaps someday the Henslow's Sparrow, Grasshopper Sparrow, Vesper Sparrow, Northern Harrier, and Eastern Meadowlark will raise their young among the native New England grasses at Arcadia.

7   East Meadow

Closest Town: Northampton

Best Time To Visit: Spring, Late Summer, Fall.

Method Of Birding: Road Walking, Car.

Birds Of Special Interest: Shorebirds, plovers and sandpipers, (late Summer), Ducks, Hooded and Common Merganser, Common Goldeneye (November), Warblers (May), Savannah Sparrow, Field Sparrow (spring to fall), Fish Crow (variable).

Advice/Rules: Use your car to watch shorebirds and ducks, but walk the roads for fall sparrows. Respect crops and farm property.

East Meadow, also called the Northampton Meadows, stretches along the banks of the Connecticut River and is well known for grassland species and shorebirds. It is adjacent to the oxbow and not far from Arcadia Wildlife Sanctuary. Unlike Arcadia, East Meadow is not a true grasslands, but it attracts some of the same species. Most of the acreage here is planted in corn, which, following the harvest in the fall, provides cover and food. In between these fields there are attractive hedge-rows of wild flowers and wayside weeds, sheltered beneath 20-foot high sumac trees.

Giant cottonwoods and forked-trunked silver maples add an aesthetic charm to the vastness of this sprawling flatland, while beyond them on the opposite side of the riverbank, the summits of the Holyoke Range rise up. Standing at the bank of the Connecticut River beneath these impressive trees, you can clearly see the division of Holyoke Range -- Mount Holyoke on the east side of the river and Mount Tom on the west.

Here in East Meadow, the land is flat and mostly open. Birders come from all over the Pioneer Valley to find the grassland species they might have missed at Arcadia. In late summer, shorebirds are of interest, and in winter, birders hope for rare visitors such as Snowy Owls, Short-eared Owls and Northern Shrike. Probably the best time to visit this site is late summer and fall. As mentioned, winter is well worth a trip, and spring can be productive, too.

Northampton's

East Meadow

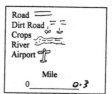

Road
Dirt Road
Crops
River
Airport

Mile
0 _____ 0.3

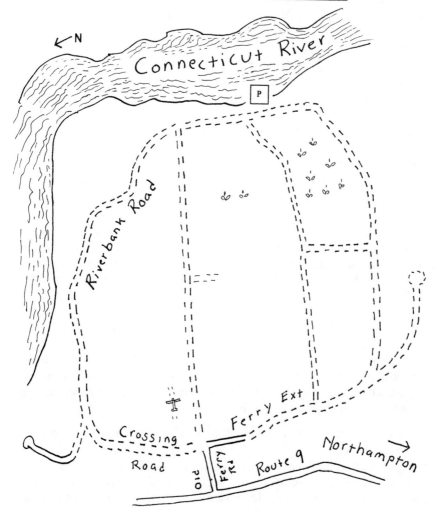

N

Connecticut River

P

Riverbank Road

Ferry Ext

Crossing

Road

Pio

Ferry Rd

Route 9

Northampton

Getting There

Coming from the south on I-91, take exit 19, turn left on Route 9 west (toward the center of Northampton), and go 0.4 mile. Just past a recreation field on the left, turn left onto Old Ferry Road. Go about 0.4 mile through an intersection with Crosspath Road. Continue straight ahead, passing LaFleur Airport on your left and the Tri-County Fairgrounds on your right.

Birding East Meadow

Just past the airport, where the road becomes dirt, begin looking for Killdeer on the right. Killdeer are not uncommon; they are sometimes joined by Semi-palmated and Black-bellied Plover in late August. Just a few tenths of a mile past the airplane hangers on your left, there begins a weedy hedge-row where numerous sparrows are finding cover. Before getting too close, park your car and walk up along the weeds, checking for shy sparrows before they flush out and fly across the field. If it is summer, expect to find Field, Chipping, and Tree Sparrows. Savannah Sparrows are usually found in the summer, but Vesper and White-crowned Sparrows are uncommon. They are more likely in the fall, when Lincoln's Sparrows pass through with many others, and the whole business of sparrow watching becomes a real challenge.

At 0.9 mile from the airfield, flocks of Snow Buntings can be seen (November to January) on the ground or dispatched in flight. A short distance further (1.1 miles from the airfield), a road enters at your right, but continue going straight for another 0.7 mile until you reach a T in the road -- turn right here and proceed along the banks of the Connecticut River (which is on your left). When you have traveled 2.0 miles, there will be ample room for pulling over to the left and examining the shoreline that begins just beyond a short drop. This is where you can find a good view of the opposite shoreline, which frequently harbors shorebirds in late summer and early fall. Birds to be expected are: Solitary, Least, Semipalmated, Pectoral, Stilt and White-rumped Sandpipers. In years when the river's water level is low, the exposed sand can yield more of the same birds or some rare sights. Such rarities include Ruddy Turnstones and Black-bellied Plovers. In the river itself, a wide variety of waterfowl or gulls may be seen, depending on the time of year.

Gulls that have been seen include the Black-backed and Lesser Black-backed. In winter, common Ring-billed Gulls and Herring Gulls are sometimes found along the melt waters. Numerous ducks will be resting during spring migration. These may include (but are not limited to) Common Goldeneye, Common and Hooded Mergansers. From here, leave your locked car, and walk to where the dirt track turns right, but go straight, slipping behind the brush and an island of trees. Before you is yet more open space -- some of it grassy and some of it in cultivation. Meander back here, checking carefully for the occasional nesting Indigo Bunting, and circle around the island of trees back to your car.

Eastern Meadowlark

Indigo Buntings are among the most site-faithful of all perching birds. They will return to breed at the same site each year, even when the site has changed physically from succession. Thus, they are often seen in atypical places where weedy fields and shrubs have turned woody. If you find an Indigo Bunting singing in the spring, be sure to spend some time listening to it and others in the area. Each male has a unique beginning to his song, and each cluster of buntings has their own singing dialect.

Back in the car, drive up a short embankment to where you can see a red barn off to the left, and slowly proceed onto your first right. Continue on this road until you must turn left or right. Go right and back to the road that parallels the river. Now take a left back the way you came in. Soon you will pass the road you arrived on from the airport on your left. Proceed along the far edge of the field and head up to the airport which will now be on your left. All along this road, you should be carefully checking the open field in fall and winter. In spring, your attention will be in the other direction.

In spring, the trees that line the river bank are often filled with migrating warblers. From April until June, the warblers frequent these trees, but the bulk of them will pass through in mid-May. Most common are Yellow-rumped, Yellow, American Redstart, and Black-and-white Warbler. You can count on seeing the Yellow Warbler during the breeding season.

Once past the airport, turn left to get back where you came in. If you turn right, you will travel along the river for about 0.2 mile and will eventually have to turn around. Sometimes, such short detours can produce unexpected sightings. At the very least, this turn will allow for another view of the river where the current is stronger. Canada and Snow Goose are possible. Sometimes these geese are also found feeding in the cornfields. The Snow Goose is an uncommon-to-rare visitor, while the Canada Goose can be assumed. Other birds besides waterfowl, shore, and grassland species are found here as well.

These weedy cornfields often set the stage for exciting finds during the fall migration. Numerous species have been recorded by local birders, who have popularized the site. Since much of the land produces weedy tangles, there are healthy numbers of American Goldfinch and Tree Sparrows. Sumac attract robins and other wintering berry-dependent birds. Bluebirds cannot be ruled out, nor can the retiring Wood Thrush.

Presently, there are no serious concentrations of crows, but the cornfields and surrounding environs will eventually attract a regular flock for overnight roosting. Tall trees make the site a good candidate for communal roosts. The Connecticut River is a popular roosting site all along its course. The Fish Crow, a newcomer to the Northampton region, is now established. Look for them along the river and identify them from the common American Crow by their more nasal call.

8   Wildwood and Orchard Hill

Closest Town: Amherst

Best Time To Visit: Spring, Fall.

Method Of Birding: Walking Trails or Dirt Road, some viewing from Car.

Birds Of Special Interest: Warblers, Cape May Warbler, Chestnut-sided Warbler (April to June), Willow and Yellow-bellied Flycatchers (May only).

Advice/Rules: Arrive early in the morning and use the Audubon Bird Call. Birders are allowed here, but must exhibit respectful behavior at Wildwood.

Wildwood

The Wildwood complex of Amherst has been a popular birding site for many decades because it is easily accessible and has a variety of plant life that attracts migrants. The complex consists of open lawns, shrubs, woodlands, field, brushy meadows, a pond, and large shade trees. In the heart of the Amherst suburban area, this site offers local birders a quick fix for their birding urges. In summer, common garden birds and colorful songbirds are abundant. The "old timers" know about Wildwood's history of yielding some exciting rarities, including many warbler species and a rare flycatcher. In the 1980s, an unusual visitor turned out to be a Mississippi Kite!

Getting There

Heading north from the center of Amherst, drive on East Pleasant Street for about 1.0 mile, and turn right on Strong Street. You will find the entrance to Wildwood Cemetery on your left. You may also enter at the Wildwood Complex Entrance or Conservation Area off of Village Park, which is further north on East Pleasant Street.

Birding Wildwood

Much of the complex consists of the Wildwood Cemetery and needs little in the way of orientation because small roads criss-cross the entire place and are self-evident. Behind the cemetery there are several acres of woodland that gently slope down toward Brown Field. At the back of the Cemetery, where there is a slight incline and a road turns to the right, an easily distinguished trail enters the woods. From here it is a walk of about 900 feet to the edge of Brown Field. Immediately before Brown Field, a trail can be found branching off to the right.

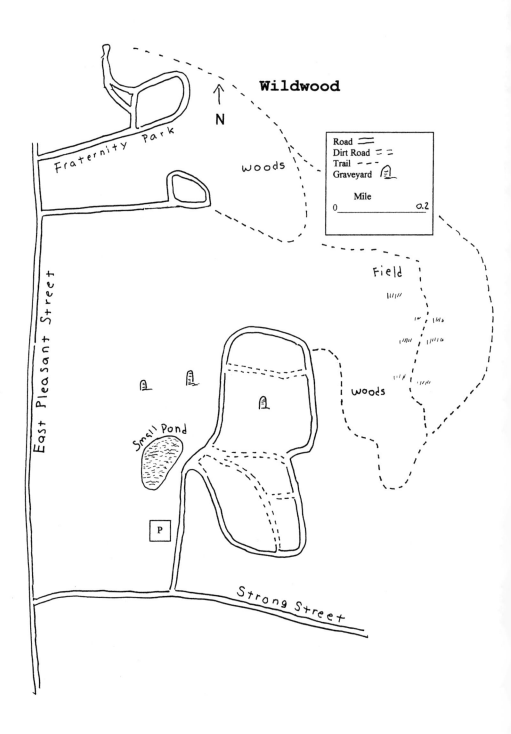

Wildwood

Woods

N

Fraternity Park

Road
Dirt Road
Trail
Graveyard

Mile
0   0.2

Field

Woods

East Pleasant Street

Small Pond

P

Strong Street

This trail (to the right) is recommended. (You may explore Brown field on the way back.) Turning right will take you through some dense brushy areas and back behind some shrubs. After completing a semi-circle around the field, take a sharp left and walk back across the grass. There are trails which head down to the railroad tracks halfway around the circle (on your right). You can also continue up the hill away from the field and come out at Fraternity Sorority Park while traveling through some deciduous woods mixed with pine. However, backtracking will be necessary, unless you wish to walk through town along East Pleasant back to the Cemetery.

Cemetery

This is a great place for beginners to "test their wings." During the spring migration, the birds can be seen flying from tree to tree without effort. Warblers are especially noticeable, flitting from shrubs or among the shade trees. There is also a good representation of common yard birds.

At the entrance to the park, large conifers often attract Black-throated Green Warblers and Cape May Warblers during their migration in May. Another good spot is near the caretaker's house and along the shrubs near the pond. Yellow-rumped and Yellow Warblers are regulars in the cemetery, starting in late April and departing in late May. One of the most celebrated warbler sightings was a Kentucky Warbler. However, Cerulean, Golden-winged, and Hooded Warblers have also been seen. These three species are more likely to be encountered along the perimeter of Brown Field.

Woodland and Brown Field

The Blue-winged Warbler is a fairly reliable species that can be found opposite the rail tracks. It may appear with the reasonably common Chestnut-sided Warbler. The birding is not limited to warblers -- the woods and open sections east of the cemetery have long been known for Yellow-bellied Flycatchers in late May. Some of the more interesting breeding birds in this section include Eastern Bluebird, Field Sparrow, Tree Swallow, Eastern Towhee, Ruby-throated Hummingbird, Wood Thrush, Great Crested Flycatcher, Red-eyed and White-eyed Vireo, Yellow, Blue-winged, and Chestnut-sided Warblers.

Throughout the woods, there will be Eastern Wood-Pewee, Scarlet Tanager (sometimes), Rose-breasted Grosbeak, Northern Cardinal, Eastern Screech Owl, and Great Horned Owl. In the winter, there are bands of Black-capped Chickadees, Tufted Titmice, American Robins, Hairy and Downy Woodpeckers and White-breasted Nuthatches. Red-bellied Woodpeckers are seen on occasion. An area called Gulliver Meadow can be visited before leaving (on Strong Street). This is a productive site throughout the year.

Orchard Hill

At the edge of the University of Massachusetts campus is a small area known as Orchard Hill. Appropriately, it was named after the apple orchard that once thrived here. Later it became the home of several horses; but now it just remains unto itself as a quiet corner on a hill away from the hustle and bustle of the University. The Orchard Hill Dormitories can be seen at the far top of the hill, and an old observatory is apparent as well. Popular among student birders, the Orchard Hill site is underestimated for its number and variety of spring warblers. It has remained an open and shrubby habitat consistent with an orchard, where multiflora rose, alder, and berry brambles meander freely.

Getting There

From Amherst center, go north on East Pleasant Street to the corner of Eastman Lane. Orchard Hill is on the left and borders East Pleasant Street. Park on the side of Eastman Lane (to the left facing down hill). UMass buses travel to the dormitories at the southwest corner of the orchard. Trails extend from there and Eastman Lane.

Birding Orchard Hill

No less than 100 species have been observed over the years at Orchard Hill. The scattered woods and open, orchard-like setting seem especially attractive to warblers, but many other species contribute to this impressive number, which is unusual for such a small hilltop. Common species of warblers found here are Yellow-rumped, Yellow, Pine, and Chestnut-sided. The wooded edges often produce Black-throated Green, Bay-breasted, American Redstart and Black-throated Blue Warblers on May mornings. The Cape May Warbler is a good find for the novice, and they are somewhat reliable at the orchard. They can be very specific, often staying close to conifers.

Common and easily identifiable birds are available here. Look for Northern Cardinal, Song Sparrows, and mockingbirds. The Northern Mockingbird is especially noticeable. These winter-sensitive birds feed on multiflora rose. The Brown Thrasher, a rare bird favoring dense thickets, is a possibility. They may even nest here. A small pond attracts nesting Mallards, but has also provided a niche for Swamp Sparrows. In addition, the Willow Flycatcher breeds along the pond, and American Woodcock are heard in the still of the fading light on cool April evenings. Although a wide variety of species can be found on those special spring days when waves of migrants settle down, the average birder will be delighted with Indigo Buntings, Carolina Wrens, and the aforementioned songbirds. An Eastern Bluebird may visit and, when nesting boxes are provided, they will breed here, too.

Baltimore Oriole

9 More Great Birding Sites near Amherst

Puffer's Pond

Habitat

Woodland: hardwoods, hemlock grove, some shrubby areas.
River: Millers River, some swift moving sections, shallows.
Pond: large pond surrounded by trees, small bathing beach.

Seasons/ Birds

Fall: waterfowl, migrating songbirds.
Winter: owls
Spring: migrating warblers, songbirds, few herons.
Summer: thrush, nesting songbirds, woodland species nesting.

Description:

This is a very popular and busy swimming spot. However, in the early morning when birding is best, it is peaceful here. This stream- and spring-fed pond is adjacent to town conservation land, and it abounds with birdlife. A well-maintained trail meanders along the river beneath hemlocks and hardwoods.

Getting There

From Amherst center, head north on East Pleasant Street. You will come to a T-crossing; turn left here onto Pine Street. Take an immediate right onto Sand Hill Road, then a right onto State Street at the bottom of a hill. Look for the Robert Frost Trail before the Pond and across from the dam.

Birding Specifics:

This is the best place for birders to observe the Louisiana Waterthrush. Look for it across the street (State Street) from the pond, where the river borders the white apartment complex (Mill Hollow). There is a trail that will take you along the river. Look for the entrance and car parking off of State Street. Louisiana Waterthrush sing loudly from branches that overhang the river. They may also be seen along the river's edge flirting with the passing water. In May, wood warblers, such as the Yellow-rumped Warbler, are frequently seen.

The pond may attract a few geese in the fall, but birders usually check the pond for Northern Pintail, Green-winged Teal, Black Duck, and American Wigeon. You can always expect to see a few Mallards. Sometimes, however, sea gulls show up here. Occasionally, a rare one may be spotted. In the summer, even with the crowds, Great Blue Heron are spotted at the far corner of the pond across form the beach. In the winter there are Golden-crowned Kinglets moving about the hemlocks. In the Conservation lands, there are Barred Owls along the streams, and Eastern Screech Owls are heard at night later on in the season.

Amherst Center

Habitat

Lawn: town green
Park Trees: variety of trees planted, spruce.
City Structures: chimneys.

Seasons/Birds

Fall: goatsuckers, songbirds
Winter: transients
Spring: migrating songbirds
Summer: swifts, songbirds

Description:

This is a town common, but more closely resembles a downtown area with some shade trees. Birders will enjoy the unique shops and restaurants.

Getting There

From Exit 19 off of I-91, follow Route 9 east to the center of Amherst.

Birding Specifics:

In the late summer, this is good spot to see dozens of Night Hawks migrating in the evening sky. In the winter, it is fairly quiet, but sometimes rare transients turn up. This is especially true on the evergreens during flight years. In the spring, a few warblers will appear, and a variety of songbirds filter through. The main attraction, however, are the dozens of Chimney Swifts streaking across the horizon.

Worm-eating Warbler

Mount Sugarloaf

Habitat

Woodland: oak woods, some northern hardwood elements.
Hilltop: traprock cliffs

Season/Birds

Fall: some hawk activity, migrating valley neotropicals.
Winter: wintering regulars, feeder birds.
Spring: migrating hawks and neotropicals.
Summer: warblers, passerines.

Description:

This site provides a wonderful view of the Deerfield River Valley. The hill is cloaked in oaks and has steep cliffs. An auto road takes you to the summit.

Getting There

From Sunderland center, take Route 116 west. Go across the river to Deerfield, and take your second right to the Mount Sugarloaf entrance.

Birding Specifics:

While there are several fall hawk watching sites, Mount Sugarloaf is one of the few decent spring sites. The view from the hill faces south and hawks can be seen on their way north. A wide variety of these birds are enjoyed. Broad-winged Hawks are common, as are Sharp-shinned, Red-tailed, Kestrel, and Northern Goshawk. Many others have been reported. Mount Sugarloaf has also been known as a breeding site for Worm-eating Warblers (*illustration*). A few Rose-breasted Grosbeaks have been seen here during the breeding season. The Wood Thrush can be heard on June evenings. The Eastern Phoebe shows up every spring for a few days, but probably does not nest.

Mount Sugarloaf

Norwottuck Rail Trail

Habitat

Fields: grassy and weedy waysides, agriculture.
Woodland: mixed woods, some spruce.
River: Connecticut River, wetlands.

Seasons/Birds

Fall: migrating warbler and sparrows, waterfowl, shorebirds.
Winter: owls, sparrows
Spring: neotropical migrants, waterfowl.
Summer: rails, larks, sparrows, shorebirds, hawks, herons.

Description:

This is a 9-mile-long rail-trail that travels through a variety of excellent birding habitat. Although there are several places to access the trail, the official entrance is on the western bank of the Connecticut River, allowing for excellent viewing of the river in all directions. Before the trail crosses under Route 9, you will pass through some shrubby and weedy sections. The trail continues through flat, generally open fields and brushy areas until it approaches the Amherst College Woodlands. You will find some spruce here. Past this, there are more woods and some wetlands. There is also a powerline cut to cross.

Getting There

From I-91 going north, take Exit 19 and proceed straight across Route 9 onto Damon Road. The beginning of the rail-trail is immediately on the right, where there is parking. The rail-trail may also be entered from places further east along Route 9, across the river. There are entrances behind the Malls on Route 9 (on the right, near Bread & Circus, Wal-Mart, or the cinemas), where there is ample parking. Another entrance is near Amherst center, off of Snell Street.

Birding Specifics:

The beginning of the trail is a great place to view the waterfowl and shorebirds along the Connecticut River. Red-necked Grebe, Snow Goose (uncommon), mergansers, dabbling ducks, Great Blue Heron, and Great Egret are sought for during spring through fall. In the fall migration for shorebirds and wading species (late August), there are a wide variety of exciting sightings. Be on the look-out for some of the rare ones while scanning for the regulars such as Semipalmated and Least Sandpipers. Spotted Sandpipers are likely as well.

In the fields alongside the rail-trail, such favorites as Bobolink, Eastern Meadow Lark, and sometimes Vesper Sparrows are seen. American Kestrels are more obvious as they are observed perched on wires. The White-crowned Sparrow can be somewhat common along the wooded-to-brushy section near the fields. This is a good site for finding them.

At the end of the trail where there are some wetlands, look for the Virginia Rail. Listen for Song Sparrows and American Woodcock in the spring. The Red-tailed Hawk is often heard calling out a hundred or more feet above its territory.

Mount Toby

Habitat

Woodland: mixed woods, extensive forest with elevation.
Pond: some wetlands, streams, small falls, large pond

Seasons/Birds

Fall: migrating warblers, thrush, vireos, hawks, waterfowl.
Winter: owls, sparrows
Spring: neotropical migrants, waterfowl.
Summer: nesting songbirds, few warblers, hawks, herons, waterfowl.

Description:

This is an extensive and deep woodland. There are streams, small waterfalls, and a region of steep cliffs. The University of Massachusetts has performed some instructional management of the woodland. There are clear-cuts and small clearings. The adjacent farmland provides variety at this site. A good part of the mountain is privately owned, and permission is granted for the Robert Frost Trail right-of-way. The University of Massachusetts, in conjunction with the state Fish and Game Department, manage the remainder. Cranberry Pond has an undeveloped shoreline.

Getting There

From the Amherst area, go north on Route 63 out of North Amherst for 3.0 miles, and take a left on Bull Hill Road. Travel Bull Hill a short ways to the Robert Frost Trail on the north side of Bull Hill Road (look for pull-over). To get to Cranberry Pond or the north end, continue on Route 63, turn left just past the town line marker onto Reservation Road. Find the pond on your left, and then the trail/service road where there is some parking another 0.5 mile on left.

American Redstart

Birding Specifics:

Although a trail leads to the summit, most birders are content with exploring the roads and shoreline areas. However, if you have the time and do not mind an invigorating hike, Mount Toby should be explored more closely. A journey through the woodland on an early June morning will provide at least one memorable bird experience. It may be an encounter with the tiny Ovenbird or a visit from the higher canopy by a Scarlet Tanager. Ovenbirds and tanagers both prefer unbroken woodlands where they remain somewhat reclusive. Add to this experience the remote and wild calls of a Northern Raven and the drumming of the Yellow-bellied Sapsucker, and you may think that you are in the Green Mountains of Vermont.

Listen for Winter Wren in clearings adjacent to hemlock stands. Anticipate Hermit Thrush, Veery, Wood Thrush, Pileated Woodpecker, Hairy Woodpecker, Black-throated Green Warblers, and Ruffed Grouse. Two kinds of hawks are common -- Red-tailed and Sharp-shinned. The Goshawk is seen from time to time, and occasionally, a Broad-winged Hawk.

Along the roads there are Arcadian Flycatcher, Eastern Wood-Pewee, Eastern Screech, and Great Horned Owls. There are Red-eyed and Blue-headed Vireo. Wild Turkey are sometimes flushed out, while the Ruby-throated Hummingbird goes about its business searching for nectar. Blue-gray Gnatcatchers are found in the brushy areas, along with an infrequent sighting of a Prairie or Black-throated Blue Warbler. The Chestnut-sided, Black-and-white, Nashville, and American Redstart Warbler (*illustration*) have all been observed nesting at different locations throughout the mountain.

Check Cranberry Pond for dabbling ducks. In the summer, expect Mallards and Black Ducks, but in the early spring and mid-fall, be alert to some interesting finds like Northern Pintail, Common Merganser, Wood Ducks, Pied-billed Grebe, and Common Goldeneye. If you see movement along the shores, scope them out for sandpipers.

10   Quabbin Park

Closest Town: Belchertown

Best Time To visit: Spring, Winter.

Method Of Birding: Walking on Trails and Paved Road, Car.

Birds Of Special Interest: Diving and Dabbling Ducks (November, April), Bald Eagles (January- early March), Golden Eagle (January, February), Northern Raven (April), Cerulean Warbler (May to July), Swallows (summer).

Advice/Rules: February is best for Bald Eagles. Ask questions at the Visitor Center. Cars or motorcycles are not allowed to cross over the dam.

The creation of the Quabbin Reservoir established a unique, wildlife-rich woodland in the heart of Massachusetts. This man-made, semi-wilderness covers 125 square miles. A massive dam was constructed across the Swift River, flooding the valley behind it to provide drinking water for the eastern part of the state. The dam was completed in 1939, and the reservoir was filled to capacity by 1945. The Quabbin is one of the larger reservoirs in the world that were created exclusively for drinking water; it holds over 400 billion gallons of water.

Throughout most of the past decades, Quabbin forestland has been hailed as some of the best managed in the Northeast. Selective cutting and logging has helped create open meadows and sun-dappled glades. The forest is diverse and contains habitats for an impressive number of both transient and nesting birds. Some 55,000 acres of woodland protect the water supply and house many species of mammals.

The Quabbin is under the strict control of Boston's Metropolitan District Commission (MDC). Over the years, some restrictions have been relaxed, and public use has increased, along with the appreciation and respect for this unique site. (Note, however, that some regulations and their enforcement have become more restrictive since the 9-11 event.) Today, the surrounding forest and the reservoir itself are used for a variety of passive recreational activities, including hiking,, biking, birding, and photography, but be sure to check the posted rules. (One rather nonsensical regulation is that skiing is not allowed.) Fishing is allowed, but the use of large motors is prohibited. In the 1990s, when deer overpopulation was negatively impacting the forest, a restricted hunt was implemented.

With its immense forest and the surrounding contiguous woodland preserves, the Quabbin offers a wide choice of birding. Birders can find everything from shorebirds to upland game species. There is a healthy population of Bald Eagles and a growing one of Common Loons. Small owls, many birds of arctic origin, and Great Blue Herons, which nest here, are reminders that the name "Quabbin" means "the land of many waters."

But birds and deer are not the only important residents of Quabbin. Black bear roam these woods, along with large carnivores, such as the bobcat and eastern coyote. Fishers, which are large members of the weasel family, are plentiful. They feed on squirrels and other small rodents. At one time, the fisher was extirpated in Massachusetts, but has since been reintroduced from the north.

Beavers are numerous here, and their activities work well with the watershed. They have created countless ponds and bogs throughout the Quabbin region, which in turn are inhabited by moose. The moose has made a steady comeback. Originally there was a modest population in Maine, but eventually these enormous herbivores worked their way west into New Hampshire and its Connecticut Lakes regions, then southwest through Vermont. Others traveled south via the White Mountains into the Monadnock Region, where they began to prosper and slowly populate the Quabbin. This appearance of moose has been both anticipated and appreciated. And while they can be found nearly everywhere, the most frequent sightings are on the reservoir's western side -- along Route 202.

Deep within the Quabbin is a peninsula of some 10,000 acres. Although this area would likely offer great birding, it is kept off-limits for exploration. Approximately 14,000 acres of Quabbin forest is never visited by the public. The Prescott Peninsula and all of the islands in the reservoir are set aside to remain in their natural state, so that wildlife can flourish and remain undisturbed by humans. Perhaps it is the mystery of this special acreage that gives Quabbin that feeling of enchantment.

The area referred to as Quabbin Park includes the Visitor Center, the Winsor Dam, the Quabbin Lookout Tower, and Enfield Lookout. The Quabbin Park area is located at the southern end of the reservoir. This is the Quabbin that most people refer to when they speak of the reservoir. Unfortunately, it is the least wild. Many people are simply not aware of the many access gates and the additional miles of hiking and birding available to them beyond Quabbin Park.

Nevertheless, beauty is everywhere. At Quabbin Park, there are wide-open lawns and spectacular views of the reservoir and its surrounding forest. From this grand perspective, you can appreciate the greatness of the Quabbin, with its vast waters and forested hills.

Quabbin Park

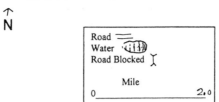

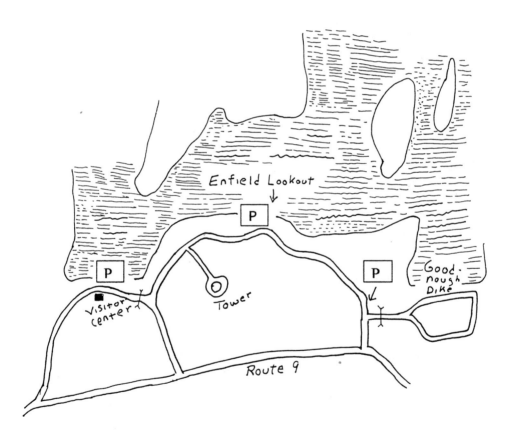

Getting There

From the Massachusetts Turnpike, take Exit 8, and travel north on Route 32 and then west on Route 9 to Quabbin Park on the right. Route 2 will intersect Route 9. For the Quabbin Park and Visitor Center, go west on Route 9 for the entrance on the right. From Amherst, follow Route 9 east for 12.0 miles to the Quabbin Park entrance on the left. From Ludlow, travel on Route 21 heading north until the junction of Routes 202 and 9. Travel west on Route 9 for the same entrance on the right.

Quabbin Park and Winsor Dam

This is a popular site for observing American Bald Eagles. However, there are other species worth visiting the site for -- Wild Turkey, Northern Raven, and the Quabbin's specialty, nesting Cerulean Warblers. Sometimes Northern Shrike can be found along the roads, and Worm-eating Warblers are seen occasionaly along Administration Road near the turn up to the Quabbin Tower.

From the entrance on Route 9, drive along the Administration Road and park next to the Visitor Center. The center is open all week from 9:00 a.m. to 4:00 p.m. (5 p.m. weekends) A volunteer is available to provide information or answer questions. This is where you can gather information about the greater Quabbin, address your concerns about the area with the professionals, and plan your visit and subsequent visits with the best resources available. All are important because of the vast size of the birding site.

You can start birding across the street from the Administration Buildings and Visitor Center. From here, there is an impressive view of the water where you may spot some feeding waterfowl. Fall is usually the most productive time for these species. September brings in a few Common Loon, and then it picks up with Horned Grebe, Ring-necked Duck, Scoter and Bufflehead. Common and Hooded Mergansers are frequently present at some point in November. Later on, you might catch a flock of Snow Geese or even on very rare occasions, a Tundra Swan.

From the Visitor Center, you may continue walking in the same direction and follow the signs across the Winsor Dam. The Enfield Lookout can otherwise be reached by passing over the dam and taking your first left toward Quabbin Hill Road, which you will later pass on your right. For years, cars were allowed across the dam, but because of tightened security established in 2001, only bicycles and foot traffic are now permitted.

If you are not inclined to walk the long distance across the dam and up to the rotary and over to the Enfield Lookout and Quabbin Hill, you can reach these sights by driving back out to Route 9 and turning left. Drive a short distance down Route 9 and turn left into the Quabbin Park or go further to the other end of Administration Road (the second left).

You will be able to drive directly to the Enfield Lookout. This is where the Bald Eagles are. Sometimes Golden Eagles may be seen here, too. Take advantage of this opportunity. Golden Eagles will not present themselves in Massachusetts at any other time or place, such as they do here. Identify a Golden Eagle by its darker (reddish brown) color and broader wings. Be sure to bring binoculars because the eagles are usually seen from a distance. Winter is the time to see an eagle, usually February and March are best.

Eagles

Unlike other winter eagle-viewing sites, the Quabbin does not necessarily rely on open ice or mid-winter thaws for good eagle watching. The eagles are often seen feeding on deer carcasses, which have been dragged out on the ice by coyotes or have resulted from falls on the slick ice in crossing. Sometimes packs of hungry coyotes chase deer out onto the ice and the deer break a leg or panic in exhaustion. Cruel as it is, nature in turn provides these carcasses to sustain other wildlife, including the eagle. In the spring, the eagle returns to its more dignified state as a bird of prey and discontinues this scavenging. But such scavenging behavior often provides birders with the experience of seeing several eagles together.

The first eagle to appear at the Quabbin was in 1948, only nine years after the dam was completed (a few years after the reservoir was filled). The numbers have been growing ever since. In the early 1980s, about thirty eagles took up winter residence here. That number has gradually increased to almost fifty individual birds. An environmental success story, the Bald Eagle is now nesting in several locations across the state. The nation's emblem, once on the endangered list, is now making a comeback.

The eagle was nearly destroyed by shootings and DDT poisoning. It is hard to believe that as recently as 1962, bounties were paid for shooting a Bald Eagle. Fortunately, attitudes have changed, and eagles are now very much esteemed here and throughout the nation. It was once believed that eagles and other birds of prey negatively affected man. And although a few birds of prey are still taken down by the ignorant, most people know that these winged predators are an asset in their own right.

As hunters feeding at the top of the food chain, eagles and Osprey were ingesting huge amounts of DDT and other pesticides back in the 1950s. The pesticides played havoc with the healthy, normal production of eggs, and the eagles could not reproduce successfully. The increase in their number is proof that the ban on DDT allows the waters to cleanse themselves. Unfortunately, it has taken decades for society to achieve this. DDT, which is still being used in other parts of the world, can now be detected in every corner of the globe.

The work done with eagles at the Quabbin is an excellent example of what good wildlife management is capable of doing. In the 1970s, a program was initiated by the Massachusetts Department of Fisheries and Wildlife to restore the Bald Eagle. They chose the Prescott Peninsula for its outstanding eagle habitat and isolation from man. An artificial eagle nest platform was constructed, and tiny eaglets were raised in a man-made box by biologists using puppets to simulate the mothers. Eagles are territorial birds, so when these chicks grew up, they returned to that nest and started raising their own offspring. The Quabbin has had nesting eagles ever since. Currently, the population has risen to five breeding pairs and is still growing.

In fact, the Quabbin eagles have spread out into adjacent suitable nesting grounds. Many of the eagles found nesting across the state are descendants of the original Quabbin pair. In western Massachusetts, Bald Eagles are now found nesting along the Connecticut River in Northfield and West Springfield. Suffield, Connecticut, also has a nesting pair, which are sometimes seen from the Fannie Stebbins Memorial Wildlife Sanctuary (see Site 1, The Meadows).

Bald eagles begin breeding-related behavior early in the year when the snow is still flying. It takes careful observation and attention to detail to spot these birds; but sometimes luck is with the viewer, and they are seen at close range. Experienced birders hope to spy something more than just a perching eagle -- they are looking for courtship or breeding rituals. More often, however, what they observe are eagles at "play," testing one another and asserting their pecking order or hierarchy of experience.

During this time of year, the eagles are especially interesting to observe. One behavior you may observe is the chasing of immature eagles by older ones. Eagles will engage in a chase over the water. When one eagle catches up with the other, just before they touch, the pursued individual will roll over and extend its talons. If you are lucky, you might see eagles lock talons and roll in mid-flight. Eventually, as spring approaches and the days grow longer, all but ten of these eagles will return north to breed, as the icy waters thaw. By spring the staff at the Quabbin Visitor Center generally have a good idea where the eagles are going to nest for the season. In 1997 a nest was visible from the Enfield Lookout. Most of the eagles nest on the islands, which were once the tops of rugged peaks that towered up from the farmland before the flooding of the four towns created the reservoir.

Other Birds

Aside from the Bald Eagle, this part of the Quabbin can offer birders a great chance to add the Cerulean Warbler to their life list. This warbler is hard to find for even the most advanced birder, and its presence at the Quabbin is worth the effort of searching. They are known to nest in the trees along the Quabbin Park Road. Walk or drive slowly up the hill leading to the tower and scan the roadside.

Another spot where Cerulean Warblers have reliably been found is near the spillway just after crossing the dam. Walking across the dam from the Visitor Center, you will see the spillway on your left. Walk past the spillway, past a little stone marker and small memorial, to ascend the hill up to the rotary. If you pass a clearing with a view, then you have gone too far.

This is a unique spot because it is on a hill, and the road is elevated on an embankment. This allows you to look into the canopy of the trees, as they are rooted below the road, growing out of the embankment and covering the slope down to the reservoir. Each year these warblers return to the site about the second week of May. In some years, they can be seen flying over the road as they go to and from the nests. Try to spend some time here, as they are not a conspicuous species and may not be seen but rather heard. If they are not seen after spending some time, try using a birdcall or the "pish" sound. With careful observation and a little perseverance, you will be successful. This is a beautiful warbler, and every birder hopes to see one at least once in a lifetime.

If Cerulean Warblers are not seen, than perhaps the larger, more obvious Northern Raven will make the short walk worth your while. Northern Ravens have been nesting on the rocks of the spillway for a few years. The raven is an extremely secretive bird of sharp intelligence, and finding a nest in such a visible and easy-to-observe location is not to be taken for granted. Try getting here early in the morning to increase your success.

Be sure to visit the Quabbin Tower, just minutes from here. From the tower, much of the Quabbin's 125,000 acres can be seen. This impressive total includes both the forest and the reservoir. There are four trails in the Quabbin Park section, and each is good for birding. One trail of interest to birders is the Hanks Picnic Area Trail. Every spring, a variety of wood warblers are seen there. These often include the Black-throated Green and Chestnut-sided Warblers. There are also nesting Eastern Bluebirds in most of the birdhouses set out by the MDC. Red-shouldered Hawks and Ruffed Grouse are also in this area. Ovenbirds and Wood Thrush can be heard singing in June.

While on the roads in the Quabbin Park-Winsor Dam area, be sure to check the lawns for Wild Turkey. The Wild Turkey is another one of the Quabbin's success stories. Turkey were completely extirpated in Massachusetts until a recovery program re-established them in the 1970s. A series of mild winters provided an opportunity for the turkey to multiply and spread throughout the Quabbin and into other suitable habitats all across the state. These Wild Turkey were originally trapped and transferred from Pennsylvania, then set free here.

Sometimes birds associated with open grasslands are seen along the lawns near the dam. Kestrels are now appearing here on occasion. There have been some increases in recent sightings of Worm Eating Warblers, too. Look for these birds in the wooded areas. In general, there are a wide variety of possibilities along the shoreline near the Visitor Center, everything from woodland passerines to shorebirds. There is also a swampy area just before the third entrance to the Quabbin from Route 9 heading east. Pull off the road here and scan the shoreline and dead snags for wading birds and flycatchers. This pond is just a small preview of the dozens that can be accessed via the numbered gates found on all sides of the reservoir. There are 118 miles of shoreline, excluding the small ponds. With a good working knowledge of these specific sites and species, time spent here will be more enjoyable.

Regulations at the Quabbin

Although regulations are posted within the Visitor's Center and on a map at the entrance to Quabbin Park, you will want to know that the area provides drinking water for 2.5 million people. This means security is tight (especially since the 9-11 event), and violators will not be given the benefit of the doubt. Specific guidelines must be strictly enforced to ensure the safety and quality of this resource. One basic rule is no fires, which includes smoking. Off-road vehicles are prohibited. Boats can be rented at gate 8, and launching larger boats with appropriately-sized motors is permitted in certain areas along the western shore. Horses and dogs are forbidden, and skiing is not allowed.

Additional Suggestions

From the middle entrance, it is one-half mile to the turn at the north end of the Winsor Dam, and one mile to the Winsor Memorial. At 1.8 miles, there is another small lookout. A few large tamarack trees are of interest at the east entrance to Administration Road. Good birding exists at the Goodnough Dike. While in the area, try the Covey Wildlife Management Area off of Route 9 (a few minutes going west from the Quabbin Park entrance). Massachusetts fishing licenses can be purchased here. A paved and dirt road will take you down 2.0 miles through some woods and fields. At 0.2 mile, there are vernal pools on the right. At 1.9 miles, just in from the road a few hundred feet, there is a beaver pond with waterfowl. Look for Mallards and Wood Ducks. Great Blue Herons and many other notable species are also seen here.

11   Quabbin Gate 40

Closest Town: Hardwick

Best Time To Visit: Spring, Summer, November, February.

Method Of Birding: Walking Trails and Dirt Road, Bicycle.

Birds Of Special Interest: American Bittern (April), Virginia Rail, Diving and Dabbling Ducks (April and November), Ring-necked Duck, Hooded Merganser, Common Loon, Cerulean and Palm Warbler (spring), Eastern Bluebird (March to July).

Advice/Rules: It is over three miles from the gate to the shoreline. Plan on spending some time at this site, exploring the side trails. Some birders ride in on bicycles as far as the pavement goes, and then they walk. Be sure to study a little Quabbin history before arriving here; it will bring added appreciation to the outing. Bicycles are not allowed on the dirt roads (This is a new rule -- check for changes). Swimming is not allowed. Do not block gates.

This section of Quabbin is notable for many smaller streams and ponds. One large pond (Pottapaug) defines the Gate 40 experience. The gate has its share of visitors, but the road is long, and there are many different forks and side paths. Early morning visitors are the happiest, as they encounter most of the wildlife. Beaver and porcupine are especially common. Those who travel silently may catch a glimpse of a coyote or fisher. Shorebirds and ducks are of particular interest here, as are Eastern Bluebirds and American Bald Eagles in summer.

The road is relatively level and effortless going in, but most birders experience a little fatigue on the return trip. Plan to spend the better part of the morning or afternoon here, as there is much to see. A thorough investigation and exploration will consume most of the day. Many birders pack a lunch and enjoy some relaxation along the shore.

Getting There

From the Massachusetts Turnpike, take Exit 8 for Palmer / Route 32. Travel north on Route 32 through Ware, and proceed to the north on Route 32A into Hardwick. Continue to the Hardwick town common and stay on 32A. Gate 40 is off of 32A, on the left, a few minutes past Green Valley Road on the right.

Gate 40

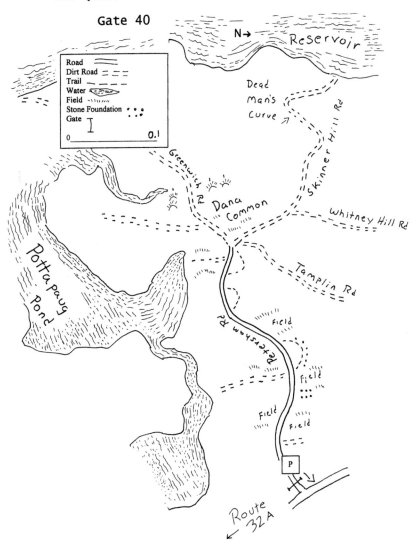

Reservoir

N→

Dead
Man's
Curve

Skinner Hill Rd

Greenwich Rd

Dana
Common

Whitney Hill Rd

Tamplin Rd

Pottapaug
Pond

Peterstown Rd

Field

Field

Field

Field

Field

P

Route
32A

Road
Dirt Road
Trail
Water
Field
Stone Foundation
Gate

0   0.1

Birding Quabbin Gate 40
and Pottapaug Pond

Petersham Road

Petersham Road begins behind the Gate 40. This road takes you down through a patchwork of weedy fields and wooded sections. After about 1.75 miles, the woods yield to the historic Dana Common. The birding down this road and around the Common area is very good all year long.

With the recent clearing of the eastern red pine, numerous new species are beginning to show up. Even before this took place, the mix of fields and forest have attracted a significant variety of birds. In addition to the usual summer resident Gray Catbirds, Northern Cardinals, and Blue Jays, there are a significant number of less common nesting species of notable interest.

At the first field on your right, there are nesting Cerulean Warblers in the trees along the back end of the clearing. To get close enough requires some work and navigating through heavy brush, but scanning the immediate vicinity with binoculars and perhaps using the "pish" sound or an Audubon bird call might provide a sighting. While in the field, notice the Eastern Bluebird nesting boxes. From a respectable distance, Eastern Bluebirds will tolerate observation. Be sure not to approach any closer than forty feet, as this could stress their nesting activities.

Further down the road, wild cherry trees attract many migrants during the fall migration. Among the long-distance travelers are flycatchers, vireos, warblers, and, within the weedy edges of the fields themselves, sparrows. The Yellow-rumped Warblers and Palm Warblers appear here each May.

At the southern end of the second big field, there is a modest trail that goes down to Pottapaug Pond, which is known as a good spot for sighting ducks. Approach the shoreline slowly, and carefully scan the flocks or individuals along the cover near the edges. Look for Black Ducks and Ring-necked Ducks, which appear less often. Expect to see Great Blue Heron and hawks during migration, too. All of this action takes place in the fall, and to a lesser extent in the spring.

The next place of interest is the Dana Common. Filled with old, abandoned cellar holes, this historic town green inspires some reflection on days past. When the reservoir was created during the Great Depression, four towns were flooded and removed from the map. The State's power of eminent domain, resulting in the loss of one's home, land and community in order to benefit the eastern part of the state, was a questionable issue at the time, and it remains controversial even to this day. Yet, as you stand on this common, the goldenrod sway in the breeze, and there is only peace.

Common Loon

Climbing a small rise on the road, just before the road forks, there is an old paved road on the left, immediately before Dana Common. The road changes to a path as it cuts through a field and ascends through white pines to the shore. Check the pond at this vantage point for flocks of Hooded Mergansers in fall and Common Loons (*illustration*) in the spring. Both Barred and Great Horned Owls live here and hunt the fields at night. In the brushy areas along the road there are almost always Common Yellowthroats in spring and summer.

Returning back to the Dana Common, observe an interesting cellar hole in good condition on the right. This was the site of the former Langley family. The history of this cellar hole, and many of the others that are clearly visible, can be researched at the Quabbin Visitor Center. The Quabbin area was once home to a few important people. It was also the retreat of a few unusual people who attained local fame. The notorious Popcorn Larson, who was buried in a glass coffin for fear of being buried alive, acquired his nickname by adhering to a rigid diet of popcorn and milk.

Greenwich Road

From the center of the Dana Common, there are two roads of interest to birders. The one on the left is called Greenwich Road; it heads out in a southwesterly direction and meanders for more than two miles to the shore of the reservoir opposite Southworth Island and Mount Zion. Along the way, there is a variety of good birding in conifer woodland, wetland, and shoreline. The first part of this two-mile journey takes you through the maple and white pine woodland that surrounds the immediate common proper. The forest changes slowly to a wetland; it is here that a number of uncommon-to-rare species can be sighted.

Look for the rare Virginia Rail and the slightly more common American Bittern. If you can find no sign of them after rigorously checking the marsh, begin to listen to your surroundings. Listen patiently for the unusual courtship call of the American Bittern. This bird is more difficult to spot than the Virginia Rail, whose call is also strange -- sounding like "whak, whak, whak" in a descending series. Those who have never heard the American Bittern will be even more amazed at its unusual quality. The call can best be described as an unusual knocking sound that climaxes into what resembles the dunking of a jug under water followed by its resurfacing. Once noted, it cannot be mistaken and can help you place this bird in any quality marsh. If your hearing is sensitive enough, you can locate the general area from which the call is coming and then with acute scutinization of the marsh, you can eventually pick out this elusive and well-camouflaged bird.

The American Bittern is known for its secretive way of holding its head erect in order to blend in with the marsh vegetation. After a few minutes, it resumes a more horizontal posture, and can be more readily seen. With such behavior, there is no confusing it with other wading birds.

The American Bittern is not common, even within the watery acreage of the Quabbin, but with skill and patience it can be found. At 0.6 mile down the road, you encounter another good site for marsh birds and ducks. Expect to see Wood Ducks or at least hear them while in flight, escaping your presence (with a squeaking sound). Hooded Mergansers have been reported here frequently. The Barred Owl is known to nest here.

Beyond this wetland, the road crosses some drier terrain under plantings of red pine. A few lush sections liven up the walk with the colors of deciduous trees, pink in spring and crimson or orange in the fall. Also check for Barred Owls here. Eventually, the road comes out to the reservoir, where there are more ducks. However, Bald Eagles are the main attraction. Sometimes they are seen cruising overhead or perched across the water at either island. Their conspicuous white head and tail can aid identification.

Skinner Hill Road

From the choice of roads leaving Dana Common, an alternative way to bird is by following the Skinner Hill Road, which is the first right-hand turn off the common. This is considered to be a better choice for birders, but be prepared for a long walk and an uphill battle on tired legs for your return. Be careful not to take a sharp right, as this will put you on Tamplin Road. Skinner Hill Road is a gradual branching off from the Petersham Road at the Dana Common, and Tamplin Road is off of it.

To start, look for Black-capped Chickadees and nuthatches. In the spring, you will see such familiar species as American Robin or Wood Thrush. Then, after a short distance there is a wetland rich in bird life of many kinds, especially in spring. The Alder Flycatcher is one bird frequently associated with this marsh. Find it with other flycatchers (Least, and sometimes Willow) in spring. It can continue to appear during the summer because many of them breed here.

You may struggle with the differences between Eastern Phoebe and Eastern Wood-Pewee, as both inhabit the immediate area. Be sure to note their size and wing markings before consulting a guide. A few reports of Black-backed Woodpeckers seem believable, but are slightly atypical. The Quabbin is known for its attraction to northern species such as the Boreal Chickadee. Evening Grosbeaks are not unheard of during the winter. Other birds seen in this part of the reservoir may include Ruffed Grouse, Northern Saw-whet Owl, and Wild Turkey.

Passing the wetland, the road begins to climb up a gradual but demanding hill. The Black-billed Cuckoo is a challenge to find here, as is the Northern Goshawk. The high-pitched calls of the Red-shouldered Hawk are easier to process among the song of summer nesting birds, while the call of a Pileated Woodpecker is also distinct to most birders.

In May, there will be Blackburnian Warblers, Black-throated Green Warblers, and tenacious Blue-gray Gnatcatchers. Closer to the reservoir, Wild Turkey continue to be seen with relative frequency. September brings in dozens of favorites and exciting firsts. These might include common birds such as Rose-breasted Grosbeaks or less common species such as Connecticut and Orange-crowned Warblers. A few weeks later, they will have moved through and will be gone.

Skinner Hill Road passes through a cluster of smaller paths, but you will continue down toward the reservoir by remaining on the road without turning. Finally, after some time and many good sightings, you will arrive at a boat landing. Grave's Landing is where Skinner Hill Road ends.

Grave's Landing is potentially the best site in the Quabbin, but it depends on the level of the reservoir in response to precipitation received during the summer. In most years, there is sufficient rainfall through the summer and into the fall. Occasionally, there are dry spells that lower the reservoir, followed by a dry fall, making the level drop enough to expose the shoreline. It is during such a time that the receding water turns this shallow neck of the reservoir into a mud flat, thus creating a temporary but very attractive habitat for advancing shorebirds in migration.

Snowy Egret

Sometimes, with the right conditions, the mud flats may extend for miles. Birders often refer to the place as the "North Dana Flats." During one good dry spell, as many as 15 different shorebirds can be seen. The year 1988 was a banner year that saw over 23 species of shorebirds! Some of the more celebrated species that occur here -- regardless of the water level -- are the Horned Lark, Snow Bunting, and American Pipit. Some of the rare ones include grassland species such as Vesper Sparrows and Sedge Wrens, which appeared during historic droughts, when the area actually dried up.

Search for American Pipit, Horned Lark, and Snow Bunting in migration. In early fall, the Northern Shrike is seen. During the winter, you can look for Bald Eagles. However, in most winters, the Quabbin freezes over, and the general area near the shoreline receives strong steady winds, so be prepared for cold. In addition, access to this part is often very difficult in January and February. Spring brings with it a good number of ducks. Enjoy an abundance of Canada Goose and American Black Duck. Try looking for Ring-necked Ducks, Bufflehead, Common Goldeneye, Northern Pintail, Hooded Mergansers, and American Wigeon.

12   More Great Birding Sites at the Quabbin

Quabbin Gate 8

Habitat

Forest: northern hardwood, conifers.
Reservoir: Quabbin Reservoir's western shore, protected bay.

Seasons/Birds

Fall: neotropical migrants, waterfowl.
Winter: nuthatches, woodpeckers, owls, eagles.
Spring: neotropical migrants, waterfowl, loons, hawks.
Summer: warblers, flycatchers, sparrows.

Description:

This is another great spot along the shoreline of the Quabbin Reservoir. Birders will enjoy the mixed species of northern hardwoods and the occasional hemlock-cloaked ravine. The shoreline is wooded, and there is a boat launch.

Getting There

This gate is on the west side of the reservoir and is found off of Route 202. It is 1.1 miles north of the Belchertown/Pelham line on your right.

Birding Specifics:

This gate provides the birder with a chance to see Red-breasted Nuthatch and Red-tailed Hawks. Birders may either walk or drive the 2.1-mile road to the shoreline, but it is closed to cars in winter. Along the way, you will see Ruffed Grouse, Great Crested Flycatchers, and many warblers in May. If you walk down the powerline to your north, there are some ponds created by beavers. Look for Swamp Sparrows and flycatchers. The Common Yellowthroat can be coaxed out of hiding with the "pish" sound. Closer to the boat launch, the road crosses a stream where there may be a Northern Waterthrush in the summer.

Quabbin Gate 45

Habitat

Forest: northern hardwood, conifers, old maples.
Reservoir: Quabbin Reservoir's eastern shore, protected bay.
Stream: small streams leading to and from beaver ponds.

Seasons/Birds

Fall: neotropical migrants, waterfowl.
Winter: nuthatches, woodpeckers, owls, eagles.
Spring: neotropical migrants, waterfowl, loons, hawks, herons.
Summer: herons, dabbling ducks, loons, flycatchers, songbirds.

Description:

This walk takes birders past an old stonewall and toward two beaver ponds. There are fields and a mix of oak and maple trees. The shoreline is especially peaceful, since few visitors bother to walk this gate. Directly across the water is an island called Mount Lizzy, one of 60 islands in the watershed. It was a hilltop before the reservoir filled.

Getting There:

From the Hardwick town common, find Greenwich Road on the left. Follow Greenwich Road 2.6 miles until gate 43. Bear left at gate 43 (this is still Greenwich Road), and travel another 1.7 miles to Lyman Road on the right. Follow Lyman Road to gate 45. Park away from the gate entrance.

Birding Specifics:

Look for Great Blue Heron (*illustration* next page), Wood Duck, Black Duck, Snow and Canada Goose, and other wading birds hiding along the edges of the ponds. You might hear the Winter Wren near the conifers or flush a Ruffed Grouse out of the field on your way in. Bald Eagles are seen over the reservoir or sometimes perched on trees (usually in the distance). Listen for the haunting cry of the Common Loon from May to September.

Great Blue Heron, female

Quabbin Gate 29

Habitat

Forest: northern hardwood, conifers, old apple trees, shrubby sections.
Reservoir: Quabbin Reservoir's northern section.
Open edge: powerline cuts, old orchard.

Seasons/Birds

Fall: neotropical migrants, waterfowl.
Winter: nuthatches, woodpeckers, owls, eagles.
Spring: neotropical migrants, waterfowl, loons, hawks.
Summer: songbirds, small owls, waterfowl, few shorebirds, hawks.

Description:

The area at this gate is characterized by a variety of semi-open habitat. There are old abandoned apple orchards and powerline cuts that offer a shrubby edge to the surrounding woodland. The walk or bicycle ride down to the shore is made more interesting by a series of stately sugar maples. At the end of the paved road you will travel through a deep grove of pine and hemlock before arriving at the quiet shoreline. This excursion offers birders a chance to enjoy the northern part of the Quabbin "wilderness."

Getting There

From Route 2, take 202 south for 2 miles to the parking area of gate 29. From Belchertown, follow 202 north 18 miles and look for gate 29 on right. (Use caution when looking for gates and turning off Route 202.)

Birding Specifics:

There are many Saw-whet Owls in the northern end of Quabbin. Look for them on this road among the conifers at the very last stretch before the reservoir. Be sure to listen for their long, wailing whistle call just before dark. Another good place is near the powerline cut right-of-way. In the spring, there will be many migrants in the shrubby areas beneath the transmission lines. American Kestrels have been observed as frequent visitors. Prairie and Blue-winged Warblers are possible under the powerlines or in orchard trees. In the apple orchard, look for Eastern Screech Owls and Cedar Waxwings. At the shoreline, use binoculars to scan the water carefully for Common Loon, Common Mergansers, and American Wigeon. Be on the lookout for Ring-necked Ducks and Common Goldeneye. Always be prepared to identify the rare visitors, which in the past have included Dovekie and Tundra Swans.

13   Highland Park

Closest Town: Greenfield

Best Time To Visit: Spring, Summer.

Method Of Birding: Walking Trails

Birds Of Special Interest: Black-throated Blue and Black-throated Green Warbler (spring to summer), Ovenbird (summer), Red-eyed Vireo (spring to summer).

Advice/Rules: For hiking the entire loop, be sure to bring your daypack with some snacks and water. The escarpment can be slippery -- keep children away from the edges. Study your vireos and other canopy dwellers before arriving. Parking is allowed in the designated parking area only. No campfires.

Highland Park offers good birding throughout the year on well-cleared trails. The habitat is primarily woodland, although a small pond can be seen near the entrance. This is an extensive urban forest fragmented by roads, but otherwise contiguous to other forested parcels. From the entrance, it appears to be a typical wooded park with joggers, children fishing, and people walking their dogs. However, hidden within the foliage are rugged rock escarpments and dark hemlock-cloaked roads. A beautifully wooded section, now commonly known as the Temple Woods, stretches for 56 acres. This acreage was given by the Women's Club of Greenfield. Together with Highland Park, the woodland totals 85 acres. To the rear of the park is the well-known site called Poet's Seat. It offers stunning views and additional woodlands. A network of poorly marked trails descends from this property to the Connecticut River Valley. The entire area is managed by the town of Greenfield .

Getting There

From I-91 north, take the Greenfield Exit (26) for Route 2A Main Street (downtown). Proceed onto Main Street, also known as 2A. Follow Route 2A for one mile, and go straight across the 5 & 10 Route crossing. Continue following Route 2A up to a point where it forks. Then leave 2A which turns left, and proceed to the right onto Crescent Street. Travel past Prospect on the right to a fork in the road. Highland goes off to the right. Take Peabody to the left. Travel another short distance and go left again at a fork in the road. Drive downhill past tennis courts and around a sharp turn to the dirt parking lot.

Highland Park

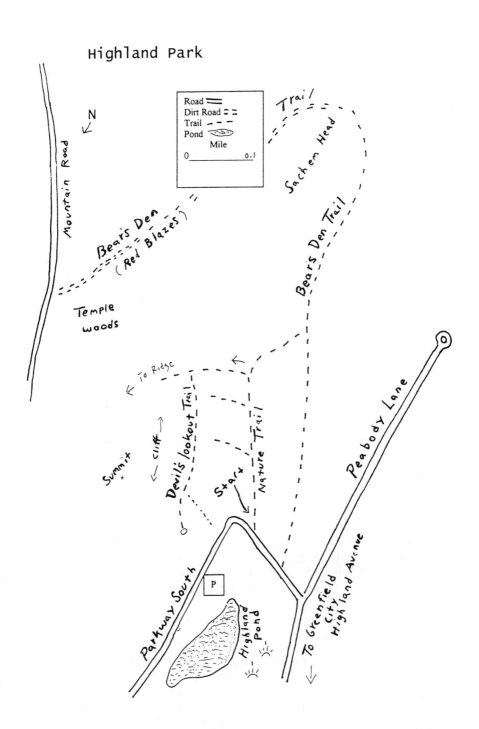

Birding Highland Park

Begin birding immediately at the parking lot, where in the tall white pines a variety of early migrating warblers can be seen in April. Expect to see Pine Warblers flitting about the high branches of the pines. In the following weeks, some Yellow Warblers might turn up on the lower branches or smaller shrubs. Sometimes the Black-and-white Warbler can be seen climbing these tree trunks in a way similar to the Nuthatch. Look for the Black-and-white Warbler about April 25th. They are often confused with nuthatches and chickadees.

Next, walk down to the pond to see more early migrants, the first of which will be the Eastern Phoebe, followed by other members of the flycatcher family. Eastern Phoebes are the hardiest and may appear here briefly as early as March. During migration, look for the Willow and the Least Flycatcher. Flycatchers are often seen perched on the discrete utility wire along the road at the pond's edge.

By summertime, this pond is usually covered with duckweed, but in the spring it may harbor a few Black Ducks, Mallards and Wood Ducks. In the summer, Mallards are frequently seen during the quieter hours along the back edge. Interestingly, the pond is lined with a healthy growth of cattails instead of the invasive purple loose strife. Red-winged Blackbirds are seen here, arriving in late February. Later in the breeding season, they are not well represented.

Another feature of this section of the park is the heavy undergrowth thriving beneath the white pines. Usually, the pines shade out plants and create a carpet of needles. It seems that here, the trees are spaced apart just enough to let in the light. Throughout the area, including the edge of the pond, herbaceous growth shelters small birds, such as Song Sparrows, Gray Catbirds, and even Common Yellowthroats.

The Bear's Den Loop

Walking back toward the parking lot in the direction from which you arrived, find a trailhead around the corner on the left. A conspicuous sign with a map of the popular trails begins the walk. Enter here, and you will find yourself in a quiet woodlot with hints of suburbia seen through the trees on the right. Soon, however, the trail turns away into a shady forest of white pine, hemlock, maple, birch, and oak. Walk an easy 0.4 mile, passing two trails branching off to the left, then turn onto the third one.

You will quickly notice some log stairs, which help to make the short climb effortless. Halfway up the stairs, a trail sneaks off to the left. Turn here and carefully step over some rocks, following the trail along the bottom of the escarpment, which you will soon see rising on your right. To your left, a hill descends back toward the trail you came in on (Bear's Den Trail). Soon, the ochre-colored cliffs will catch your eye, as they are contrasted with white birch.

At 0.3 mile after the stairs, you notice an avalanche of rocks spilling across the trail. On the left, a large boulder can be seen covered with some soil and plant growth. Continue walking this trail, and after turning to the left at a fork in the trail, proceed down a hill. This goes back toward the parking lot.

Vireos can be seen on the trail to the right called Devil's Lookout. The only devilish thing about this trail is the empty promise of a good view, but birders can scan the tops of the trees while walking atop a steep hill. While looking into the treetops, the sight of an Eastern Wood-Pewee or Red-eyed Vireo (*illustration* next page) can sometimes be enjoyed. These high-canopy-dwelling birds are otherwise very difficult to see in the summer.

An even better opportunity exists if you ignore the left turn on the stairs and proceed instead to the top of the rocky escarpment where hawks can be watched in the spring. The rocky promontory stands 100 feet above the forest below on the west side. When viewed from the south, the cliff forms a striking resemblance to both a bear's head and the face of a human (presumably Indian).

While walking the loop trail just beneath the rocky summit, birders may notice the less common songbirds that prefer an extensive woodland. Be on the lookout for Scarlet Tanagers, Rose-breasted Grosbeaks and Eastern Wood-Pewees. Wood warblers found in migration include Worm-eating, Yellow, Nashville, and Yellow-rumped Warblers. Suspected nesters include Black-throated Blue, Chestnut-sided, Nashville, and perhaps Cerulean. The Ovenbird and the Black-throated Green Warbler have been documented here. It is assumed that Pine, Chestnut-sided, American Redstart, and Black-and-white Warblers breed somewhere in the park.

Bear's Den to Mountain Road (Big Loop)

A longer hike through a quieter portion of the site can be experienced by staying on the Bear's Den Trail and following it until its end on Mountain Road. (There is a yellow-blazed trail on the left that leads back to the rock ledge.) From Mountain Road, you can find your way back to the parking area after walking 0.8 mile to the rear gate entrance of Highland Park and then back to your car. This hike takes about 90 minutes or more and is 2.3 miles long. Since this route requires walking along a busy road, you should exercise caution. It is recommended to hike early in the morning when traffic volume will be the least and birding is, of course, the best.

Birding on this route can be a peaceful experience. In late spring and summer, Eastern Wood-Pewee sing their familiar notes from high atop the trees which surround the wide trail. Similarly, Red-eyed Vireo can also be heard singing from above. On warm June and July evenings, the heavenly sounds of Wood Thrush and Veery fill these hemlock woods with a mystical enchantment. Hermit Thrush are also seen here on occasion in the spring. Birds of the thrush family are known for their evening song.

Red-eyed Vireo

Later in the summer, approximately the last week of July, the chorus begins to turn to silence. Birders then turn their attention to the woodpeckers. Downy, Hairy and even a few Pileated woodpeckers frequent this long, sylvan trail. Infrequently, Yellow-bellied Sapsuckers are encountered. In the fall foliage months, when the deciduous woods beckon the leafer-peepers looking for color, sapsuckers may be mistaken by the inexperienced for Hairy Woodpeckers. Other birds seen during this time include Red-tailed hawks, Goshawks, Canada, Blackburnian, and Blackpoll Warblers. About this time of year, Black-capped Chickadees, Nuthatches and Blue Jays become more social and conspicuous as the woods are emptied of colorful songbirds.

Species found year-round include Barred Owl, Great Horned Owl, Dark-eyed Junco, Blue Jay, Tufted Titmouse, Hairy, Downy, and Pileated Woodpeckers. Brown Creepers are regular visitors, and Red or White-breasted Nuthatches can also be expected. An occasional Northern Goshawk may stick around, and cautious Ruffed Grouse can often be found in the areas with heavy cover.

Because this woodland has many hemlock, there are likely to be Pine Siskin or even both species of Crossbills in the winter. Evening Grosbeak are sometimes seen in winter, as well. If you have never seen a Yellow-crowned Kinglet, the Bear's Den is a good place to search, especially in February. Generally, winter is quiet. But careful observation can reveal some unusual visitors.

Option to Poet's Seat

A short distance down Mountain Road from the terminus of the Bear's Den Trail is the entrance to the Poet's Seat Tower and its accompanying woodland. The Tower overlooks a bucolic view to the west, and is a popular site for romantic couples on summer evenings. Inspiring now, just as it was over one hundred years ago, the tower was constructed at this site in honor of the poets that once flocked to the Greenfield area in search of its natural beauty. Some say that the tower was built for one such poet, Fredrick Tuckerman Goddard (an unknown but talented individual), who had gained the respect of Emerson and Hawthorne. However, most believe it was constructed because of the community of poets in the region -- hence the name "Poet's Seat." The tower was first erected in 1873 and was made of wood, but in 1912 it was replaced with stone. Several decades later, the structure was renovated.

Rocky Mountain Loop Trail

To extend your hike by one mile, walk up the paved road to the Tower and continue around the turn for the way back down. Birds observed during this pleasant extension are usually hawks. In summer, check the overhanging branches on the access road for Red-eyed Vireo (*illustration*) and White-eyed Vireo, Baltimore Oriole and Scarlet Tanager.

There are several trails from this northern section that can be added on to your route. All of this land is a loose association including Highland Park and Temple Woods, and forms a corridor stretching down almost to the Connecticut River. A red-marked trail can be found past the gated clearing just to the right of the Tower parking area. This trail will take you down and along the escarpment for many more breathtaking views. Eventually it connects with the blue-blazed trail known as the Pocumtuck Ridge Trail. This trail will gain some elevation and take you through a section of pitch pine trees. There are more views along this way, but birders will be interested in finding the Northern Raven. Eventually, you will arrive back at the tower.

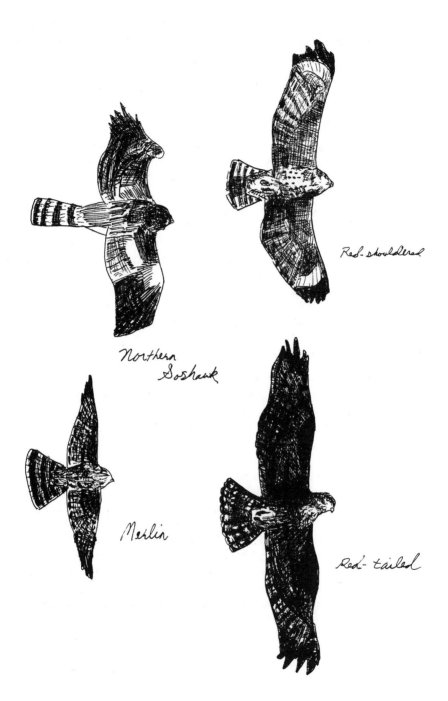

Red-shouldered

Northern Goshawk

Merlin

Red-tailed

14   Griswold Conservation Area

Closest Town: Greenfield

Best Time To Visit: Mid-Winter, Spring, Summer.

Methods Of Birding: Walking Trails

Birds Of Special Interest: Eastern Towhee (spring to summer), Eastern Meadowlark (June), Barred Owl (late winter), Indigo Bunting (summer), Black-throated Green Warbler (spring to summer), Brown Creeper (winter).

Advice/Rules: Explore the hay field, but use tick prevention. Early mornings are best. Overnight camping is permitted with permission from the town.

The Griswold Conservation Area was acquired in 1973 by the Greenfield Conservation Commission, and has been set aside for the enjoyment of the community and protection of wildlife. The site is a mix of open hay fields, thick forests and some wetlands. Virtually unknown to birders outside of Greenfield, the 71.7 acres has no birding records. Yet those who frequent Griswold claim that it offers excellent birding, the primary attraction being woodland and open hayfield species. A healthy grove of hemlock and smaller trees adds to the variety of feathered sightings.

Getting There

From I-91 north, take the Greenfield Exit 26 for Routes 5 & 10 or 2A. Travel 1.0 mile on Route 2A until the intersection of Routes 5 & 10. Turn left onto Route 5 north. Travel 4.2 miles until Log Plain Road on the right (*not* Log Plain on the left). Turn here, travel another 0.6 mile to Lampblack Road, and turn left. The Griswold Wildlife Conservation Area is 1.2 miles on the left.

Look for the yellow house and a small (easy to miss) dirt driveway and grassy parking lot. You will notice a conservation sign on the right as you approach, but continue past this. There will be fields with patches of woods on your left before the site is reached.

Griswold Conservation Area

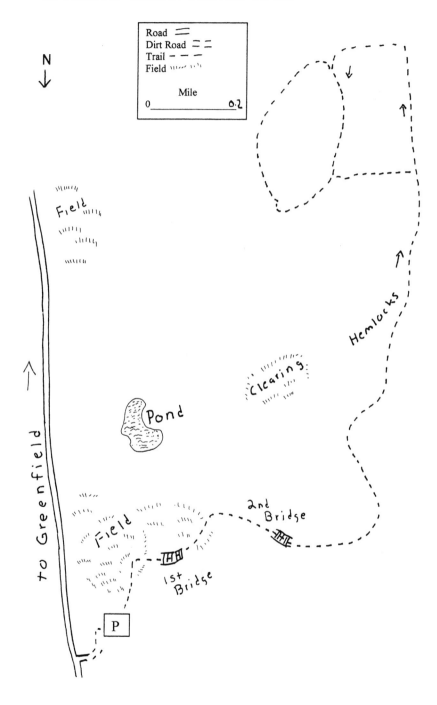

Road
Dirt Road
Trail
Field

Mile
0 — 0.2

N

Field

to Greenfield →

Pond

Clearing

Hemlocks

Field

2nd Bridge

1st Bridge

P

130

Birding Griswold Conservation Area

Enter the trail behind the big metal gate at the corner of the parking area, and be prepared for immediate sightings. Start looking for Eastern Meadowlark, Savannah Sparrows, Bobolink and Eastern Bluebird (May to July). These fields at the beginning of your walk are some of the most important parts of this experience. Be sure you remain quiet and explore the meadow thoroughly before returning back to the gate. Try not to lose the trail; it hugs the right side of this field and enters the woods after a few yards. You will then pass over a bridge and enter another field. Staying along the right side of the field will place you directly onto the trail that can be seen starting at the edge of the woods. This is where your walk begins.

As you walk the first few yards into the woods, there is an impenetrable stand of saplings on your left. This creates the perfect "edge" effect, and if you look in the muddy stream bed to the side of the trail, there will be signs of deer and sometimes moose tracks. Moose will sometimes use the wooded buffer along the edge of the highway as a travel corridor down from the north. Some species of birds tend to do the same.

The "edge" is great for birds such as Indigo Bunting, American Goldfinch, Field Sparrows, Blue-winged and (infrequently) Prairie Warblers. Look for these species in the early summer before the breeding season. Eastern Towhee can often be heard and sometimes seen scratching the leaves and debris beneath the brush and cover of saplings. In the fall, a variety of thrushes, warblers and sparrows may linger on in these thickets.

Definitely watch for Great Horned Owls in the late evening. They tend to shelter during the sunny days away up in the hemlocks, and then flirt with the open field at dusk -- sometimes gliding over it and swooping back up into the trees on the opposite side along the road. Barred Owls can also be found here, especially near the secluded ponds. Eastern Screech Owls are common, but hardly ever seen.

The birding remains good as you get deeper into the forest. The trail widens and becomes carpeted in pine needles, providing for soundless walking. This is perfect for surprising ground dwellers like the Hermit Thrush, Veery and Ovenbirds. These summer birds can still be heard singing even farther along the trail where it parallels the highway. In the winter, however, the calls of Brown Creepers and White or Red-breasted Nuthatches compete with the drone of the Interstate. Do not let the close presence of the Interstate deter you from continuing (I-91 is only yards away). A peaceful experience is somehow still gained. Perhaps it is the dark cover of hemlocks and sun-dappled, fern-covered glades that sooth the soul.

Wood Thrush

The repetitive song of the Black-throated Green Warbler is heard from start to the finish on this rewarding walk. Their call is reminiscent of the northern reaches of Vermont's Washington County, where the abundance of hemlock and birch ensure this tiny bird some breeding habitat. Although the trail is marked "difficult" in spots, it is really quite manageable by most people's standards.

Eventually, the trail crosses another wooden bridge, where delicate, sensitive fern grow up from the wetland on either side, followed by some larger ostrich fern on the right. Now the trail begins to turn and ascend a small hill. Birders can find Ruffed Grouse, Wood Thrush (*illustration*), Black-capped Chickadees, Downy and Hairy Woodpeckers, and Northern Flickers. Eastern Wood-Pewee can also be expected in summer, along with Blue Jays and vireos. Wild Turkey are known to frequent the brushy areas on the left where some pruning and thinning took place in recent years. Sharp-shinned and Cooper's Hawk are regularly seen.

At 1,000 feet from the second bridge, you will begin to see more mast-producing trees. In the fall there are more opportunities for Wild Turkey. Favorites such as woodpeckers, jays and Ruffed Grouse are frequently seen feeding on the crop. You may also flush a deer from this area. Black bears like to eat these acorns, too. Notice the large variety of trees that includes black, red, and white subspecies of oak. There are also beech, blackgum ironwood and hornbeam growing in this wildlife-rich section of trail.

You are now in the upland part of the conservation land where owl pellets are sometimes found. Keep your ears open for mobbing crows chasing hawks and owls. Stay on the main trail and ignore the trail branching off to the left. Continue walking toward the center of the conservation area. After hiking for another 2,000 feet, the trail will turn more sharply and come out to a T where you have a choice to go either left or right. You will want to turn left, and begin to head back while making a loop and joining up with the opposite end of the left-branching trail you ignored earlier. Turn left on that trail, where you will see double blue triangular trail markers. This will join with the trail you entered at the parking lot. Turn right onto it and follow it back to your car.

If you want to extend your hike, turn right at the T and follow the trail in a large loop. Achieve this by bearing left, while you circle through the woods and pass by two trails on the right. Later on, you will pass a sign with the number eleven on it. Eventually, you arrive at a tree marked with double blue markers. This is the same trail described earlier, which brings you to the entrance trail. The two trails at the turn on the loop that you passed before the numbered sign post will bring you out to a field on the left.

Throughout this section of the sanctuary, there is an increase in thinned or logged sites. Brush and snags have been left in place, so as to add cover for birds and other wildlife. Among the birds found in this area are sparrows such as Field, White-throated, and (in migration) the uncommon Fox Sparrow. Closer to the fields, birders have a chance of finding White-crowned Sparrow.

The Griswold Conservation Area is good for finding a variety of warblers. In this section, especially where the woods meet the fields, there are quite a few Yellow-rumped Warblers each spring, which are thought to be present in the breeding season. The Black-throated Blue warbler is a nester; look for them in the brushy areas and where there are logs and branches or snags. This is a great place for finding the Canada Warbler, which prefers moist, mixed woods with heavy underbrush; they are believed to nest here and are often seen in July.

A visit in mid-May to any part of this site will produce lots of warblers in migration -- Nashville, Wislon's, Morning, Cape May, Chestnut-sided, and American Redstarts. Chestnut-sided is a suspected nester, and the American Redstart is often seen late in the spring. Flashes of yellow in the thick growths of saplings and overhanging branches near the fields will indicate the Yellow Warbler; a few must nest on the property. Unfortunately, few birders are aware of this site, and consequently much is still to be learned about the nesting species and unusual migrants. There are, no doubt, many birds that frequent these forests and fields that have so far remained unseen.

In the fields and woods not described here, there are American Kestrels on occasion. They have been seen using the nest boxes. The site also contains some habitat for visiting Great Blue Herons and flycatchers. The Eastern Kingbird has also been a casual visitor. This large flycatcher is often seen along the road that brings you from Greenfield. The Purple Finch is another resident. Find this bird near the fields or along the road or sometimes at the far exterior of the forest. Another favorite finch is the Evening Grosbeak, which may appear in the winter. Winter usually offers sighting of many common feeder birds and sometimes Pine Siskins .

Birding should improve here over the next few years, as more people become aware of its value to wildlife. The town has placed a "multiple use" emphasis on the property. The desires of the Griswold family, who donated the land, and the town residents, are not in conflict with this. If the land is managed responsibly, the site should only become more attractive to birdlife. Thus the fields will continue to be maintained and harvested late in the season, so as to protect the nesting activities of the Bobolink and other birds within it. Logging will be an on-going activity to keep the diversity in the age of the forest, as this will increase its productivity for wildlife.

GTD Land

Adjacent to the Griswold property is an additional 122 acres of conservation land known as the GTD site. This site consists of heavy pine woods and mixed forest in prime logging condition. Trails have been developed, and birding is good; but the site is virtually unknown to most people in the community. There are deer, coyote, bear, and fox. A rabbit population must help sustain some birds of prey, and the pines probably support many warblers (Pine Warblers).

15 More Great Birding Sites near Greenfield

Greenfield Community College
and Local Agricultural Fields

Habitat

Woodland: hardwoods, some shrubby areas.
Lawns: manicured grass.
Agriculture: expansive hayfields and crops, open country with some trees

Seasons/ Birds

Fall: sparrows, songbirds.
Winter: larks, buntings, sparrows, owls.
Spring: larks, buntings, owls, sparrows, songbirds, flycatchers.
Summer: songbirds, sparrows.

Description:

The campus of GCC is endowed with large rolling lawns and shade trees. The campus is bordered by woods in the rear, and on either side there are hundreds of acres of hayfields and agricultural crop land.

Getting There

From I-91, take Exit 26 and follow Route 2A for the sign on the left at the intersection of 2A and Colrain Street (lights). Follow for 0.7 mile, and bear left for the college (marked by a sign). Proceed across Colrain Road from Colrain Street to College Drive.

Birding Specifics:

The birds include songbirds and open country-loving species. Savannah, Field, and Song Sparrows can be seen, spring through fall. There are Eastern Phoebe and other flycatchers. On the road (Colrain Road) going right and left of the main entrance to the campus, look for grassland species such as Bobolink, Eastern Meadowlark, and Northern Harrier (rare). In winter, look for Horned Lark and American Tree Sparrow.

Erving State Forest

Habitat

Woodland: hardwoods, hemlock groves, mountain laurel tangles, oaks.
Lake: Laurel Lake.

Seasons/ Birds

Fall: ravens, owls, waterfowl.
Winter: ravens, owls, woodpeckers.
Spring: ravens, neotropical migrants, waterfowl.
Summer: ravens, hawks, owls, songbirds

Description:

The Erving State Forest consists of 4,479 acres, most of which is northern hardwoods. Laurel Lake provides a break in the densely-foliated hills of birch, maple, oak, hemlock, and pine. A short, upward-climbing nature trail brings visitors to a stunning view of Mt. Monadnock. White- and pink-flowering mountain laurel grow along the way.

Getting There

In Erving, from the intersection of Route 2 and Church Street, travel north on North Street to Swamp Road on the right. Take Swamp Road and follow the road northeast into the State Forest. Travel 1.7 miles from Route 2 to the State Forest boundary. This road becomes Laurel Lake Road, and then in another 1.2 miles, brings you to the ranger station and the parking area on the left.

Birding Specifics:

Northern Ravens and migrating hawks can often be seen from the summit of the trail. In the woods, there will be Black-throated Blue Warblers and Wood Thrush (spring). In summer, the trees are filled with a variety of songbirds, including a few Rose-breasted Grosbeaks. At the lake, there could be dozens of diving and dabbling ducks. November and April are usually the best time to check for waterfowl.

Great Blue Heron

Barton's Cove and Turner's Falls Airport

Habitat

River: a cove or still water produced by a dam.
Airport: grasses along runways.

Seasons/ Birds

Fall: waterfowl, shorebirds.
Winter: eagles, waterfowl, owls, sparrows.
Spring: waterfowl, eagles, sparrows, grassland species.
Summer: eagles, grassland species.

Description:

The Turners Falls dam has created an area of still waters on the Connecticut River called Barton's Cove. A fish ladder has been constructed to assist some 40,000 fish to get upstream to spawn each year. Boaters and canoeists launch their way into the cove from a public boat launch that also provides good views of the river's birdlife. The Turners Falls Airport is a few miles away.

Getting There

From I-91, take Route 2 east and proceed to the Turners Fall Bridge. Turn right to cross the bridge and follow Avenue A. Immediately over the bridge, go left on 1st Street. Look for the parking area on the left. The boat ramp is 0.5 mile east of the Route 2 traffic lights.

To find the airport, travel along Route 2, heading east over the Turners Fall bridge, and take an immediate sharp right. Follow this to Mineral Road until an intersection with Millers Fall Road. Turn right here and follow toward the industrial park. The airport is on the right (park and walk along dirt road).

Birding Specifics:

Although the fish ladder is open between 9 A.M. and 5 P..M. from Wednesday to Sunday in May and June, birders will look first to the waters of Barton's Cove. Bald Eagles and diving ducks can be seen here throughout the spring and fall. Two eagles, a male and female, may be seen all summer, as they maintain a nest nearby. In the late summer, the juveniles may pose an identification challenge for the inexperienced. The best time to see the ducks is in the fall or spring. Many dabbling ducks are also observed. These include the teals, Mallards and Black Ducks. At the airport, you can see Grasshopper and Vesper Sparrows, along with Bobolink (spring to fall).

16   Notchview Reservation

Closest Town: Windsor

Best Time To Visit: Winter, Spring, early Summer.

Methods Of Birding: Walking Trails, Cross-Country Skiing, Snow-Shoeing.

Birds Of Special Interest: Roughed-legged Hawk (spring to fall), Sharp-shinned Hawk (spring to summer), Chimney Swift (summer), Barred Owl (late winter), Warblers (May), Blue-winged Warbler, Magnolia Warbler (spring to summer), Hermit Thrush (June), Red and White-winged Crossbills (winter), Pine Siskin (winter), Savannah and Field Sparrows (spring to summer), Bobolink (June, July).

Advice/Rules: Pay attention to weather forecasting, as temperatures are usually several degrees lower here than in the Pioneer Valley. Snow is usually present throughout the winter, even when it has melted in the valleys. Do not hike the Drowned Land alone, and be sure to use a topographical map and compass. Be careful during hunting season -- stay within the Reservation. Pack all basic hiking supplies, including water bottle and snack. Dogs must be on a leash. No camping or camp fires.

The Notchview Reservation looks, smells, and feels like sections of northern Vermont because most of the reservation is above 2,000 feet elevation, and the climate is cool enough to support the spruce and birch that thrive here. Geologically speaking, Notchview is part of the Taconic Orogeny Mountains, which are an extension of Vermont's Green Mountains. Therefore, much of the bird life here is characteristic of the northern hardwood/boreal transition forest which is found sporadically throughout Vermont's northern counties. This means that there is a healthy number of nesting warblers and thrush.

Notchview also has some open fields and bog habitat, increasing the variety and excitement of birding at this wild but accessible reserve. In this 3,098-acre site, approximately 10 percent is open country. Within the site there is enough variety of habitats to support at least 56 nesting species. Everything from woodland passerines to wading birds is represented here.

Notchview Reservation

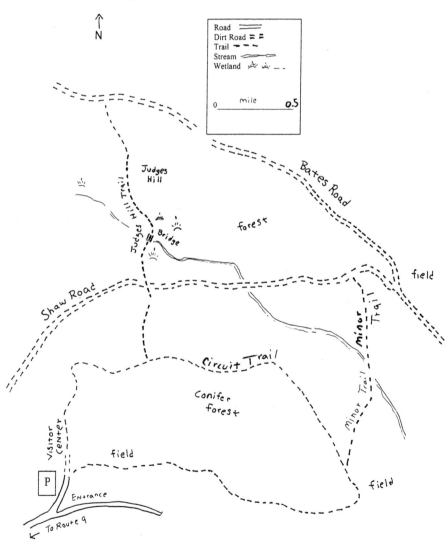

Getting There

Traveling from the east (Northampton), go west on Route 9 past Cummington and Windsor State Forest. Look for the "Trustees of Reservations" sign on the right. From the Pittsfield area, go east on Route 9, look for the intersection with Route 8A, continue 1.0 mile east on Rte. 9, and enter the site on your left.

Birding Notchview

The Circuit Trail

The Circuit Trail, as its name implies, is a loop that connects several smaller trails. It ends where it starts -- at the parking area adjacent to the Budd Visitor Center. This easy-to-moderate trail is 1.8 miles long; to complete the circuit takes anywhere from an hour and a half to a little over two hours, depending on the birding and one's rate of walking. The Circuit Trail can be hiked by itself or in combination with other connecting trails. Birding at Notchview is considered very good by most authorities, and since these connecting trails are relatively hassle-free, it is recommended to include any of them.

There is enough to see on this loop trail to make any visit to "the Notch" worthwhile. Begin birding the moment you get out of your car. The Circuit Trail begins here in an open field with wild apple trees and nesting boxes tacked to old clapboard fences. An old favorite, the Eastern Bluebird, nests in this open hay meadow. In May, the bluebirds are busy dropping from perches to snatch insects hidden in the grass below. In early July, they can be seen flying to and from the nesting boxes.

The sweet song of the Bobolink is heard in the spring. At Notchview, this grassy meadow-loving bird is cherished, and its return is always a special event. Bobolinks are remarkable migrants. They chart their way over the vast ocean from South America, arriving each spring at this same field to nest and raise their young. Perching on fence posts, Bobolinks sing with great vigor.

Plenty of common summer nesting species inhabit this part of the reservation -- Gray Catbirds, American Robins, and Northern Cardinals. Interestingly, the less common Chimney Swift nests in the chimney of the Budd Visitor Center. Blue-winged Warblers are found among the apple trees and wooded edges. In early spring, check for Winter and Carolina Wren. In the fall, look for Cedar Waxwings that may be seen feeding on small bits of this delicious fruit.

Wild apple trees are found in various places where there were once old farmyards. A hundred years ago, these trees provided food for troubled farmers trying to work the rocky, unforgiving soil. Today, these trees provide food for Ruffed Grouse, deer, and many other species of both mammal and bird. Ruffed Grouse are reasonably common in the many abandoned farms, where secondary growth and weedy fields meet.

Where the Circuit Trail quickly becomes shaded beneath a healthy mix of conifers and northern hardwoods, the Sharp-shinned Hawk can be found speculating a nest site in the spring. This bird is a rare nester in Massachusetts, but has been seen in July and somewhat regularly during migration. The Broad-winged Hawk is a confirmed nester in deciduous groves like the one near the start of the Circuit Trail. Red-tailed Hawks may also be encountered near the open hay meadow, and with some luck, the Rough-legged Hawk can be seen in winter.

A few minutes into the hike, just before a side trail on the left, you will see the remains of an old stone wall. Check the wall for ground-loving species such as Dark-eyed Junco in the summer or winter. Red spruce and balsam fir become more common here. The side trail cuts over to a wide dirt track called Shaw Road. You will see an abundance of moosewood or stripped maple in this area. Moose love to feed on this low-growing tree -- hence the name. Moose frequent the reservation, and cows with young are an annual treat each spring. You can bird the road just a bit before returning to the Circuit Trail; sometimes the edge or open sun-splashed ambiance here provides the sighting of a warbler or songbird. In winter, when the trees are bare, you may notice the nest of a Red-eyed Vireo. These birds love to nest above roadsides.

Trace your steps back from Shaw Road to return to the Circuit Trail; go left to continue on this loop. The forest is now a mix of birch, maple, and red spruce. Stonewalls cross the trail several times. After about 0.8 mile, there is a bench on the left. Wood Thrush and Hermit Thrush can be expected here. In the thick groves of spruce, the trees grow in competition for the light, shedding branches on their journey upward. The forest floor is deep with sticks and needles. In such places, be on the lookout for inhabitants as rare as the Ruby-crowned Kinglet. Golden-crowned Kinglets are confirmed nesters in this area. Another prize are migrant Cape May Warblers, which are equally fond of thick spruce stands. There are also Magnolia Warblers, which are nesting here each year.

The Anthill, Bridge, and Whitestone Trails are short cuts going back to the visitor center; these will reduce your hike substantially. The Quill Tree Trail will only cut your hike in half, but for the best birding, stay on the Circuit Trail. Eventually, the trail begins to descend. Where it opens up to a field, there is a shelter and a view of Shaw Brook Valley. Occasionally in winter, a Northern Shrike may make an appearance, and sometimes Snow Buntings present themselves. Otherwise, expect to see American Goldfinch, Savannah Sparrows, and Field Sparrows. Kestrels have also been recorded.

Past this field, the landscape begins to close in again. More conifers envelop the trail, providing more opportunities to spot Black-capped Chickadee, Dark-eyed Junco, and White-throated Sparrow. Many Red-breasted Nuthatch inhabit the Reservation and are seen in these conifers. This is an uncommon bird in the lower Pioneer Valley. Look for this bird year-round.

Red-winged Crossbills

Eventually, the trail opens up again to a beautiful meadow on the left. Check the undersides of a maintenance shed (also on the left) for nesting Eastern Phoebes or American Robins. On the right side of the trail, a series of old steps mark the site of an old abandoned homestead. What little is left of these stairs leads up into a dense grove of rhododendron that is virtually impenetrable, stands about twenty feet high, and covers about one quarter acre. Surrounded on either side by giant Norway spruce, this grove makes an attractive place to spend some time coaxing whatever birds may be within it. A Black-throated Blue Warbler ought to be inhabiting this little micro-habitat from late May until end of July.

Just beyond this grove, the birding changes from cover-seeking, shy, ground-dwelling species to ones of the open meadow. Try again for Bobolinks. Snow Buntings are seen here, too. On the left, there are some impressive-looking Norway spruce, where there is often a great deal of action. Carefully scope these out, as there are frequently Pine Siskins each winter. These trees are also a good place to look for Purple Finch and Notchview's specialty -- the Red Crossbill (*illustration* previous page). Crossbills are nomadic and erratic visitors, but have been recorded in the years termed " flight years," when severe weather and/or cone seed shortages in the far north force them to go south. The spruce and fir forest at Notchview offers excellent habitat. Look for the crossbill flocks throughout the reservation among the conifer stands.

Judges Hill Trail

Immediately past a stone wall and almost across from the entrance to the Anthill Trail is the trailhead of the Judges Hill Trail. Turn left off the Circuit Trail here, and begin your hike to the higher slopes of the reservation. This trail goes deeper into Notchview's forest. The Judges Hill Trail takes you up to Judges Hill and then back down to the Bates Road. Once on Bates Road, turn right, and bird along this rutted dirt track until it intersects with the Shaw Road. This is recommended as an extended loop.

After a few minutes, the trail crosses the dirt road known as Shaw Road. Directly ahead is the entrance or continuation to the Judges Hill Trail. Apple trees grow on either side among goldenrod and a variety of succulent green weeds and grasses. They are a hint of the wetlands that lie ahead. Although this trail is known to be steeper than some of the others, before it climbs up to Judges Hill, it first slopes down and traverses a wetland and brook. A variety of attractive ferns grow here, including lady, Christmas, wood, and spinulose.

Pay close attention as you move through the wet area, where high grass and slippery wood planking used to cross the mud can make for challenging walking. Beyond this area, thoughts return to the birds that in spring will be singing loudly. Listen for Veery and Hermit Thrush, both eloquent singers.

This is a good place to look for spring migrant warblers. American Redstart and the Blackpoll Warbler have been sighted. Neither of these species nests at this site. At 0.5 mile from Shaw Road, the trail crosses the beautiful Shaw Brook, where a new bridge is about to go up. The land begins to dry out after crossing the brook. Finally, the trail begins its ascent up toward Judges Hill.

There is a mix of beech trees, spruce, maple and some birch varieties. At 0.7 mile from the start, look for the Windsor Trail to branch off toward the east, where it meanders into the Minor Trail. Continue straight on the Judges Hill Trail, and get ready for a manageable but steeper rise. Enjoy the larger mature stands of beech and maple. After a short while, the maple drop out of the climb, and the trail becomes surrounded by smooth-trunked broad-leafed beech. One tree shows scars of a bear's claws and is large enough for such a creature to climb. Congratulations -- you are now in black bear country, but don't worry -- they are more afraid of you than you are of them.

The trail soon passes by a very old beech tree on the right. This historic beauty sits in a small clearing and resembles something out of a children's story. Passing through another clearing with attractive white birch growing out of the ferns, the trail brings you to the peak of Judges Hill and an old stone foundation. Huge stones sit balanced upon one another, squared off on three sides; it was once the four-sided foundation of an 18th century farmhouse. With one side open, wild flowers such as goldenrod are welcomed in and protected by the stone arms of the old house. A chimney can be noticed precariously rising up on the north side of the house. A young maple grows behind it in eager anticipation to shade and shelter the homestead, but no one lives here now except busy little chipmunks that scurry through the rocks.

Cool breezes bring in fresh air from the Berkshire Mountains to the west, and suddenly some of the precariously perched slabs look like inviting seats upon which to ponder the passing of ages. This part of the trail is at 2,297 feet above sea level, and there are species here that cannot be found in the Pioneer Valley to the east.

In fact, many of the birds at "the Notch" cannot be found in the numerous valleys throughout the Berkshires. This is what makes Notchview special -- its altitude and Canadian flora. Therefore, check the spruce patiently as you descend back down the other side of this hill, going north toward Bates Road, for the northern affinities abound. The conifers at the top of hills in this part offer more chances of seeing Pine Sisikin, as well as White-winged and Red Crossbills (usually fall or winter). Evening Grosbeaks and Northern Ravens can be seen on this hill infrequently in colder months.

In warmer weather, this is a place to find a Swainson's Thrush. Although this bird is not confirmed as a breeder, the habitat seems inviting for it. Listen for its call during May and early June. Any sightings of this bird past the first days of summer could indicate a breeding pair. June is also best for sighting secretive wood warblers that are singing for their territory. Hunt for the Black-throated Green Warbler high up in hemlocks, red spruce, or birch in early spring. Find the Morning Warbler near cuts and brushy hillsides. The Nashville and the Black-and-white Warblers both nest in the deciduous trees.

On the way down to Bates Road is an interesting plateau where beech grow almost exclusively. In this particular grove, the trees are only a few decades old, unlike the bear-clawed beech you saw back at the turn for the Judges Loop North Trail. Below this turn, at roughly 0.2 mile from the summit, are numerous Wood Thrush singing. Where the trail traverses through ferns and widens or opens up a bit on each side, look for Red-eyed Vireo. Spruce make a reappearance past the beech grove and continue to add beauty to the excursion down to Bates Road. Eventually, larger maple and white birch tower over old stone walls that line either side of the road for short distances before crumbling back into the forest floor.

Canopy-dwelling species will grab your attention. The Eastern Wood-Pewee and the vireos are chief among them. Walk 0.8 mile until a field appears on the left, and then go right, almost backtracking, down another rutted dirt track; this is Shaw Road. This opening with the large meadow is where General Bates once lived. Look for Indigo Bunting; they are common in this meadow, especially along the edges. The Savannah Sparrow is regularly seen here and has been recently documented nesting. Bobolink and Eastern Meadowlark may be spotted, too.

From Shaw Road, there are two choices: return to the Circuit Trail via the Minor Trail (0.3mile from Bates Road), or continue walking down Shaw Road and take the Judges Hill Trail back to the Circuit Tail. The latter choice allows for more time on the Circuit Trail if you turn left and not the way you came. Utilizing the Minor Trail shortens the walk, and provides equally good birding. However, the more time and ground covered, the greater the odds of seeing something special. If you continue down to Judges Hill Trail, expect to see or hear Red-eyed Vireo, Pileated Woodpecker, and most of the common northern hardwood summer species. Perhaps, a Rose-breasted Grosbeak may reveal itself and dazzle you with its striking black, white, and red plumage.

A walk down the Minor Trail takes you through ferns and spruce with very little other undergrowth. At 0.2 mile, a small stream flows peacefully beneath a footbridge, and then the understory begins to fill up with more vegetation. Spruce yield to maple, and the conifers share the area with the deciduous trees. Veery and Hermit Thrush are also very vocal here.

Birding the Minor Trail may provide a chance to see warblers such as Bay-breasted, Cape May, Parula, and Black-and-white. The most likely to be seen, however, are nesting Blackburnian, Yellow-rumped and Black-throated Green. Louisianna Waterthrush are present, but are seen infrequently along this and other streams.

The Drowned Land

Beyond the reach of any existing trails is the region known as the Drowned Land. It is approachable for those ambitious enough to bushwhack through the rudimentary footpaths that appear and disappear. Another possibility for those more cautious and less adventurous is to drive up along Route 9. Take your first right onto Savoy Hollow Road, and then bear right at the V-fork in the road (immediately after crossing Bates Road intersection). This takes you near the Drowned Land. Park where practical, and either start birding from the road, employing your ears, or find a trail and venture in on foot. Birding by car may provide a few good sightings, but be prepared for poor road conditions. The Drowned Land can also be accessed via Route 8A by following the Drowned Land Brook or utilizing the State Access on the left (Look for the sign).

Birds to be expected are Wood Duck, Alder and Willow Flycatchers. The Great Blue Heron is nesting in Windsor and may visit the more open spaces of this region. The Northern Waterthrush may be here in the breeding season. Barred Owls have been heard and probably nest nearby. Unconfirmed but likely at times are the Green-winged Teal and Olive-sided Flycatchers. Black-backed Woodpeckers have not been recorded and are unlikely, but are worth being aware of as a possibility. Listen for the distant cry of the Red-shouldered Hawk, as the Drowned Land offers suitable habitat.

17 Eugene D. Moran Wildlife Management Area

Closest Town: Windsor

Best Time To Visit: Winter, Spring, Fall.

Methods Of Birding: Walking Trails, Cross-Country Skiing, Snow-Shoeing.

Birds Of Special Interest: Broad-winged and Red-tailed Hawk (spring to fall), Boreal Chickadee (winter), Ring-necked Pheasant (year-long), American Woodcock (April), Warblers (spring to summer), Nashville Warbler (June), White-winged Crossbill (winter), Pine Siskin (winter), Evening and Pine Grosbeak (winter), Bobolink (June, July, Early August), Eastern Meadowlark (June, July).

Advice/Rules: A winter visit is recommended, even without skis or snow-shoes. Unfortunately, many people have been removing some of the rare plants. Do not disturb or remove sphagnum moss.

The Moran Wildlife Management Area is very good for open-country-loving birds and northern species. This is a unique site little known to casual birders. Because of the variety of forest and open meadow in succession, there exists an incredible "edge" effect here. The result is a list of 194 different birds recorded on site. An unbelievable 99 species have been breeding here since 1970. There is an impressive conifer grove and several acres of mixed hardwood forest. Fobes Hill is a gentle rise that has gained a reputation as a good site for fall hawks in migration. The Moran Wildlife Management Area consists of 1,147 acres contiguous to much undeveloped land. Its setting -- upon the heavily wooded Berkshire Plateau -- gives it a wild appearance.

Getting There

From the west (Pittsfield), travel on Route 9 east and look for the junction of Routes 9 and 8A north. Turn left onto 8A. Fobes Hill is on the right, and the Bosma Road spruce grove is on the left after 0.75 mile. From the Northampton region, take Route 9 west, and 8A is on the right after passing Notchview Reservation.

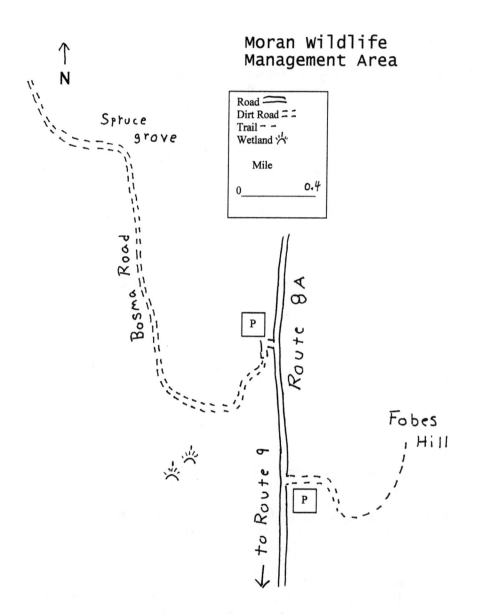

Moran Wildlife
Management Area

N

Spruce
grove

Bosma Road

Route 8A

to Route 9

Fobes
Hill

Road
Dirt Road
Trail
Wetland

Mile

0   0.4

P

P

Birding Moran Wildlife Management Area

The Open Country

Beginning with the spring return of neotropical migrants to Massachusetts, the grassland harbors a wide number of avifauna. Although Red-winged Blackbirds and Common Grackles are first to arrive in late February, early spring migrants include everything from American Woodcock to Tree Swallows. From then on, there occurs a constant influx of birds returning from the tropical reaches of the West Indies and Central and South America. The Nashville Warbler nests here and is considered a specialty in June.

Bobolink and Eastern Meadowlark are both here from May to October. The Bobolink is the more tolerant of higher elevations, and therefore more abundant at Moran. The Eastern Meadowlark, however, arrives earlier and has generated late winter sightings. At Moran, the Bobolink is a very reliable species, and each year in late August, there are hundreds seen in the canary grass.

Female Bobolinks may be confused with sparrows by less-experienced birders. Besides common sparrows like White-throated and Field, check for the Swamp Sparrow and the Lincoln's Sparrow. All of these may be seen in summer while they are busy nesting. Look for the Lincoln's in the sedge tussocks. Sometimes the fall is better for sightings. The Dickcissel, a rare grassland species, was reported here in 1996 -- a confirmed sighting of a territorial male singing and defending what was assumed to be an active nest.

Such rare documentations make the Moran an exciting place at the start of each breeding season. Birders still talk about the Upland Sandpiper of 1989 -- a rare summer species for Berkshire County. A Northern Harrier was believed to have nested here in 1999 and was the first in memory to have established itself through the nesting season. Perhaps even more exciting was the presence of a Henslow Sparrow, lingering here in early August, 1984.

Short-eared Owls are another thrilling experience at Moran. Birders have not reported seeing them nest here. Short-eared Owls are extremely shy. The Northern Saw-whet Owl is a confirmed nester.

Moran is also recommended for those looking to add the American Kestrel to their life list. Common here and nesting in various spots around the area, kestrels are seen perched on power lines or chasing after their smaller prey -- everything from songbirds to insects. In winter, another aggressive species of similar size and wit enters the silent landscape. Northern Shrikes (*illustration*) show up faithfully each fall during the second week of November and remain until the end of March. They are solitary birds and easy to miss.

Northern Shrike

Other species of interest in this open part of the management area include Sedge Wrens (summer), Horned Larks (winter), Rough Legged Hawks (winter), and a possible nesting Savannah Sparrow. Ring-necked Pheasants add a little excitement with their long, exotic tail feathers and flashy colors. The State releases these birds for sportsmen regularly each October.

Spruce Grove and Bosma Road

The most exciting time to visit this part of the Wildlife Management Area is winter. Access is possible during snow cover along cross-country ski trails. The use of snowshoes is required when the snow is fresh or unusually high. But of course, be sure to take advantage of snow melts or snowless winters. Bosma Road can be picked up at the far south end of the second parking area on the left of 8A going north. The Bosma Road twists around (north) and heads downhill. Eventually, it narrows out before climbing up another hill and turning to the left. From here it travels through field and forest, passing a spruce grove and arriving 2.0 miles later on Cheshire Road.

Birders from across the state come here every year to find winter finches. Red Crossbills and White-winged Crossbills can be found in healthy numbers in flight years. During non-flight years, birders are still able to find a few. In 2001, White-winged Crossbills actually spent the summer. Ironically, this does not suggest breeding activity; rather, these members of the finch family are able to nest during the winter. They are opportunistic in the sense that if food is abundant they will be stimulated to mate, incubate and raise young, even in the sub-freezing winter elements. Local researchers believe that the cone crop at Moran is productive enough for this to be taking place.

Pine Siskins are also eagerly sought after here. There can be large flocks making their way through the red spruce during flight years. Evening Grosbeaks are more noticeable; their contrasting black and gold plumage stands out against the dark green boughs of these evergreens. It is the Boreal Chickadee, however, that attracts birders from all over the state each winter. The Boreal Chickadee is a casual visitor to the Moran. This species is nearly identical to our common Black-capped Chickadee, but this northern variety is smaller and has some brown feathers instead of the black. The call of the Boreal Chickadee is more nasal than that of the common Black-capped Chickadee.

The Pine Grosbeak sometimes graces the spruce grove with its majestic, stocky build. Painted red and burgundy, this giant seed-eater is quite a sight. When viewed for the first time, their beauty is astonishing. They are a much hoped-for visitor from the boreal forests of the far north. These large finch are also seen in December along Bosma Road, where they feed on the bright red berries of cranberry viburnum.

Common Redpolls and Hoary Redpolls are more difficult to view and to identify. To be acceptable, sightings of the latter must be taken at close range. In decades of recorded winter census-taking, only nine sightings in Berkshire County were convincing.

Fortunately, confirmed sightings of rare birds need not concern those who are truly involved in birding for the enjoyment and tranquility. Any time spent at Moran is an intrinsic experience. From the open meadow to the thick cover of the conifers, this site is rewarding, no matter what birds are sighted.

Fobes Hill

Fobes Hill can be reached in twenty minutes by foot from the first parking area on the right while traveling north on 8A. A spectacular view of Mount Greylock can be enjoyed here amidst a forest in succession. The summit of Fobes Hill is 2,080 feet high and provides good hawk watching during the fall migration. Broad-winged Hawks are common, but others include Sharp-shinned, Northern Goshawks, and Red-tailed Hawks. The remaining forestland contains much the same species as across the street.

18 Dorothy Frances Rice Sanctuary for Wildlife

Closest Town: Peru

Best Time To Visit: May, June, September

Methods Of Birding: Walking Trails.

Birds Of Special Interest: Ruffed Grouse (year-long), Least Flycatcher (Spring), Warblers (May), Rusty Blackbirds (variable).

Advice/Rules: Be alert for black bears. Cross-country skiing is allowed.

The little-known Dorothy Frances Rice Sanctuary offers six well-marked trails and over 40 nesting species of birds. This hidden sanctuary receives few visitors; nearby Moran Wildlife Management Area and Notchview Reservation receive most of the attention. However, the Rice Sanctuary offers good birding.

In the late 1920s, Oran and Mary Rice established this sanctuary in memory of their daughter. Decades later, it was entrusted to the New England Forest Foundation. The Foundation acquires land and sets it aside for wildlife and people. NEFF is unique in that the land is working land, managed for the twin goal of natural resource use and protection. Their forests are available for logging and small-scale farming, with the idea that such practices can enhance habitat while uplifting economic livelihood for rural residents.

The site offers birders a healthy representation of typical Berkshire woodland species. Largely unexplored as a birding site, there are no known specialties or unusual sightings. Instead, it offers trails through logging fields, meadows, beaver ponds and densely wooded hills where nothing but the soothing sounds of nature await the visitor. The Sanctuary protects 276 acres contiguous to State land on the north boundary. Black bears are seen here frequently, and moose are becoming more common each year.

Getting There

From the center of Peru, take Route 143 west, toward Pittsfield. Turn left on South Road. Travel 1.0 mile to the gate and the sign for the Sanctuary. Park outside of the gate if possible.

Rice Sanctuary

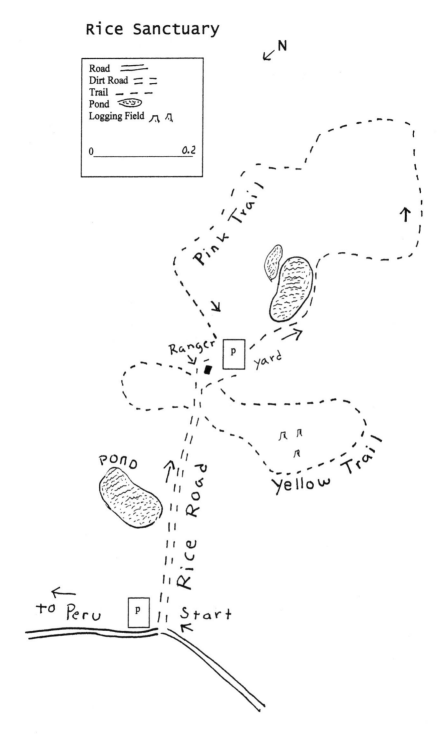

Road
Dirt Road
Trail
Pond
Logging Field

0   0.2

N

Pink Trail

Ranger

P

yard

Yellow Trail

POND

Rice Road

to Peru

P

Start

Birding Rice Sanctuary

Rice Road

While Rice Road can be driven all the way to the posted map and trailheads, many people choose to park at its beginning. This allows for a nice walk down Rice Road, where there is much to see. Almost immediately on the left, tucked away from the road, there is a long beaver marsh. Every spring, on the dead trees or bushes along the circumference of the marsh, members of the flycatcher family abound. There may be Willow, Alder, and Least Flycatcher from spring into September. Yellow-bellied Flycatchers have been seen occasionally in migration. Look for Great Crested Flycatcher along Rice Road, they will be found high up in the trees. Occasionally, they will descend and this is when they can be matched with their distinct *dweep-dweep* call, which is different from all other flycatchers.

Check the marsh along the road for spring warblers. Further down Rice Road, along the open roads and fields by the cabin, look for Yellow Warbler. Sometimes Common Yellow Throat and Northern Cardinals can be found in the cover or "edge" habitat. Just before the caretaker's cabin, there is a field on the left; Ruffed Grouse and Wild Turkey are seen here almost daily. Blue Jays, American Robins, and Goldfinch are well represented, but less common birds may include Blue-gray Gnatcather, Eastern Bluebird, Cedar Waxwing (winter) and Tree Swallows.

The Ruffed Grouse is known for its drumming of feathers while displaying itself on a decaying log. The log is usually that of an older tree and of large size. Logs hidden beneath brambles or low hanging evergreens are frequent choices, as there is a preference for a covering of debris and moss. Birders have been known to elicit a response by cupping hands and beating one's chest in order to imitate the sound. In the silence of the woods, the beating of the grouse's wings may often sound like the beating of one's own heart; especially at the beginning, when the drumming starts off soft and slowly increases in speed and intensity. If you here a drumming grouse, it is probably closer than you might think. Try locating it in the direction of where there may be some old, decaying logs.

The Pink Trail

Rice Sanctuary is criss-crossed with well-marked, properly maintained, color-coded trails. From the large map posted at the rear of the parking area, go directly to the left to find the trailhead of the Pink Trail. This trail will take you along the edge of an active beaver pond, through some woods, and up into a forest, where you will ascend gradually to a lookout.

Rusty Blackbirds

At the very start, along the trailhead, look for Blue-gray Gnatcatcher, Gray Catbirds, Common Yellowthroat, and Wood Thrush, from May to October. If you travel quietly toward the beaver pond, you may see a Great Blue Heron feeding patiently along the water's edge. Although this is a small body of water, these majestic wading birds are frequently caught off guard while taking advantage of the beaver's hard work by stealing a dinner of small fish from their carefully engineered reservoir. They are often seen flying from this pond over the lawns and fields of the Nature Center toward the pond on Rice Road.

This beaver pond is also a great place to enjoy a less noticeable species -- the Rusty Blackbird (*illustration*). It is sometimes seen along the shoreline. This bird is in decline and becoming increasingly rare. They are usually mistaken for Common Grackle or other blackbirds, but they are a distinctly separate and interesting species. Found here during migration, this bird may be highly erratic in its appearance during both journeys north and south. They are largely confined to their travels between mid-March and mid-April, but they travel alone and show up in unlikely places. Sometimes they are found nesting in this region, but for the most part, this bird is a boreal black spruce bog inhabitant.

Rusty Blackbirds are an unobtrusive species, presenting a considerable challenge to even the best birders. They feed along the shore of densely covered ponds and bogs. Song is the best way to locate them; listen for an unmusical squeaking or a wavering whistle-like call. If you're close enough, a pair of yellow eyes will give away their identity.

The Northern Waterthrush is similarly reclusive and occupies the same shoreline zone. They cannot be mistaken for Rusty Blackbird, for the waterthrush is a smaller bird with a different build. Other birds of specific interest at the pond are the flycatchers. Look for the same ones mentioned under the Rice Road section. Of the group, the most likely flycatcher at this pond will be the Least. Eastern Wood-Peewee and Eastern Phoebe are in the surrounding trees. Other insect-eating birds will include Tree Swallows and Cedar Waxwings. The Belted Kingfisher is another possibility, but it prefers to nest inside sandy embankments and is not a confirmed nester here.

If the prospect of encountering black bears makes you nervous, you may not wish to visit the Dorothy Frances Rice Sanctuary. During the early spring, when they emerge from hibernation, black bears visit the wetlands at this sanctuary, and then return again in the late summer to gorge themselves upon the abundance of wild blackberries and raspberries. During the summer of 2001, the resident caretaker, who lives in the cabin, saw eight bears. (He also saw a moose and her calf on a regular basis.) Black bear sign is evident all along the pond and in the "cuts" where logging has allowed for a healthy sun-drenched succession of berry-producing plants.

The Berkshire Hills are rich in history, and the Rice property is no exception. Evidence of the settlers that once worked the land is seen in the stone walls that add an aesthetic charm to the property. Abandoned parts of old tools suggest a time when life was a bit tougher, and there are remains of an old colonial trade route. Hidden deep under twisting trees and a blanket of leaves are the remains of old carriages that probably belonged to the Rice family. These relics await your analysis. Although travel off-trail cannot be recommended, you can usually stray a few hundred feet from the trail without getting lost. Look for these carriages between the little beaver pond and the beginning of the Pink Trail. Do not take any "souvenirs." Remember that everything here belongs to the sanctuary.

Down by the little stream set back in the woods, opposite of the caretaker's cabin, there once spanned an impressive stone arched bridge. It eventually collapsed, releasing a burden of stone off its back and apparently dumping them like weary travelers into and across the stream. If such interesting remains like these can still be found, consider the myriad of other treasures that have yet to be revealed or discovered. When the settlers left New England for places in the West, they left many things behind, which have remained, reclaimed only by the growing forest and its countless layers of leaves.

Shortly after passing the pond, you begin to ascend toward the peak. The woods are mixed deciduous with some spruce and white pine. Listen for canopy-dwellers such as Scarlet Tanager and Red-eyed Vireo. In fall, the Philadelphia Vireo is possible. Blue-headed Vireo may nest at the summit.

The summit offers a magnificent view to the north. There are plans to take down an acre or more of trees to enhance the view and allow for the pond to be seen. This will bring in Morning Warblers, which favor slash growth in logged areas along hillsides. In the meantime, check for Nashville Warblers. There may be a few Black-throated-Green Warblers in the higher canopy.

After spending some quiet contemplative moments at the summit lookout, you will exit to the right and begin a quick descent. In about fifteen to twenty minutes you will arrive in the rich woodland opposite to where you began. Cross over the grassy area while keeping a hopeful eye out for Blue-winged Warblers. An uncommon woodland nester, the Black-billed Cuckoo is believed to breed here. One might reveal itself in a brushy area.

Downy and Hairy Woodpeckers frequent the base of trees, along with the Red-breasted and White-breasted Nuthatches. Screech Owls have been heard at this point where the Pink Trail terminates. In the dead of night, Great Horned and Barred Owls fill the air with their distinct hooting calls. The Barred Owl's call is commonly known "who cooks for you ... who cooks for you all." Great Horned Owls emanate a less baritone or resonating call, consisting of long hoots.

Yellow Trail

The Yellow Trail begins a few yards off to the right of the beginning of the Pink Trail. Walk back toward the cabin and across Rice Road to reach the trailhead. This is where the black bears are frequently found feeding during late August to early September, when the berry crop ripens. Make your presence known if you see recent evidence of their presence. They do not like surprises.

If the bears have not eaten all the berries, this is a great time of year to find early migrants adding some fruit to their diet. Cedar Waxwings are a possibility at this time of year and even more so later into the fall. During the fall migration, Hermit Thrush, Wood Thrush, and even a few Swainson's may turn up. Certainly flocks of American Robins will make quick work of the fruit if they happen upon it. Aside from migrating members of the thrush family, there will be dozens of sparrows, primarily the White-throated Sparrow. Their whistle calls are a welcome and peaceful tune at the end of the summer or on crisp cool fall evenings when dusk falls and mists begin to rise.

At this same time of day, just after sunset, Dark-eyed Juncos can be heard with their chipping, high-pitched, short notes. Juncos nest on the higher hills at this site, but will flock in the fields during fall. Canada Geese might be heard in the distance; but in general, after a noisy summer of song, this wildberry-filled log field is mostly quiet until spring.

Follow the Yellow Trail down a hill along the "cut," enjoying a wide variety of birds from spring through summer. Look for Carolina and Winter Wren. Common Yellowthroat are hiding all about the regrowth, while nesting Wood Thrush fly in and out of the clearing. Ruffed Grouse walk concealed beneath the tangles of saplings and brambles. An occasional Northern Flicker may settle here and try for a meal of carpenter ants in the decaying logs buried beneath the dense vegetation. Indigo Buntings may nest -- singing males have been seen in the summer on occasion.

The Yellow Trail cuts back up along this log field and then shoots off to the left. From there, it dips down across some wet regions and eventually comes out to the Rice Road. Here, it continues across the road. If you choose to continue on this trail, it will take you back into a woodland.

Throughout this part of the Sanctuary birders can expect to see a healthy representation of typical mixed deciduous forest bird species. Although this site has no known rarities of its own, it offers a quiet birding experience where a birder can enjoy a typical New England forest.

19   Mount Greylock Reservation

Closest Town: Lanesboro, North Adams.

Best Time To Visit: May, June, July, September.

Methods Of Birding: Walking Trails, Car.

Birds Of Special Interest: Hawks (September), American Kestrel (summer), Yellow-bellied Sapsucker (Late April, May, June) Red-breasted Nuthatch (year-long), Olive-sided Flycatcher (late Spring), Gray-cheeked Thrush (spring), Swainson's Thrush (spring to fall), Hermit Thrush (June, July), Eastern Bluebird (March to July).
Warblers (May, spring to fall) -- Mourning Warbler, Blackburnian Warbler, Blackpoll Warbler, Black-throated Green Warbler;
Boreal Chickadee (winter), Northern Saw-whet Owl (variable), Evening and Pine Grosbeak (winter), Red and White-winged Crossbills (winter), Pine Siskin (winter to spring, sometimes breeding season), Bobolink (summer).

Advice/Rules: Be sure to visit The Hopper. Do not forget the good birding near the Visitor Center and the open fields along the way to it. The hiking can be demanding and requires preparation. There is camping well into the fall. Do not park cars overnight along roads. Rockwell Road is open 24 hours. The auto road closes in winter.

Mount Greylock is 3,491 feet high, is accessible by car, and offers views of five states. The Massachusetts Division of Forest and Parks maintains this, the state's highest peak, and has successfully acquired a total of 12,500 acres to the Mount Greylock Reservation. It fell into state ownership in 1898 and was the first state park. Nearly a wilderness, the Reservation provides 68 miles of trails. The Appalachian Trail winds its way over and around the summit, bringing hikers to and from Vermont, just a few miles to the north.

For years in the past, birders came to the mountain to spend the June evenings on the summit listening to the spiritual flute-like notes of the Bicknell's Grey-cheeked Thrush (now known as simply Bicknell's Thrush -- a separate species). The secretive bird would ascend from a perch in an acrobatic flutter and then retire back to its perch, all the while singing loud, ethereal notes, lasting long into the sunset and even past dusk. Today the Bicknell's Thrush is no longer found here -- birders may see one only in migration. Yet the haunting beauty of a Greylock sunset is still inspirational.

Mount Greylock

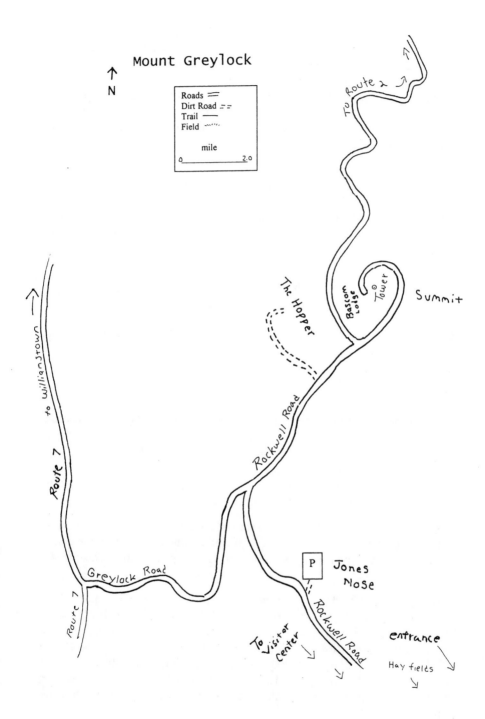

N

Roads =
Dirt Road = =
Trail ——
Field ~~~~

mile
0   2·0

To Route 2

to Williamstown

Route 7

The Hopper

Bascom Lodge

Tower

Summit

Rockwell Road

Route 7

Greylock Road

P   Jones Nose

To Visitor Center

Rockwell Road

entrance

Hay fields

Greylock is a unique experience for birders who may not otherwise have the opportunity to travel further north. Visitors travel a ten-mile-long auto road to the summit, passing through a variety of plant communities. Ascending 1,000 feet in elevation is equivalent to traveling about 200 miles north. At 3,491 feet, the summit is comparable to a boreal forest in northern Maine or central Quebec! With just a short ten-mile drive, birders can experience the change from oak woods to red spruce, where species like Northern Mockingbird give way to Evening Grosbeaks.

Getting There

From Pittsfield, take Route 7 North to North Main in Lanesboro, turn right and follow this road to the entrance. From North Adams, take Notch Road south to a sudden left turn at a reservoir (this is still Notch Road), and then follow Notch Road to Summit Road and the lodge on the peak.

Greylock through the Seasons
Auto Road and Trails

Since there are 68 miles of hiking trails, and birding by car along Rockwell and other roads is productive, the individual trails have not been listed here. More information about the trails is available at the visitor center at the summit.

Winter

Although the auto road to the summit is open 24 hours a day, the reservation closes in the winter and the road is blocked off to visitors at the first substantial snowfall. Snow usually begins falling on Greylock as early as October, with accumulations occurring in November. However, with the unseasonable winters we have had periodically over the past two decades, it is entirely possible the auto road may still be open in December. Be sure to call first to confirm.

It is worth mentioning a few of the exciting birds that are often found on the mountain during the winter. For the brave and ambitious, these birds can be accessed, as the region is open for winter sports such as snow-shoeing and cross-country skiing.

In winter, the White-throated Sparrows and Dark-eyed Juncos depart, flying down from the summit and settling in weedy fields and waysides. Birds such as Blue Jays and Chickadees may also work into small loose flocks and find feeders in the warmer valleys below. Other flocks from areas to our north may fill in behind them along the 2,000-foot elevation mark. Thus, above 2,000 feet in winter, things become quiet. The sound of snow falling and the wind are only temporarily broken by the calls of a few Brown Creepers or Red-breasted Nuthatches.

The Boreal Chickadee is a possibility, but rare. Near the peak, the firs and spruce sometimes become decorated with Pine Siskins, White-winged and Red Crossbills. Red Crossbills should be expected at some point during the season, as they are attracted to the red spruce growing here. Other birds of the north may also be found, including the brilliantly colored Pine Grosbeak.

This attractive bird of the boreal forest finds itself at home among the red spruce and fir of Greylock. A tame bird, the Pine Grosbeak is exceptionally rare in Massachusetts. It usually appears during winter for brief visits and mostly at the summits of our higher peaks, where some boreal or spruce/fir forest can be found. Here they feed on the cone seeds that are sometimes in short supply further north. Some birders tell of walking to within feet of these large docile finches.

The only summer record of this giant finch is from the town of Florida on August 22, 1985. Erratic records of their presence shows as many as 192 on scoresheets during the 1971 Pittsfield Christmas Bird Count, and then again in 1972 when 125 were counted, but since then, their occurrence has dropped off considerably. In the past few years, none have been sighted during the CBC. However there were some small flocks in Becket during the late winter of 2002.

The Evening Grosbeak is another bird to look for during the winters on Greylock. This handsome gold and black bird enjoys feeding on maple seeds but will also be found at the higher points of the mountain. They almost always travel in small flocks, usually noted first by their clear, liquidy notes and habit of grouping and dispersing. Prior to 1950, these starling-sized finches were very unusual in Massachusetts, but slowly, they began to make more appearances. Like the other northern finches, their arrivals are unpredictable and very erratic. A healthy 1,993 were documented in 1971, but years later there were none.

Purple Finch and Hoary Redpolls remain rare throughout the state, but winters on Mt. Greylock are good times to check. The Redpolls are difficult to identify. Occasionally they settle down at feeders near the mountain and are reported. Theoretically, they should be looked for at all feeders during January and February cold spells.

Northern Saw-whet Owls are assumed breeders. These tiny owls stay close to cover and never allow themselves to be vulnerable during their afternoon roosts in the sun. Like other small owls, they must be prepared for attacks from their larger cousins. While crows mob the Barred and Great-horned Owls, it is Black-capped Chickadees that often rob these owls of their peace. Long-eared Owls can, on rare occasion, be found in the thicker groves of young spruce and fir during the day. Unlike the other owls that become vocal in the winter breeding season, they remain quiet all year long.

Great Horned Owls and Barred Owls are common. The Great Horned prefers the lowlands, and the Barred is perhaps more common near the wetlands. Ravens are often heard; they give the winter landscape a true feeling of wildness as they call to one another with remote and unusual sounds. Stony Ledge is good place to watch and/or listen to them.

Generally, winter is a quiet time when nature is unkind, and the struggle to survive is most dramatic. Black bears hibernate, the days are short, and the woods see few human visitors. The persistence of winter's icy chill lingers long on this high mountain. Snow may still be found on the summit even in late May. Some of Greylock's winter specialties may be found in the late spring. Evening Grosbeaks continue, and sometimes Pine Siskins are reported through the breeding season. This small bird of northern affinity may find the evergreen-covered peak suitable for nesting.

Spring

In March, when the snow is still deep on the top of Greylock and just beginning to melt down below, American Robins can be heard singing in the yards and pastures that surround the mountain's base. Soon they appear in the deciduous forests up to 2,000 feet, where the snows give way to the earth soaked in icy drainage. Here the skunk cabbage poke their heads up through the mud, and marsh marigold add the first hint of color. A few weeks later, these robins move higher up the slopes into the mixed deciduous forest of maple, yellow birch, and hemlock.

The progress of spring is displayed for you in reverse as you take each step higher, for it seems that you travel back into winter, and every stage of this season can be enjoyed. It is as if time stands still for a moment, allowing you to go back and experience a part of the season you had missed in your hectic life. When the leaves first appear at 2,500 feet, the days have already grown warm in the green valleys across western Massachusetts.

A spring favorite is the Yellow-bellied Sapsucker that frequents the northern hardwood region about midway up the mountain. Sapsuckers have a peculiar call that has a whining sound. When the woods are still quiet and barren in early spring, these noisy woodpeckers are easy to identify. Black-and-white Warblers may appear as early as the sapsuckers in April. Generally, warblers will arrive in concentrated waves between May 15th and June 15th. The spruce forests are filled with northerners in migration.

Summer

Many of the migrating northerners will choose to nest. Look for the Yellow-rumped Warbler preparing to nest and remain for the summer at the summit (above 2,700 feet).

Blackpoll Warbler

Blue-winged, Chestnut-sided and Common Yellowthroat Warblers are found along or near Jones Nose Trail and a bit further down. They prefer open or brushy places, so also check for them near the visitor center from May until early September. Good concentrations of Blackburnian Warblers show up every year in a region of mature spruce within The Hopper (see map). You can reach this area by heading south on Route 43; simply bear left onto the Hopper Road (a hike is required). Black-throated Blue, Black-throated Green, American Redstart, and the waterthrushes are found throughout the forest. Black-throated Green is common at higher forested points, and the Yellow Warbler at lower. Cape May (uncommon) and Canada Warbler (common -- several often seen in one day) are seen on Saddleball Mountain (Appalachian Trail) just a short hike in from the Summit Road near the last sharp turn.

The Blackpoll Warbler (*illustration*) is another wood warbler that nests on Greylock and is perhaps Greylock's most celebrated specialty. This species is much sought after, and birders come from all over Southern New England and beyond to add this bird to their life lists. You can see this black-and-white-colored bird near the summit. Try the last few miles of Notch Road. Here they breed in concealment among the spruce and fir. Blackpoll Warblers nest nowhere else in the state!

Among birders, the second in popularity to the Blackpoll Warbler is the Mourning Warbler. On Sperry Road, heading toward to the campground, there are several acres of regenerating cut-over timber in succession. In this brushy area are the prized Mourning Warblers. On Rockwell Road, along Jones Nose Trail, there is another site of nesting Mourning Warblers. This site was once full of these little birds each summer, but over the past few years some of the saplings have gained considerable height, which makes the area less ideal for the warbler. Some cutting is planned and this will restore the warblers' prefered habitat.

There are additional sites where the land has been recently logged and the warblers thrive in the regrowth. These can be found along the Appalachian Trail at the point where it crosses the Summit Road, and also at the junction of the Sperry and Rockwell Roads. All of these sites are convenient. The Jones Nose region can be accessed by a pullover. A sign will mark the site.

Other nesting warblers are found at various places throughout the mountain. There are 15 species of wood warblers that nest on Greylock. Finding just a few of them shouldn't be too much work, even for beginners. One of the best places is along the upper part of Notch Road , and Rockwell road is also very good.

In fact, a drive up Rockwell Road is recommended for sampling the variety of birds found on Greylock. Driving up to the lodge with the windows open as the sun is rising will fill the soul. Skilled birders can pinpoint precisely which species are present along different points of the ascent. For instance, the Veery can be heard singing up to about the 1,500-foot mark, and then the Wood Thrush is heard at 2,500 feet. The melancholy song of the White-throated Sparrow is a good indication of the change from northern hardwood to a more boreal community. Listen for its unmistakable, evocative song that sounds like "old Sam Peabody, old Sam Peeeaabody." This bird's counterpart, the Dark-eyed Junco, is also common near the summit.

Be sure to stop every so often and listen more carefully. Where it is safe, get out and bird along the side of the road, or use the designated pullovers that allow for more parking space. Some birds of interest living from the lower elevations up to about 2,300 feet are Great-crested Flycatcher, Pileated Woodpecker, Brown-Creeper, Hairy Woodpecker, Scarlet Tanager, Baltimore Oriole, Blue-headed (Solitary) and Red-eyed Vireo, Hermit, Wood, and Swainson's Thrush (up to the summit), Winter Wren, Eastern Wood-Pewee, Cedar Waxwing, Northern Goshawk, Sharp-shinned, Red-tailed, and Broad-winged Hawk.

The aforementioned Swainson's Thrush is an unobtrusive bird that is quickly becoming less common. You might see one in the boreal forest, which begins about 2,600 feet. This reclusive and seldom seen bird is a talented singer, but soon it may disappear from the peak, as did the Bicknell's Thrush.

Both the Bicknell's and the Grey-cheeked Thrush (formerly considered subspecies) may be seen in the spring or fall during migration. Both are uncommon and difficult to identify in the dense conifer growths. The last breeding pair of Bicknell's Thrush was documented in 1972.

The Olive-sided Flycatcher is a locally rare species that does not breed in many places within the state. It is sometimes found on Mt. Greylock in an area known as Wilbur's Clearing along the Appalachian Trail. This is a boggy section located a few miles up (toward the summit) from where the trail crosses Notch Road. Near the summit, where Notch Road joins with Rockwell Road, another locally rare flycatcher can be seen on occasion. Follow the Appalachian Trail 1.2 miles in (south) from where the trail crosses Summit Road to find the Yellow-bellied Flycatcher in a boreal bog setting.

Both the Black-backed and Northern Three-toed Woodpeckers are rumored to exist in the remote bogs within the boreal zone. These are very rare boreal species that inhabit spruce bogs with dead standing timber. They have been very infrequently documented in the Reservation. Every once in a great while, a birder reports a Black-backed elsewhere in the state.

Fall

Fall is time when birders come to see hawks in their migration. The Broad-winged, Sharp-shinned and Northern Goshawk are likely. There are several places that offer hawk watching, but probably the most convenient are the Adams Lookout and the War Memorial Tower on the summit. The Adams Lookout is located off the side of the Summit Road. From here, there are spectacular views to the east. From the tower, there is a 360-degree view. Stony Ledge offers another vantage point and is considered the best. The views from there are the most dramatic, but also require caution. This view can be reached from the Sperry Road Campground.

Visitor Center and Adjacent Open Country

Few people think of this reservation as being good for anything other than woodland birds; but the wide-open fields and meadows adjacent to the visitor center attract a variety of birds each spring and are home to such open country-loving species as Bobolink, Eastern Meadowlark, and Eastern Bluebird. Other birds in the open country are American Woodcock and a variety of sparrows including Vesper, Savannah, Chipping, and sometimes Field Sparrows. Kestrels perch on wires and posts above the hay fields.

20   Berkshire Lakes

Lake Pontoosuc, Lake Onota, and Cheshire Reservoir

Closest Town: Pittsfield

Best Time to Visit: April, November

Methods Of Birding: Walk on shoreline, Rail-Trail (bicycle), Car.

Birds Of Special Interest: Snow Goose (winter), Common Loon (April and November), Diving and Dabbling Ducks.

Advice/ Rules: Mornings and evenings are best. Motorized boats are not allowed on Cheshire Reservoir.

Three Berkshire Lakes are excellent for birding -- Lake Pontoosuc, Lake Onota, and Cheshire Reservoir. Although other lakes in the region have been good for birding, these three get the most attention and are among the most rewarding sites. Furthermore, they are convenient, accessible, and within minutes of downtown Pittsfield. Also within a reasonable drive are Pleasant Valley, Canoe Meadows and Mount Greylock. The Berkshire Lakes are also attractive because of their affinity to the greater Housatonic River Valley.

Birding the Lakes

The best birding is achieved from October to November. This is when migrant waterfowl land and rest on their way south through the Housatonic Valley. They consistently produce a healthy representation of loons, ducks, geese, and grebes. In addition, Lake Onota has evergreen trees of a considerable age and size growing through its adjacent park. Sometimes during flight years, Pine Siskins and both kinds of crossbills can be sighted. Evening Grosbeaks turn up on rare occasions from fall through spring. Tree Swallows, and an occasional Barn Swallow have also been noted. Grackles are often found nesting in the tops of the white pines. The action begins in early September and peaks in the early days of October with the increasing chance of migrant loons. By this time, Common Loons have finished with breeding on the lakes to our north and have settled in at the Berkshire Lakes for extended visits.

Berkshire Lakes

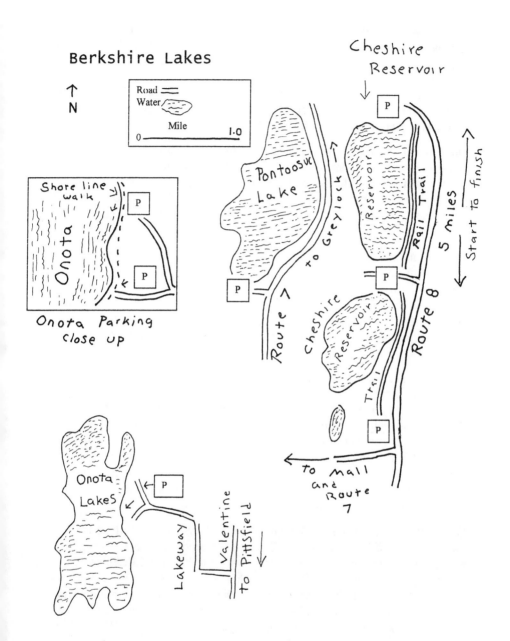

Road ═══
Water ⬭
Mile
0 ——————— 1.0

N ↑

Cheshire Reservoir

Pontoosuc Lake

Reservoir

to Greylock

Cheshire Reservoir

Rail Trail

5 miles

Start to finish

Route 7

Route 8

Trail

Shore line walk

Onota

Onota Parking close up

Onota Lakes

Lakeway

Valentine

to Pittsfield

to Mall and Route 7

Loons have been recorded on all three bodies of water, but check Onota Lake especially. Loons prefer the presence of white perch and the good visibility of Onota. Sometimes, a wayward Red-throated Loon may appear, and a Northern Shoveler might be possible. About the same time of year, Pied-billed Grebes turn up in small groups. They may stay a few hours or a few days, but then move on. The future is questionable for the grebe, which requires extensive wetland marshes to prosper -- so enjoy this rare experience.

The Canada Goose, on the other hand, is prospering. Common on all three lakes, they tend to appear in flocks from September until the waters ice over. Occasionally the beautiful and majestic Snow Goose appears with them. During winters, when the ice has not formed before January, Snow Goose may find these lakes very attractive. Canada Goose can be expected to nest on all three Berkshire Lakes.

The Mallard and American Black Duck are constants here as well, breeding at one time or another on all three of these lakes. Blue-winged Teal, American Wigeon (*illustration*) and Northern Pintails, Common and Hooded Mergansers are also well known visitors throughout the fall. The lakes are best known, however, for their ability to produce unusual bird sightings -- such exciting species as Red-necked and Horned Grebes, Ruddy Duck, Brant, Goldeneye, and Bufflehead.

There is a special time just before sunset known as the "window" when Canada Geese slide in after circling in great clamorous, honking tirades. Listening to this classic fall sound in the fading light is reward enough for any birder, but more delights follow with other overnight visitors flying in from all directions. Mallards and Common Mergansers are just as noisy. The Mallards quickly swim into weedy shores, and the mergansers stay out in the deeper water. Mergansers swim through the night, without diving. Resting from time to time, they are generally alert and ready for take-off at sunrise. The lakes remain overnight shelters for these birds until the ice begins to form.

When the lakes are frozen, a few gulls may be found wherever there is some melt water or surface depressions. The gulls generally stay out a ways from shore, but with spotting scopes or binoculars, even their age differences can be discovered. Be on the lookout for Iceland Gulls -- a rare possibility. As the days grow longer and the ice recedes, gulls often show up only in the morning while on their way to other more "gullish" sites. Yet these late winter days during ice-out are probably the best time for seeing one. The Ring-billed and Herring Gull are common, but the Lesser and Black-backed can arrive here unexpectedly -- only on rare occasions. April is the best time to see the Black-backed Gull, but even then it is unlikely. Spring typically brings with it the increase in Black Duck and Mallards. Sometimes, the sightings of Gadwall, Northern Pintail, or Bufflehead may also increase in the spring (early April).

170

American Wigeon

Rare terns may be sighted by those looking to the skies above or those lucky enough to see one skim across the lake's surface. Records dating back to the early twentieth century show that Black Terns regularly pass over these lakes and sometimes fly down low to storm the shorelines at high speeds. The chances of seeing one are very slim, but nevertheless the thrill of knowing that terns may be seen is compelling. Especially worth noting is the sighting of a Foster's Tern at Onota Lake on June 2, 1986. Sightings of Common Terns are recorded for Onota in 1996. A very common species along the coast, its presence inland is extremely rare. The Caspian Tern has also been seen, with one on Pontoosuc in June of 1994. These sightings are anomalies, but worth mentioning because sometimes there are hurricanes, which historically force these birds into the Berkshires, where they gravitate to the lakes.

Shorebirds are rare on the Berkshire lakes. Prior to 1976, when the Pittsfield Sewer Beds were operating, these birds were common visitors in the area in late summer and spring. Now, since the sewer beds have been replaced by modern wastewater technologies, these birds are hardly ever reported. They sometimes appear on the lakes when drought coincides with their migration time. One likely spot to try is the north end of Pontoosuc where a feeder stream (Town Brook) enters. Look for Killdeer, Greater Yellowlegs, and Pectoral Sandpiper.

In summer, these lakes become busy places with motorboats, canoes, hikers, swimmers and sun-worshipers, but they may be worth checking out if you are in the vicinity in the early morning. The only birds to be found with any reliability are Mallards. Belted Kingfisher are also possible. The Cheshire Reservoir is quieter, but even there the birding slows down until late August, when conditions slowly improve.

Pontoosuc Lake

Getting There

Take Route 7 north from downtown Pittsfield and turn onto Hancock Road, which is at the southern end of the lake. There is another access point just a few yards further on the left off of Route 7.

This lake is 480 acres and has an average depth of 14 feet. Transparency of the water is normal at about 11 feet. Some fluctuation of the water level does occur, and during drought there is some exposure along the shores. A great deal of aquatic vegetation can be found growing from its mucky bottom. The northern end of the lake is especially rich in vegetation, but the south end is very gravelly. A very small marshland can be found at the north end from Bull Hill Road by heading west off Route 7. Unfortunately, like many waterfronts, the shoreline is fully developed. Although some nesting species are absent and summer is uneventful, the birding is nevertheless sustained at a high level.

Of the three Berkshire lakes, Pontoosuc Lake offers some of the best fall birding. Access to the lake consists of a few hundred feet near the southernmost end, across from the boat launch area, and along a grassy hillside adjacent to the launch itself. The grassy lawn across from the launch has an attractive clump of towering Norway spruce. Anglers enjoy the unobstructed access to the water.

There is also a walkway that can be reached from the second parking lot across from the launch. This can be taken for 0.5 mile, and it runs along the curbside of the southbound lane of Route 7, which is only a few yards from the shoreline. Otherwise, viewing may involve using watercraft, with a kayak or canoe being most practical for the job. Next to the boat launch, there is an attractive hill cloaked in evergreens. Picnic tables are found here, and there is a nice view of the lake with mountains rising up behind.

Onota Lake

Getting There

Onota Lake is accessed from Burbank Park. From Park Square in Pittsfield, travel west on West Street for 1.3 miles to a right onto Valentine Road. Travel north 0.7 mile to Lakeway Drive on the left. Follow this road to Burbank Park. Inside the park, bear to the right at a fork. This will bring you to the walkway.

This lake is a model for recreational use and natural resource protection. Just past downtown Pittsfield, its 617 acres is nicely landscaped on all sides. About 25% is parkland, which is heavily used. People come from throughout the Pittsfield area to enjoy the clear water and the cool, evergreen-shaded woods. Because of its convenient location, boating and fishing are rather consistent, yet the lake remains in good condition, capable of sustaining 18 different species of fish. The deepest part of the lake is 66 feet, with an average depth of 22 feet. Aquatic vegetation is heavy in the shallow regions. On an average day, the visibility is about 17 feet, making the lake attractive to diving species. Most anglers visit this lake in hopes of catching trout. The brown trout is of primary interest, as Onota has a reputation of producing record sizes. Ice fishing is popular during the winter.

For birding, Onota Lake offers easy access and viewing. After entering the park, there is a fork in the road at 0.2 mile. The road to the right takes you down to a fishing pier and parking lot. Birds can be viewed from the long fishing pier or by walking the paved trail that slips off to the left beyond an embankment of large rocks topped off with white birch and evergreens. This paved walkway hugs the shoreline, providing excellent viewing of the lake for about one mile. The walkway terminates at the far end of the beach house parking lot. Past that, there is a dirt road that leads to private property.

This end of the park provides some grassy areas and an actual sand beach. There are a few tiny ponds with weeds and cattails here and there, as the lake is shallow at this northern end. During dry spells, as in 2001, some extended sandbars can appear. Actually, these are more muddy than sandy, and they help make the site acceptable for shorebirds.

The park itself may be worth checking out. Most of it consists of typical park-like woods, except that the trees are old, and many are white pine or hemlock. White birch is also prominent. During flight years, winter finches have been seen. In early spring, Pine Warblers and Yellow-rumped Warblers are mixed in with groups of chickadees.

Ashuwilliticook Rail Trail
to Cheshire Reservoir

Getting There

From Pittsfield, travel north on Route 7 to the entrance for the Berkshire Mall in the town of Lanesborough. Follow the long road to the mall, and within the mall parking lot, exit via the Route 8 entrance/exit. Turn left for the trailhead of the Ashuwilliticook Rail-Trail.

To reach the Cheshire Reservoir from the Route 8 entrance, continue to the intersection and follow Route 8 northeast (left turn) until reaching Farnams Road on the left. This will put you near the other access. Views of the lake can be had in front of parking area. A left onto the trail brings you beside the water and along wooded side. If you go right, the trail will bring you along smaller bodies of water and wetlands back to the mall. Drive past Farnams before leaving and check for new developments on the trail, as it is being extended north.

A delightful setting has been created by the completion of a five-mile rail-trail along the shoreline of the Cheshire Reservoir. At the beginning, located at the Route 8 entrance to the Berkshire Mall, an assortment of young successional trees compete for a place in the sun. Towering above many of them, red maple and aspen trees grow freely, giving this converted old railroad bed a bit of character consistent with a bottomland. And indeed, water is everywhere -- a series of wetlands work their way along the right and left side of the rail-trail for the first few miles before giving way to the three impoundments that make up the reservoir system.

Separating the two southernmost basins is a causeway that allows access. These access areas are utilized by car-top boaters. With the boating limited mostly to non-motorized crafts, and development present only on the north reservoir's western shore, a birding visit can be enjoyed undisturbed. The reservoir is 418 acres and contains an impressive fishery. Largemouth bass and northern pike are the two most sought-after fish, but a healthy population of yellow perch and pumpkinseed provide much recreation for young anglers. The three basins are shallow with a maximum depth of just nine feet. Consequently, four-pound bass are not uncommon, and even a few exceptionally large pike have been taken.

For birders, there are exciting possibilities along the rail-trail. Wood Duck are common on the first two miles of the trail. The wooded shoreline along the first two impoundments provides an inviting habitat for them, and on some occasions, for the small Blue-winged Teal. Unfortunately, the view is largely obstructed from the rail-trail, and it is not until you reach the second body of water that you can find good viewing sites. Some birding can be conducted off the first causeway where the access boat drop is located.

By the time you have reached the third impoundment, the rail-trail has been sandwiched between Route 8 on the right and the reservoir on the left. Although only a few acres separate the trail from Route 8, there is much birding to enjoy on that side of the trail as well. The distant sound of traffic may be noticed at some points along the journey, but this does not seem to discourage the redwings, flycatchers, or warblers. Red-wings appear about the end of February, but otherwise there is not much action taking place after this until about the end of March, when the Eastern Phoebe may be spotted. They are usually seen perching and are immediately noted by their tail bobbing

Later, in late April and early May, scores of brightly-colored little warblers appear. These may arrive in waves, with dozens of them adorning the bushes and trees. As is the case in most places, the Yellow-rumped is most often seen. Chestnut-sided and Yellow Warblers are also common. Black-throated Green Warblers have been noted, too. Many of these tiny birds are undoubtedly on their way to Greylock, where they will be absorbed into the forest.

Throughout the summer and into the winter, birders will continue to enjoy seeing the common species. In the fall, the migration may bring down some interesting songbirds or flycatchers. The warbler action is less, and the birds are far more difficult to identify. While the main attraction is the lake, the woodland birds on the right hand side of the rail offer continuity during the lulls. And there is certainly enough natural beauty in this small strip of land to enhance the journey.

The trail directly parallels the water from Farnams Road (the second causeway dividing the reservoirs) down to the end. There is virtually no spot along this 1.6-mile stretch of the trail where you do not have a completely open view of the entire reservoir. You are literally right on the shoreline looking across the water to the mountains beyond -- and what a refreshing sight it is! Off to the north, it is especially scenic, as Mount Greylock rises up behind a classic New England white church steeple. In the autumn, the multitude of yellow-leafed white birch and distant crimson-cloaked maples create the perfect picture of this much esteemed rail-trail.

The birding also peaks here in the fall, from about the end of September and into early December (November is best). Come here with binoculars and walk the trail along the water either in the early morning or in the evening. Feeding in flocks or small groups may be Red-necked Grebe, Pied-billed Grebe, and Canvasback. Mallard, American Black Duck, and Canada Goose are easy to find everywhere. In spring, you may encounter a mother goose with her fuzzy chicks in tow. Approaching them noisily may suddenly transform the mother into a hissing snake-necked monster. Geese are very serious about protecting their young.

The Ashuwillticook Rail-Trail is a former railroad corridor that runs through Cheshire, Lanesborough, and Adams, Massachusetts. When fully completed, the rail-trail will extend another six miles and flank along the Hoosac River and associated wetlands. The name Ashuwillticook is derived from a Native American word meaning "in-between pleasant river" or "the pleasant river in between the hills." The hills referred to are the Mount Greylock Range and the Hoosac Range. The trail was a product of lobbying by concerned citizens. The right-of-way was acquired in 1993, and construction began in 1998.

21   Pleasant Valley Wildlife Sanctuary

Closest Town: Lenox

Best Time To Visit: Spring, Summer, Winter.

Methods Of Birding: Walking Trails, Bird Feeder.

Birds Of Special Interest: Blue-headed and Yellow-throated Vireo (spring and summer), Northern and Louisiana Waterthrush (spring to summer), Alder, Least and Olive-sided Flycatchers (spring to summer), Scarlet Tanager (early July), Pine Siskin (winter), Evening Grosbeak (winter).

Advice/ Rules: The trails near the brook require mosquito repellent. Visitors have free access to Lenox Mountain. Over-played as a site for Green Heron.

Pleasant Valley Sanctuary rests beneath the east side of Lenox Mountain. This peaceful 1,150-acre sanctuary protects forested hills and a beaver pond, and is home to eighty breeding species. There is a small field near the nature museum. Operated by the Massachusetts Audubon Society, the Sanctuary is open year-round. The most convenient of places to observe the rich bird life is at the bird feeder behind the sanctuary office, or down the trails near the beaver pond.

Getting There

From the Springfield area, travel west on the Mass Pike to exit 2 and then turn right on Route 20 (west). From the intersections of Routes 7 and 20 in Lenox, proceed 3.0 miles north to West Dugway Road on the left. Follow Signs 1.6 miles to sanctuary entrance.

Birding Pleasant Valley

Pikes Pond Trail

A network of clear trails exists in close proximity to the Education Center and Office. Choosing from among the trails is difficult because each has something different to offer. The best choice for someone short on time is probably the Pikes Pond Trail. The staff in the office, who can provide you with informative birding literature, often recommends it because it takes you through a variety of habitats. Thus, you are able to encounter a greater variety of birds in a short period of time and with minimal effort. This trail never leads you too far from the parking lot and adjacent field.

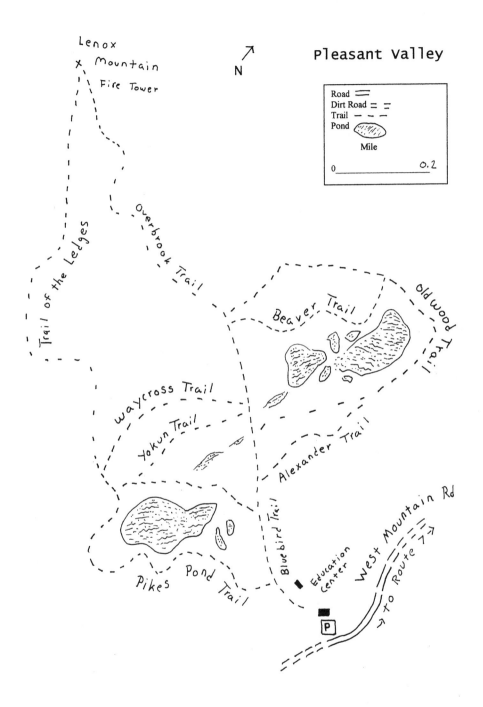

Lenox
x Mountain
Fire Tower

N

Pleasant Valley

Road
Dirt Road
Trail
Pond
Mile
0   0.2

Trail of the Ledges

Overbrook Trail

Beaver Trail

Old wood Trail

Waycross Trail

Yokun Trail

Alexander Trail

Pikes Pond Trail

Bluebird Trail

Education Center

West Mountain Rd

to Route 7

P

Begin near the Office, heading left and into the woods, and you will soon arrive at a body of water. Continuing on, you will walk another two hundred feet and cross over some more water, then enter into a wetland. Stay aware of the trail, as it now forks; but you will want to go right until encountering another fork and turning right again, away from the wetland and back toward the parking area. Another right takes you to the parking area, or turn left and walk to the open field and Education Center. How long this takes is of course dependent on the birding. Without stopping to bird (if you can imagine such a thing), the walk takes about forty-five minutes.

The birding is good all year, but spring and summer are best. During winter, American Tree Sparrows are often seen here while contemplating their return to forage at the feeder a few hundred yards away. Look for them at the start of the trail. Chickadees and Blue Jays are seen in small winter flocks and are abundant along the Pikes Pond Trail. Other winter species include White and Red-breasted Nuthatches. Ruffed Grouse are also encountered on occasion as you approach the wetland.

On Pikes Pond itself, not much will be happening in the winter. Sometimes, if the season is mild and there is some open ice, a Mallard or Black Duck might be found. Spring is completely different, however. Beginning with the ice-out, the pond comes to life with a few interesting birds. For starters, March may usher in Rusty Blackbirds with common Red-winged Blackbirds. The Rusty is rarely seen here, yet bogs and ponds in the higher hills often yield a few.

Later in March, Common Grackles begin to frequent the shorelines of these little ponds. The Tree Swallow is next to arrive, but it is the presence of Wood Duck that distinguishes these ponds. Look for this brilliantly-colored, tree cavity-nesting duck about mid-April. The Wood Ducks become more numerous in migration before completely fleeing the region in early November. The Belted Kingfisher are also present after the ice melts.

In early spring, before the foliage blocks the sunlight from the forest floor, painted trillium plants break through the debris with a flower of red crimson. Marsh marigold add color in the soggy areas where the ground is saturated and walking is forbidden.

In May and June, these damp woods around Pikes Pond are filled with singing Wood Thrush, Veery, and Hermit Thrush. Their songs are the essence of peace and tranquility. The Veery is especially fond of the dense undergrowth along the edges of wet areas. In late May, the air fills with the sweet aroma of mountain azalea. The pink blossoms of this shrub are brilliant, and each spring, they bestow their intricate beauty all along the Pikes Pond Trail.

Olive-sided Flycatcher

In summer, the trail is teeming with life. The pond becomes the center of attention and is giving life to a variety of species. Visiting birders can poke along the shoreline looking for turtles while sending frogs jumping for safety. All the while, Rose-breasted Grosbeaks sing loudly from secluded perches above the lower canopy. Baltimore Orioles dance above you, precarious in every posture, and Swamp Sparrows slip away under cover in the thickets.

Yokun & Beaver Lodge Trail Loop

This route is longer than the Pikes Pond Trail. It brings you into the Yokun Brook lowland. Birding is good, and like the Pikes Pond area, it gets better in spring and summer. Access is easy, and there is even a comfortable bench where you can birdwatch.

Follow the Blue Bird Trail down past the office and through the weedy field that slopes into the woods. On this trail, you can enjoy less common species, such as Eastern Bluebird and Ruby-throated Hummingbirds. In the fall, a few interesting sparrows may be present. Be ready for Lincoln's (September) and White-crowned Sparrows. Field Sparrows are known to nest but are not well represented nor easy to find. Indigo Buntings have also nested here, but more so along the field edges. At the bottom of the hill, after walking for about 0.3 mile, you will find the Yukon Trail on your right. The Yokun Trail will bring you along the edge of the pond and across the Yokun Brook onto the Beaver Lodge Trail, which will loop around and return to the Blue Bird Trail.

This part of the sanctuary is where most of the birds are spotted. Birdsong is intense from late April until mid-June. While the trail is certain to produce all the common woodland songsters, it is also possible to see an attractive warbler. The Yellow-rumped Warbler is easy to recognize with its appropriately colored behind. The little Ovenbird poses more of a challenge; but enough of them nest here to give inexperienced birders a unique chance to study this bird.

Along the pond, be on the lookout for Northern Waterthrush. These birds work the muddy shoreline. Their close cousins, the Louisiana Waterthrush, will be present along the streams. Swamp Sparrows may share some of these areas, but they prefer the cattail marshes. Rumors of Green-backed Herons (now known as Green Herons) abound. Unfortunately, they are not as common as everyone would like to think. Pleasant Valley has had very few reports of Green Herons.

The Olive-sided Flycatcher (*illustration*) is a rare find; but Pleasant Valley provides the opportunity in either spring or fall. However, the general public misses most of the Olive-sided Flycatchers, as they inhabit a wetland accessible only off-trail. They occasionally visit the Yokun Trail area. A Yellow-bellied is even more difficult to find, and identification is somewhat impossible for the beginner. Both Alder and Least are nesting, with the Least Flycatcher being the more common. The Willow Flycatcher does not find suitable habitat here.

The Great Crested Flycatcher frequents the woodland. Expect to see these large flycatchers at the tops of tall trees. The Eastern Wood-Pewee and the Eastern Phoebe are both common. The Eastern Wood-Pewee is absent by September in most years. While the pewee and phoebe have distinct differences, the best way to become adept at identification is to learn the songs of these flycatchers. This can be accomplished by listening to audiotapes; but be sure to follow through with observation.

One of the most striking features of this nice loop hike is the sheer abundance of common songbirds. Cherished species such as Gray Catbird, Wood Thrush, Veery, Northern Cardinal, Song Sparrow, Rose-breasted Grosbeak, and Scarlet Tanager are very common in the breeding season. Northern Cardinal numbers are thin in winter, but a few may be seen.

The Woodland and Lenox Mountain

The woodlands of Pleasant Valley sanctuary are not especially noteworthy for birding. Yellow-bellied Sapsuckers are a northern species found in abundance, and this offers birders who live in the flatlands a chance to see one. There are giant Pileated Woodpeckers to note here, as well. Swainson 's Thrush is often sought for, but they are only an occasional visitor. Red-tailed Hawks are the most prevalent, but be alert for the ghost-like Broad-winged. They are sometimes found nesting on the slopes of Lenox Mountain. Otherwise, the birder is left to the old reliables -- expect healthy numbers of Hairy and Downy Woodpeckers. The Tufted Titmouse has been established at Pleasant Valley for at least two decades. This bird has expanded its range north into Massachusetts via the milder conditions of the Connecticut River Valley.

The best way to experience the woodland is to ascend the peak of Lenox Mountain via the Overbrook Trail. Walking up this long, sylvan path, you can experience the change in bird and plant life with the rise in elevation. At the very top of the mountain, there are nesting Dark-eyed Juncos and White-throated Sparrows, each species endemic to more northern climes. In winter, these birds settle down from the cooler summit to frequent the bird feeder near the office. Throughout Southern New England, they do the same and settle in along hedgerows -- especially those in suburban lowlands, where they love to frequent feeders.

Abundant here are White-breasted Nuthatches, Blue Jays, Chickadees, Hairy and Downy Woodpeckers. Summer residents include such common species as American Robin, Wood Thrush, Hermit Thrush, and Red-eyed Vireo. The Brown Creeper can be considered a specialty, and Evening Grosbeaks are a favorite each winter. Pine Siskins can sometimes be viewed feeding during winter flight years.

There are many warblers at the summit. These include the Black-and-white, Canada, American Redstart, Blackburnian, and the Black-throated Green Warblers. The Black-and-white and American Redstart are common. Chestnut-sided and Yellow Warblers have also been documented as nesting. The Black-throated Blue Warbler seems a bit out of place in this northern hardwood mountain slope, but it has been reported to nest. Black-throated Blue Warblers are generally associated with the thick laurel growths of oak forests found in the Connecticut Valley, but Pleasant Valley has a considerable mountain laurel grove sufficient enough to harbor a few.

The Red-eyed Vireo is a common inhabitant of the woods at Pleasant Valley. Sometimes they are seen in close proximity to the road. Blue-headed and Yellow-throated Vireos are less conspicuous, but are present nevertheless, and in equal numbers. All three of these long-distance migrant species nest at the sanctuary.

The summit of Lenox Mountain is not actually a part of the sanctuary, but is owned by the State, whose protection will ensure the future enjoyment of this forest. Wildlife consists of more than birds; and as grand as the view may be, none of the important little dramas can be appreciated from the celebrated vista. Beneath the canopy of trees, hidden among the ferns, baby bobcats play with one another. Red and gray foxes are also seen here, and every now and again a black bear may be a cause for commotion. Beaver are plentiful and keep the wetlands thriving. These nocturnal animals are easy to see swimming along the Yokun Brook at dusk.

Bird Feeder

The bird feeder behind the sanctuary office is always worth checking because sometimes vagrants from the north show up. Any unusual species traveling through the Berkshire hills may find their way to the feeders along the populated valley; these are birds that you will *not* see coming to the feeders in the Pioneer Valley along the Connecticut River. Here, you will see black and gold Evening Grosbeaks in the dozens. Crossbills, Pine Siskins and Common Redpolls, while not predominant, are possible. Even Purple Finch are a treat for some bird-deprived individuals living in the cities or suburbs. The familiar antics of perky little Black-capped Chickadees, Blue Jays, White-breasted Nuthatches, and Downy Woodpeckers will warm the soul on any cold winter day. Black-capped Chickadees never fail to show for the easy pickings of big striped sunflower seeds and fat choice slices of peanut-laden suet cakes.

Although not attracted to the feeder, dazzling bright red Scarlet Tanagers do show up the first week of July to feast upon the red mulberry fruit-covered trees near the office. Often, orioles and thrushes will come in to make a quick meal of these tempting berries. If any are left a few weeks later, the Cedar Waxwing will take its turn and finish the yield.

22 Canoe Meadows Wildlife Sanctuary

Closest Town: Pittsfield

Best Time To Visit: Spring, Summer, early September,
early November, Late Winter

Methods Of Birding: Walking Trails.

Birds Of Special Interest: *Shorebirds* -- Solitary and Spotted Sandpipers (late summer), Wood and Black Ducks (spring to summer), Black-crowned, Green, and Great Blue Herons (spring to summer, Early September), Willow and Alder Flycatcher (spring)
Warblers -- Pine and Palm Warblers (May, spring and fall).

Advice/Rules: Plan repeat visits in the spring. This is a good place for the Audubon Bird Call. Trails are color-coded.

Time passes quickly along the trails of Canoe Meadows. Birders can find plenty to see deep within the walls of impenetrable vegetation along the Sacred Way Trail or while journeying along the flowering meadows on the Service Road. Whichever way you choose, the walking is easy, and the birding is busy in this quiet retreat just outside of Pittsfield.

This sanctuary is a composite of many different plant communities compacted within a small, 262-acre parcel. A wide variety of birds can be seen, even on the worst birding day, because the sanctuary has dense thickets, open woods, hay fields, wetland marsh, ponds, natural meadows, and acres of bottomland deciduous forest. The site is located along the Housatonic River, making it even more attractive to birds using the river as sort of a corridor or "flyway." It is no wonder that 175 species have been recorded here.

The sanctuary is one of the many Massachusetts Audubon Society properties. There are no facilities other than a wildlife observation shelter (bird blind) and a primitive outhouse. Inquiries or administrative work associated with the Canoe Meadows sanctuary or its use by the public is conducted at Pleasant Valley, which is located nearby. The purchase of Canoe Meadows is a blessing for both birders and mother nature, as its location within a critical wetland area associated with the Housatonic is one that has often been destroyed by human development. Safe now from destruction, the sanctuary will continue to bring birds and birders together where both can be nourished.

Canoe Meadows Wildlife Sanctuary

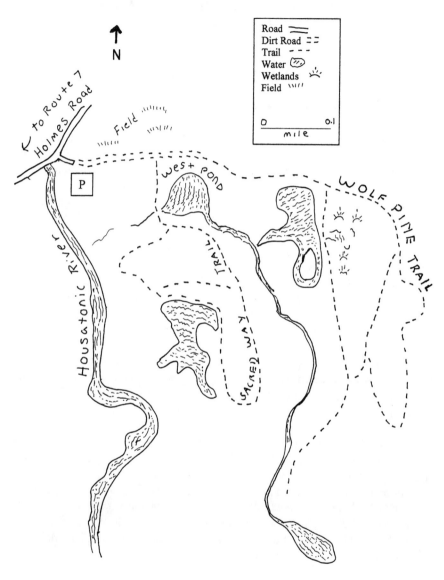

Getting There

From Route 7/20 in Lenox, look for the Massachusetts Audubon sign on your right, and take Holmes Road on the same side for 2.2 miles to the entrance on the right. Ample parking is available.

Birding Canoe Meadows

West Pond Area and Service Road

Just beyond the parking lot, a grassy field rises up onto a ridge covered by mature white pines. On the right, the shiny waters of West Pond are seen against the backdrop of the distant peaks of October Mountain State Forest.

A wide maintenance road can be seen going straight, while off to the right, a trail cuts through the shrubs and weeds, winding its way to West Pond. Begin your birding trip by taking the Service Road so as not to disturb any wildlife on or near the pond. Walk down from the parking area and keep your focus on the field where there may be a Bobolink or Eastern Meadowlark. Soon, you will see a red barn and behind it, a trail leading to a small wooden structure. This bird blind, or wildlife observation shelter, will provide you with a good clean view of the wildlife going about their business undisturbed. You might catch a glimpse of a red fox, beaver, or a common garter snake.

Any good naturalist knows to arrive early in the morning for best results. In the dim light of early morning, birders can expect to find Great Blue Herons standing motionless, waiting to strike the water with their spear-like beaks. Shorebirds may be seen on early August or September mornings before they take off in migration. Usually the Solitary or Spotted Sandpiper is observed, and rare sightings of Osprey occur around the same time of year. They are known to suddenly appear and crash down into the quiet little pond and steal a fish. Without question, however, the Belted Kingfisher's constant and cheerful rattling makes any birder's visit a success. Whatever fish this little pond gives up, it usually belongs to the Belted Kingfisher. On the surface of the pond, expect to see dabbling ducks at any time of year. In the fall, whispering wings of the Canada Goose draw the curtain on the sun each evening. The Mallards' presence is a sign that it is safe for landing.

Green Herons would be a treat to observe, but on most days they are hiding back along the oxbow waters. Explore the back section of the West Pond wetland. Sometimes Black-crowned Night-Herons are reported at the pond or elsewhere on the wetlands. Arcadian Flycatchers are unusual, but have been seen here, too. Both Willow and Alder are more common. They prefer different kinds of habitat in which to nest. Canoe Meadows is best suited for the Willow.

Boardwalk at Canoe Meadows

Wolf Pine Trail

After a few discoveries at West Pond, continue along the Service Road. Find the blue-blaze trailhead marker near the red barn, and you can proceed on the Wolf Pine Trail. This part of the sanctuary will take you into roosting areas of the Barred Owl and Great Horned Owl. Look for their small fur-ball pellets. These pellets are expelled orally after digestion is complete. They are comprised of the compacted remains of the indigestible fur and bones of the owl's prey. Small vertebrae and tiny skulls indicate a diet of mice or voles.

Also among the pines, the high pitched calls of the Pine Warbler may be heard in June. Pine Warblers are difficult to find in the Berkshire region, but here they are seen repeatedly. In winter, the tiny Red-breasted Nuthatch is more often appreciated. Overlooked in the breeding season, this quiet, little bird is present nonetheless.

The Wolf Pine Trail is named after an enormous White Pine found just after the point where the trail splits. Go right to see this natural wonder. You will complete a loop by taking a right and arriving back where the red barn is. This walk often provides birders with sightings of Ruffed Grouse, Wild Turkey, Northern Flicker, and Tufted Titmouse.

The Sacred Way Trail

The Sacred Way Trail starts on the right after entering the Sanctuary from the parking lot. It takes you around the bank of West Pond and beyond. Immediately, a variety of birds are flushed up from the weedy patches on your right and out from the shrubs to your left. If it's spring, you will be greeted by American Goldfinch, Indigo Buntings, and Swamp Sparrows. Indigo Buntings are more visible in groups during the middle of July. American Goldfinch begin to breed in August in order to take advantage of the weed seeds such as thistle. The Swamp Sparrow, however, is content to lay hidden among the weedy cover near the pond. Unmistakable encounters with Tree Swallows near their nesting boxes are also an experience to enjoy at the start of the Sacred Way Trail.

One special feature of the Sacred Way Trail is the Yellow Warbler, found in abundance here each nesting season. The Palm Warbler is another highlight on your walk down this trail through the brushy, weedy fields. The plant life along this first part of the trail is characterized by speckled alder, pussy willow, and patches of canary grass. Continue walking into the wooded section. After crossing the little slab dam and heading into the trees, a new set of possibilities await the observant birder. The habitat changes and the trail closes in, almost making one feel like this is about to become a maze. Not to worry -- the trails are well marked and simplified to just a few routes.

In this section of trail, watch for shy, secretive birds. Some rare species sought by experienced birders include the Brown Thrasher and the imperiled Yellow-breasted Chat. The characteristic black and yellow Common Yellowthroat is an easy one for beginners. This abundant little bird is very shy, but can be seen by catering to its curiosity with the "pish" sound or Audubon Bird Call. They are typically the first species to respond to these methods at this site. Gray Catbirds are the next to reveal themselves, and will generally not let you forget their presence, as they will repeat their cat-like meowing call (from which they get their name).

This stretch of trail is also good for sighting the Warbling Vireo. On a good spring day, the sound of birds singing is overwhelming. The wet element of this site allows for such eloquent singers as the brown and buff-white Veery. Common species such as Northern Cardinal, Wood Thrush and American Robin keep the chorus going well into the summer.

If you want to add either the Alder or Willow Flycatcher to your checklist, then you must visit the sanctuary before the second week of July, as the birds cannot be identified in the field by any way other than by their song (Check the field guides). Look for these birds at the oxbow, where the trail swings to the right and meanders along the Housatonic River. Another exciting attraction on the trail is the possibility of finding the large Olive-sided Flycatcher in the spring during the May migration through the region.

Immediately before the oxbow, there is another wet area where flycatchers and Eastern Phoebe are seen each spring and summer. Sometimes the Northern Waterthrush may be surprised while it feeds along the shoreline of this beaver pond. Beaver are prolific throughout the site, and their damming activities help maintain the integrity of the wetland and the bird life. They can be seen in the evening dusk before the onset of true darkness.

This section of trail begins to reveal signs of a typical floodplain habitat. The common trees found in such a habitat include the sycamore, red maple, box elder, and silver maple. However, many other young successional species grow in the drier sections. Gray birch is common in dense growths with red oaks, white pine, and white birch. In other parts, red-twigged dogwoods grow in attractive clusters.

The oxbow is an excellent place to sneak up on and observe birds or mammals. Great Blue Heron are common, but do not nest. Solitary and Spotted Sandpipers are seen in the late summer. Winter proves good for Mallards and sometimes Black Duck. The breeding season is alive with gorgeous Wood Ducks. River otter have been reported and are very entertaining to watch. There are even sightings of ermine and the seldom-seen gray fox. If you have brought children, they will take delight in the numerous painted turtles and the ominous snapping turtles that occasionally surface.

23   Bartholomew's Cobble

Closest Town: Sheffield

Best Time To Visit: Spring, August, Winter.

Methods Of Birding: Walking Trails.

Birds Of Special Interest: American Bald Eagle (winter), Bank and Rough-winged Swallows (spring to summer), Least Flycatcher (spring), Eastern Phoebe (spring to summer), Warblers (May, June, July, August), Eastern Meadowlark (summer). *Shorebirds* -- Black-bellied Plover has been seen (Late summer); Least, Semipalmated and Solitary Sandpiper (Late summer).

Advice/Rules: Stay on designated trails. Allow plenty of time for each visit -- there is a network of trails and interesting plants. Caution -- rare plants.

Since its acquisition in 1946 by The Trustees of Reservations, Bartholomew's Cobble has been considered a premiere birding area of Western Massachusetts. Bartholomew's Cobble is located in the southwestern corner of the state within the Housatonic River Valley lowlands. Because of its location in the valley, the reservation contrasts with its mountainous surroundings and therefore experiences a milder climate. Together with the river and accompanying flood plain, this climate creates an oasis for birds.

For birders, this 275-acre reservation offers the very best in shorebird sightings within the Berkshires. Its diversity of habitats, consisting of river, flood plain, mud flats, oxbow ponds, streams, beaver ponds, pasture, pine/hemlock, and mixed deciduous forest, combine to attract a remarkable variety of water birds, raptors, neotropical migrants, songbirds and passerines.

Birding is considered very good all year long, and with the milder climate, winter birding does not lag. In fact, one of the reservation's winter specialties is a large population of Eastern Bluebirds. In spring, the warblers are abundant, as are other migrants moving up the river valley. Other major attractions include a decent hawk migration over Hurlburt's Hill in the fall and a large concentration of Bank Swallows nesting in the steep mud cliffs along the river. In addition, the fields attract a good representation of meadow species.

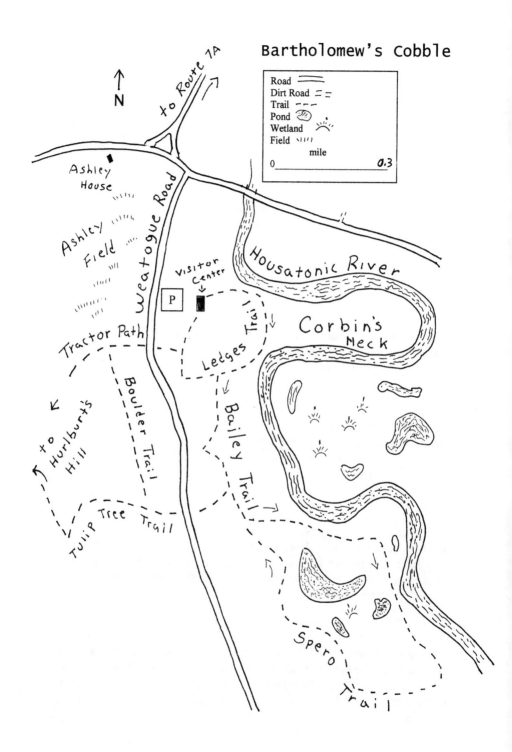

Bartholomew's Cobble

Road	
Dirt Road	
Trail	
Pond	
Wetland	
Field	

0 _____ mile _____ 0.3

↑
N

to Route 7A

Ashley House

Ashley Field

Weatogue Road

Visitor Center

P

Tractor Path

to Hurlburt's Hill

Boulder Trail

Tulip Tree Trail

Ledges Trail

Bailey Trail

Housatonic River

Corbin's Neck

Spero Trail

A total of 240 species has been documented here since the reservation's conception. Birders claim an abundance of nesting birds; nearly 100 can be found breeding here each season. There is a long list of rare species which have unexpectedly turned up here, including Red-throated Loon, Black-crowned Night-Heron, Rough-legged Hawk, Iceland Gull, Sanderling, one Western Kingbird, and a Lapland Longspur. The reservation is considered an exciting place to bird because of the high probability during migration of such unexpected or unusual sightings.

Getting There

From Sheffield center, follow Route 7 south 1.1 miles. Turn right on Route 7A and follow directional signs to Weatogue Road. The entrance and parking area are on the left.

Birding Bartholomew's Cobble

The Cobble is a natural rock garden with some 700 types of plants and 100 different kinds of trees and shrubs. The Cobble is also famous for its collection of ferns and small plants. People come from all over the East to see the vast number of ferns that grow along the Housatonic, in and around what is a series of rock outcroppings known as a cobble. Bartholomew's Cobble is adorned with 450 wildflowers and 53 fern types.

An alkaline soil, which is rare in southern New England, allows for this unique abundance and diversity of ferns and flowers. Further from the actual cobble, hemlocks shed their needles and blanket the alkaline or base soil with a layer of acidic soil. This and many other unusual circumstances allow a diversity in trees and shrubs that includes a total of 700 different plant species. Birding reflects the diversity. With so many different trees, a continuous crop of nuts, seeds, and fruits helps to attract the variety of species that birders dream of.

The land was formerly owned by George Bartholomew, whose grazing cattle probably removed many plants. Thus, an even greater number of plant species may have once thrived here, before he handed over the land to the Trustees of Reservations. Prior to its ownership by the Bartholomew family, the land was farmed by Colonel John Ashley.

There is a virtual maze of trails through the immediate cobble, but unless you have plenty of unclaimed time, consider the suggested route. While the plant life is a significant attraction, birds will be your foremost pleasure, and you will want to make the most of your visit. To bird the "Cobble," begin at the Visitor Center. Start by walking through the center, slowly building up your awareness of the area's diverse wildlife while enjoying the exhibits. Before departing, ask questions; there will likely be a biologist present or at the least a knowledgeable volunteer ready to help you.

Ledges Trail

The Ledges Trail winds its way through the heart of the cobble. Rock walls are found on your right, and the Housatonic River is on your left. Look for nesting Eastern Phoebes and Rough-winged Swallows. They nest in some of the hollowed-out pockets or little crevices found up and down the rock wall. These little crevices convey the power of water acting as a solvent upon the marble. This trail provides opportunity for up-close inspection of the delicate ferns growing out of the crevices and pocket holes. Interrupted Fern grow here -- look for the brown fertile stems interrupting the green sterile leaflets near the center of the blade. There is also a rare plant, covered with intricate and dainty patterned leaves, which grows out of the crevices; this is called the herb Robert. The herb Robert covers the wall in a decorative bloom of tiny flowers every June. Be careful not to stumble on the many roots protruding out of the soil and crossing the trail. Some roots can even be seen grappling the rock ledges. Most belong to the big hemlocks, supporting their precarious position.

After a few minutes of initial amazement, you will arrive at a place where the trail turns away from the river and into the embankments, at the same point where the rock wall recedes back into the woods. You now climb a small rise in the land and proceed to descend back down into flood plain and out into an area called Corbin's Neck. Slide through a convoluted, gated opening in the barbed wire, and walk out to the bank of the Housatonic River. This area is grassy and often harbors a wayward cow that got past the old barbed wire fence posts. This point offers a chance to encounter wading birds, ducks, and shorebirds. Baltimore Oriole may also be seen doing their acrobatics, hanging from silver maples along the river's edge at either side of Corbin's Neck. In the summer of 2001, Corbin's Neck was home to a Little Blue Heron, and others of its kind are occasionally reported here during spring and summer.

Yellow-crowned Night-Herons are recorded here, and Great Blue Heron are common. In early spring, expect to surprise Snowy Egret and Cattle Egret. Infrequently, a Green Heron may turn up. In the late summer, these birds become more likely in migration. Sometimes ducks such as Green-winged Teal, Blue-winged Teal, and Ruddy Duck are viewed from Corbin's Neck. There are always Mallard and American Black Duck, but Canada Goose are sometimes joined by Snow Goose in spring or fall.

Birders who are especially attracted to shorebirds will find Corbin's Neck and the general flood plain regions along the Housantoinc a treasured resource, as such habitat is uncommon in the hilly or mountainous Berkshire County. This is the best site for shorebird birding -- each spring and fall (including late summer), hundreds of shorebirds migrate down through the river valley and stop at the Reservation. Each year, there are the regulars that show up here as predicted, but sometimes very rare vagrants settle down out on the Neck -- unexpected species that help popularize the site among the experienced birders.

Bank Swallow

Black-bellied Plover, Lesser-golden Plover, Semipalmated Plover, Western Sandpiper, White-rumped Sandpiper, and Dunlin are rare finds in the Berkshires. Other, more common shorebirds that are worth checking for are Solitary Sandpiper, Semipalmated Sandpiper, Pectoral Sandpiper, and Least Sandpiper. The Semipalmated Sandpiper is occasionally seen even in the middle of the summer, when most of these shorebirds are breeding far to the north. The other exception is the Spotted Sandpiper that nests here in healthy numbers. Kildeer are also nesting out on the Neck.

A rare visitor is the Dunlin, formerly known as the Red-backed Sandpiper. This species was never more than occasional in the Berkshires; the maximum seen at one time was 31. Dunlin are among those unexpected birds sought after at the Cobble. Wilson's Phalarope is another. A confirmed sighting of a Phalarope in the county has not been recorded since 1959, but alleged sightings have occurred at the Cobble. Perhaps the Red-necked Phalaropes are confused with this bird. At any rate, such rumors and legends only help give credence to the excitement this site can generate.

Gulls can always be found along major rivers, and the little Housatonic is no exception. Reported with good confidence are Ring-billed Gull and Herring Gull. There have even been sightings of Great Black-backed Gulls, and an Iceland Gull has been seen here each winter since 1998. If all this is not exciting enough, then consider the following. Every spring, the silt-strewn banks along the river become home to dozens of energetic nesting Bank Swallows (*illustration*). Although a locally common bird, its abundance and conspicuous presence makes it a cheerful "specialty" at the Reservation.

Purple Martins have been seen here in the summer. They do not nest, but their presence during the nesting season is cause for optimism. This skilled flyer has suffered population losses in the state because of competition for nesting cavities from the aggressive European Starling .

Upon returning to the Ledges Trail, continue to the left and head down toward the intersection of the Bailey Trail. Immediately, the trail smoothes out and passes many more hemlocks to arrive at a bench with a casual view of the flood plain. Continue on, climb up another small set of steps, and rejoin the actual cobble or rock wall. All the while, you are heading toward the right, and will soon confront a steep 25-foot rock wall which follows the trail for a few hundred feet. In a short time, the trail joins up with the Bailey Trail.

Bailey Trail

Take the Bailey Trail by turning left off of the Ledges Trail. This trail is much longer, but less bumpy and more comfortable to travel. It begins by approaching the Weatogue Road and then crossing a foot bridge. Across the bridge, there is a great section for warblers. Here the trail heads back out toward the river, away from the road and eventually into a more open woodland. Paralleling the river for 1,000 feet, the Bailey Trail now offers another chance to see migrating warblers -- the Tennessee, Nashville, Northern Parula, Yellow-rumped, Black-throated Green, and Pine Warblers. On rare occasions there are Prairie Warblers, Cape May, and Orange-crowned Warblers in migration. Several warblers nest at Bartholomew's Cobble; they include the Blue-winged Warbler, Yellow, Chestnut-sided, Magnolia, Black-throated Blue, Black-throated Green, Blackburnian Warbler, American Redstart, and Black-and-white Warbler. Most of these warblers are very few in numbers, but a few are substantially represented. The Yellow Warbler is probably the most common. They can be found here along the river on the Bailey Trail in May.

Beyond this point, the trail strays from the edge of the flood plain and becomes the Spero Trail. This intersection occurs beneath a cool hillside cloaked in hemlock. Some of these trees are very old and quite impressive in size. Check here for the nesting Black-throated Green Warblers. This may also be a good place to find Red-breasted Nuthatch or Pileated Woodpecker, and in the evening, a Barred Owl may be spotted, perched high overhead.

Hemlock are not the only trees that have done well here. Exactly at the turn for the Spero Trail, where the trail signs are posted, there is an enormous cottonwood tree of unforgettable dimensions. This tree stands 126 feet high. Amazingly, the tree stands secure and healthy above -- even with its center rotted out at the base.

Spero Trail

The Spero Trail is considered to be the best trail for birding. At the junction of the Bailey and Spero Trails, take a left. This trail begins by running through a swampy area with overhanging trees above its shore. Numerous weeds and grasses are found on either side of you, as your walk takes you past some large grapevines and into a beautiful grove of silver maple. Ovenbirds are known to be hiding here. Louisiana Waterthrush are seen here, too. Least Flycatcher and Eastern Phoebe are often reported feeding over the stagnant water of Half River. Half River is one of the many oxbow ponds formed when the river's main course broke free during a high water period and reconnected to flow straight, leaving the bend as an isolated body. This oxbow is on the right.

The Chestnut-sided Warbler is considered a Cobble favorite. This common, attractive little bird is difficult to observe, but here in the protected understory of this flood plain near Half River, the warbler is readily seen from spring through summer. With a little effort, most birders can locate this intricately-colored bird in the deep thickets along the Spero Trail.

Although the Bailey Trail is excellent for seeing warblers, the Spero Trail is even better. Each year, rare warblers are discovered on the Spero Trail. These include Golden-winged, Hooded, Connecticut, Tennessee and Worm-eating Warbler. During the spring, look for these and other warblers from late April until early June. Surprisingly, the Yellow-rumped Warbler is uncommon in spring and fall; it is almost always found in good numbers elsewhere. Instead you might see a Morning Warbler or a Pine Warbler.

The beautiful Wilson's Warbler is another possibility. The thickets and weedy fields found along this trail beside the river is preferred habitat for the Wilson's Warbler, an active bird (but found few in numbers). They appear here from the first week in May through the first week of June. In the fall, they begin to move south (usually September). Of the 25 different warblers that have been recorded, around 12 to 15 nest on the site, and most of these are found on the Spero Trail.

The Common Yellowthroat is here in abundance, but the secrecy of this bird is a difficult obstacle to overcome. The Blue-gray Gnatcatchers also frequent the thickets and are likewise difficult to observe. Another bird that is often mentioned at the Cobble is the Yellow-breasted Chat. This is a rare one, but it is fond of the Housatonic Valley.

A few miles to the south, the Yellow-breasted Chat maintains a last stronghold for southwestern New England -- it nests in northeast Connecticut. An endangered bird, the Yellow-breasted Chat was once a regular in the valley as late as 1950, but it is now an erratic visitor. There are some reports of this bird at the Cobble.

After passing the oxbow, the Spero Trail turns toward the right and follows the river, while keeping a distance from it. Within the woods, between the trail and the river, a number of common summer songbirds may be expected. Scarlet Tanager, Rose-breasted Grosbeak, and Baltimore Oriole fill the upper canopy with magical song. There may even be a few Great Crested Flycatchers, but definitely an Eastern Wood-Pewee. During the late summer and fall, Cedar Waxwing may be found along the river's edge.

Further down the Spero Trail, the landscape changes to favor Eastern Bluebird and an occasional Indigo Bunting. Now the trail has become a rutted road-cut through a grassy field. For about a half-mile, the journey is open -- fields of grass and wild weeds spread out all around you. American Goldfinch can be seen flying across this meadow, and sometimes even an Eastern Meadowlark. While Bobolink are abundant at the Cobble, only a few may turn up in this particular area.

The trail will pass the southern end of the oxbow and cut through a nice weedy area that separates you from the river. Soon, the weedy area dissipates, and you can walk along the bank of the Housatonic. Watch the sandy riverbank across the river for Bank Swallows and Belted Kingfisher. Notice the nesting boxes provided by the Trustees. Check for Tree Swallow and Eastern Bluebird. In the winter, the Cobble is known to have the highest Bluebird population in the Berkshires. One other well-known wintering bird at the Reservation is the Bald Eagle. Sometimes as many as 12 eagles have spent the winter along the river. In the fall, Golden Eagles have also been seen here, and eventually Bald Eagles may nest, as there have been previous attempts by at least one interested pair.

From this point, until the trail heads back into the woods, the birding is outstanding. A great combination of river, shoreline, woods, weedy fields, grassy meadows, thickets, and fruit-bearing shrubs/vines provides an "edge" effect that is outstanding. One local bird expert saw a total of 100 different species in just one hour of birding, and most of those were seen at the far end of the Spero Trail. Everything from American Woodcock to Red-shouldered Hawks are seen in this diverse section of the Reservation.

Listen for Woodcock in early spring about the middle of April. Around the same time, there may be a few Common Snipe in these fields. Their call is a distinct, low-toned, climaxing whinny, and they engage in a courtship flight. These birds are best seen during the early spring, as are American Woodcock.

Above the wet fields and thickets where the American Woodcock reside, birds of prey dominate the sky. During the day, the Red-shouldered Hawk may be seen with Red-tailed or Sharp-shinned Hawks. Occasionally, a Broad-winged Hawk is encountered, usually in the fall. During spring, it may be possible to detect a nesting Sharp-shinned, Cooper's or even a Northern Goshawk. As dusk settles over the Spero Trail, nocturnal predators come to life. Both Eastern Screech Owl and Northern Saw-whet Owls (uncommon) are found here. Great Horned Owls are not abundant here or in the forested acres, but they are known to nest. Listen for them at night in late winter.

Eventually, the trail turns away from the river and enters a pine grove. Proceed through the trees and back out into another meadow. Be careful here, as the trail splits. Bear to the right and up a small rise, under some trees and out into a vast meadow with a view. Do not be lured too far into the meadow without first realizing that the Spero Trail turns a sharp right just before the woods. Bobolink and Eastern Meadowlark may be heard singing at this point, as this meadow is expansive.

Now the trail goes back into the woods, and you leave the open grassy country along the floodplain. Hemlocks shade the entire loop back to the massive poplar you saw earlier. Along the way, the forest floor is almost completely covered in hemlock needles. There is very little understory except some Christmas ferns. Approaching the giant poplar, you arrive along an elevated ridge with a view of Half River down on the right. Stop here at this vantage point, and spy those flycatchers or perhaps surprise a brilliantly-plumed Wood Duck.

You will back-track 200 feet on the Bailey Trail and turn left up to the Tulip Tree Trail. After climbing a hill out of the river basin, you will cross Weatogue Road. Find the rustic steps up into the forest and follow the Tulip Tree Trail one mile to the Tractor Path. These steps are directly across the road. Turn left onto the Tractor Path and ascend the summit of Hurlburt's Hill.

But there is also an alternative route. Depending on the species of birds you may be most interested in finding, a walk back to the Nature Center may be more rewarding, as this part of Weatogue Road transects some excellent "edge" habitat. Turning right on the road will bring you past several juniper trees, shrubby thickets, and some more interesting cobble rock walls. Birders recommend this route rather than the Tractor Path Trail. Doing so brings one through more "edge" habitat and out into the fields across from the nature center, whereas the Tulip Tree Trail is just more mixed deciduous woods.

In spring and summer, expect more migrating warblers along the Weatogue Road, and in the fall, enjoy the possibility of a dozen or so Cedar Waxwings. In the winter, this road provides an accessible route to find American Robins and Eastern Bluebirds.

Remember, the Cobble is known for unexpected wintering species. Acute observation of this area may produce a wintering Wood Thrush or related passerine. Otherwise, during the breeding season, expect House Wren, Gray Catbird, Eastern Kingbird, Eastern Phoebe, and House Finch. Sometimes a Black-billed Cuckoo may reveal itself. Northern Cardinals are abundant, while the Eastern Towhee remains elusive.

Hurlburt's Hill and Hay Fields

To get to Hurlburt's Hill, find the opening in the fence or hedge row and walk across the big field spreading to the left. Carry on for a short distance. Soon the trail ascends and wraps around to the left, entering into the mixed deciduous woods. Eventually the trail arrives at the open area upon Hurlburt's Hill.

From here you can enjoy a panoramic view to both the south and northwest. The bucolic vista includes Mount Everett and Mount Race. In fall, mornings may bring in southward-moving warblers and songbirds. After the air has begun to warm, expect a few hawks to glide over the horizon. Broad-winged and Red-tailed Hawks will be common, but Merlin and Kestrels are also possible, especially in the early fall. Fall hawk watching reaches its peak here at the same time as most other places (mid-September to early October), but many hawks continue to filter through as late as early November.

Do not confuse the enormous wingspan of the Turkey Vulture for an eagle or hawk. Turkey Vultures are seen riding thermals all year long, and recently the presence of Black Vultures has added some excitement to their large silhouette. This is the only place where the locally-rare Black Vulture is presently accounted for. On occasion, a few can be picked out from the circling groups of Turkey Vultures. Black Vultures are regularly seen across the state line at the John Boyd Thatcher State Park in New York, where they have been expanding their range from the south upward along the Hudson into the Hudson Mohawk region.

Upon your return down from the modest peak of Hurlburt's Hill, look for the many Scarlet Tanagers that may be seen flying from nearby woodlands over the trail. A Red-eyed Vireo may also be noticed along woodland edges. In the fields at the bottom of the hill, be sure to enjoy the brilliant blue wings of the Eastern Bluebird.

Many open-country species can be found out in these hay fields. Most birders are able to see the Bobolink, Eastern Meadowlark, American Kestrel, and Tree Swallow. It should be easy to find one of the 50 nesting boxes that attract bluebirds, kestrels, and Tree Swallows. Be sure to give these birds their space, and follow the rules of ethical wildlife watching. Obeying these rules will ensure years of good birding and the continued presence of more such cavity-nesters for future enjoyment at the "Cobble."

24   Tyringham Cobble

Closest Town: Tyringham

Best Time To Visit: Spring, July, September, Late February.

Methods Of Birding: Walking Trails, Car.

Birds Of Special Interest: American Kestrel (spring to summer), American Woodcock (Late March, April), Tree and Barn Swallows (spring to summer), Eastern Bluebird (March - July), Brown Thrasher (May, June), Blue-gray Gnatcatcher (spring to summer), Winter Wren (spring), Eastern Towhee (spring to summer), Bobolink (June, July), Field Sparrow (summer to fall), Tree Sparrow (winter), Vesper Sparrow (summer)

Advice/ Rules: You will see more birds in the meadow on the way up and on the way down from Cobble Hill. Do not disturb plant life.

This 206-acre sanctuary is the feature attraction of the bucolic Tyringham Valley, where Cobble Hill rises some 500 feet above the village. The birding is outstanding and is considered by many in the Berkshires to be second only to Bartholomew's Cobble. The valley has a milder climate and hundreds of contiguous meadows and pasture that attract a wide variety of birds all year long. The site is also significant for its scenic, geologic, and historic features.

Tyringham Cobble offers a 2.7-mile loop hike along the side of Cobble Hill and back down through rolling pasture land. There are dense wooded thickets, open meadows, and mixed northern hardwood forest. The site can also be enjoyed from a leisurely stroll through the meadow or by driving down Jerusalem Road, an old lane in open country.

Tyringham Cobble is another fine example of the many lands protected by the Trustees of Reservations. The land was given to the Trustees in 1963 from Dr. Rustin McIntosh, Francesca Palmer, and Edward Perkins. In 1986, the Trustees allowed the National Park Service a right-of-way over the Cobble for the Appalachian Trail. The Trail can be hiked via Cobble Hill and offers a quiet experience through many wildflowers.

Tyringham Cobble

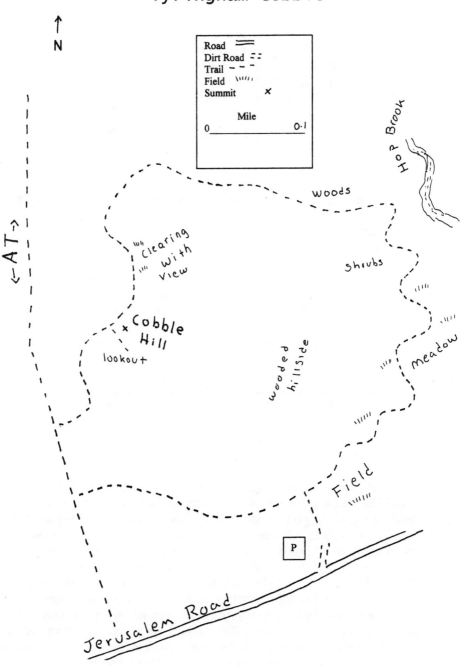

Road	═══
Dirt Road	= =
Trail	- -
Field	\\\\\
Summit	✗

Mile

0 _____ 0.1

N

<- AT ->

Hop Brook

woods

Clearing with view

shrubs

✗ Cobble Hill

lookout

wooded hillside

meadow

Field

P

Jerusalem Road

Getting There

From the Mass Pike, get off at Exit 2, and turn left onto Route 20. Travel a short distance and turn right onto Route 102. Immediately, take a left onto Tyringham Road. After 4.2 miles, this will bring you to Tyringham Village, where you will turn right for Jerusalem Road. Travel 0.2 mile, and turn right into the Trustees of Reservations parking area.

Birding Tyringham Cobble

Cobble Hill Loop Trail

From the parking area, begin the loop hike by crossing the pasture via the path that begins at the wooden gate. Flashes of blue feathers will greet you immediately upon walking across the pasture, as Eastern Bluebirds are everywhere. The sweet smell of meadow grasses adds to this pleasant beginning. Swift-moving Tree Swallows zig-zag in fearless swoops above the grass, while less common Barn Swallows follow suit. The distant moo of a cow or the drone of an old tractor may be the only sounds you hear before the influx of spring songbirds fills the valley in early May. Before such time, Eastern Bluebirds are usually present. Many of these birds choose to winter in the valley. In late March, they begin to sing in soft, fluid-like, bubbly notes.

After a few hundred feet, the trail will fork -- Bear right and across more open country. Scope the distant trees and fence posts for American Kestrels in the spring. Check the tops of the many nesting boxes for Eastern Bluebirds in April, and watch for signs of nest-building and pairing of mates. Look carefully for open country and brushy cover-loving species down near Hop Brook, which runs near the road, but is tucked away out of sight.

Eventually, you will pass a large maple tree with a nest box tacked to its mighty trunk. The trail will begin to work its way up the shrubby side of the cobble before it enters the pine woods. Now the trail is shaded and begins to rise further up the cobble. After about 0.5 mile, the woods become more typical of a mixed northern hardwood forest. Note the deep green Christmas ferns along the edge of the trail, named appropriately because they retain their color even through the winter. The trail passes through a few hemlocks and then into a unique zone that has both a canopy and lower underbrush. These shaded thickets are full of birds, so go slowly and watch carefully for shy birds such as Brown Thrasher (rare). Pileated Woodpeckers are present year-long and can often be heard drumming. Black-capped Chickadees and White-breasted Nuthatches are common, as are both Downy and Hairy Woodpeckers.

At 1.0 mile, the hemlocks regain dominance, and the trail becomes very rocky but still manageable. Listen for the tiny Winter Wren. You will know you are close to the halfway point after passing a large, "animated,"and conspicuously knarled tree branch, which reaches out across the trail. Shortly after this, the woods yield to a magnificent pasture with views of the meadow below. Look for Red-eyed Vireo and Baltimore Oriole at the top of the trees. Occasionally, a wayward swallow may float up and streak across the grassy hilltop in search of winged insects. Across the valley, you can see the sun glisten off the feathered backs of crows flying past. This is a great place to stop and lay back on the grass, while keeping a watchful eye for a passing raptor or a secretive woodland bird stealing across the valley toward another wooded hill.

Eastern Towhee

The trail runs across the spine of the open hilltop and then dips down to re-enter the woods. Follow the trail up a steep, rocky, hemlock-covered hill. This is the last upward climb. Barred Owls can be heard hooting from the hemlocks late in the day. Look for and take the side trail on the left that leads to the top of Cobble Hill. After stepping over more rocks, you will soon see the view of the Tyringham Village center with its classic white church and colonial structures. Wooded ridges rise beyond the gentle, rolling meadows that spread out in all directions from the village center.

Cobble Hill is good for viewing migrating hawks. It is not a famous hawk watching site, but it will produce a few good birding adventures during ideal weather conditions in mid-September. Bring binoculars to see Sharp-shinned, Coopers, Broad-winged, and many others. Turkey Vultures will also be seen, as they are common here. Take time to enjoy the view. To the North is Lenox Mountain (not to be mistaken for Greylock). In the south, the rolling crests of the Southern Berkshire Plateau are visible most days.

Continue following the white-blazed loop trail down from the premonitory and out from the forest onto a steep slope dotted with islands of juniper. To the left is perhaps the greatest view of the entire hike -- the three-mile long Tyringham Valley stretches far to the distant horizon. Here you can see how fertile and sheltered this little mountain valley really is.

From this point, the hike is all downhill. Look within the brushy thickets for the Eastern Towhee (*illustration* previous page). You may hear their "drink your tea" call from deep within the cover. The trail follows the edge of a large pasture along Jerusalem Road, passing by a thirty-foot outcropping of rock (recrystalized limestone). This giant outcrop is characteristic of any true cobble (hard quartzite rock hill) and may remind you of the escarpments at Bartholomew's Cobble. Just past this geologic wonder, there is good "edge." Move slowly and search for Blue-gray Gnatcatcher, Eastern Towhee, and perhaps a Yellow Warbler. Before you is the pasture where you saw the Tree Swallows and Eastern Bluebirds. The parking area can now be seen, and the loop is complete.

Jerusalem Road and Tyringham Valley through the Seasons

Winter

Things do not slow down in the winter at Tyringham Cobble. In fact, it is considered by many to be the best winter birding site in the Berkshires. This is due to its low-lying elevation, milder climate, and the numerous fruit-bearing plants, which provide food for birds that are primarily insect-eaters, thus sustaining them through the winter.

This is the place to find American Robins, Eastern Bluebirds, and even some common members of the thrush family such as the Wood and Hermit Thrush. Sometimes, Northern Flickers try to make it through the winter here. Very rarely, there may be a report from this valley of a wintering oriole or wood warbler. Golden-crowned Kinglets are frequently seen in the woods. Among the non-migratory, year-round New England species that increase here during the winter are the Red-bellied Woodpecker and the Northern Cardinal. Northern Mockingbirds are also seen during the winter.

The mockingbird was once an exclusively southern species. When restricted to the southern states, it became the state bird of Florida, Georgia, and Alabama, where its presence was almost symbolic of the southern way of life. Slowly, the bird began to appear further to the north. It is believed the mockingbird first appeared in Massachusetts in the late 1950s. The first record of established mockingbird populations in the Berkshires occurred in 1965. It is unclear as to what the primary factor was in their expansion; but it seems that an increase in the plantings of ornamental fruit-bearing trees and shrubs across an increasingly suburbanized landscape, along with a gradually warming climate, must have played a significant role in this bird's widening range.

"Mockers" are fiercely territorial and will aggressively defend a favorite tree or shrub that is heavily laden with fruit. This behavior ensures the bird's survival during the harsh winter, when competing for fruit becomes intense. This behavior is often observed with scorn by homeowners who have planted fruiting trees to attract a variety of birds. But for an insect-eating species whose primary substitute is fruit, such actions are merely a natural expression of their dependency. In this way, they survive through the cold Massachusetts winters and have successfully established themselves across most of the Northeast.

Other year-round residents of the valley are Red-tailed Hawk, American Kestrel, Wild Turkey, Mourning Dove, Great-horned Owl, Barred Owl, Belted Kingfisher, Downy and Hairy Woodpeckers. The Pileated Woodpecker is also present here during the cold, dark days of January and February, when the woods become quiet and only the sound of Black-capped Chickadees or White-breasted Nuthatches can be noted.

Look for the American Kestrel in the hay fields and pastures. Along the edges of these fields, you will find the White-throated Sparrow and (if you're lucky) the Tree Sparrow. In the thickets and brambles, expect to see some Dark-eyed Juncos and Ruffed Grouse. Although most of the winter birding action takes place out in the open or along the edges, the woods are visited each winter by small flocks of the breathtaking gold and black Evening Grosbeak. These notable birds of the north settle down from higher peaks and ridges to spend some time in warmer valleys. Sometimes, the finely-streaked, thin little Pine Siskin visits from the north. Rarely, these two species may be found during the summer at high elevations.

Evening Grosbeaks are known to nest sometimes along the quieter high peaks. Another member of the finch family is the Purple Finch. Purple Finch are reasonably common, but somewhat difficult to pinpoint. They often appear at feeders and then leave, not to be seen again for weeks. American Goldfinch are abundant and present all year long.

Spring

Spring is an intense time at Tyringham Cobble. Beginning in March with the return of the Red-winged Blackbirds to Hop Brook, and ending in June with the arrival of Brown Thrashers, there is no day without excitement for visiting birders, as thousands of birds work their way up the valley into familiar nesting sites. While there is no actual flyway (as in the lowlands of the Connecticut River Valley), the Tyringham Valley funnels birds through the Berkshire Mountains. The mix of farmland and woodland along the Hop Brook draws in birds like a magnet. Soon after the arrival of the redwings, dozens of Tree Swallows swarm across the fields and daringly flirt with the surface of Shaker Pond. Swooping down over water, these expert high-speed flyers are able to actually skim the surface of water by opening their beaks and dragging them across the surface of still lakes and ponds. Their arrival is a treasured moment after a long, cold winter. They emit a cheerful note or two as they flash across the sky in total disregard for the anxious birders waiting with scopes. They are best observed at the nest box, where they remain still enough to exhibit their iridescent feathers.

April brings more action as the insect world is reactivated. Several migrations take place during this month. Local migrations are now heading out, and other species are returning. Dark-eyed Junco begin to head back up the slopes into the deep forests, aloft for the summer. Chickadees and Tufted Titmice break off from their small flocks and return to favorite breeding areas or seek new ones. An initial push of early wood warblers travels through in late April.

Tyringham Cobble a good place to see the Blue-winged Warbler and the intricately-colored Magnolia Warbler. Black-and-white Warblers appear in April, but are moving through into more of a conifer-type setting. Two birds to look for this month in the pastures adjacent to wet soils are the American Woodcock and Common Snipe. High above, a Sharp-shinned Hawk may be seen circling around in search of a snack.

May is the best time to bird, as most of the breeding species have arrived by the end of the month, and the foliage is not yet thick enough to conceal them. At this time of year, the woods are filled with the notes of hundreds of birds singing. To enjoy the chorus, birders must arrive early with the first rays of sunlight. About mid-month, dozens of flashy Yellow-rumped Warblers pass through. They can be seen flitting from branch to branch along the edges of the woods or near water or roads. Palm Warblers, which are less common, are equally as attractive and may be seen mixed in among the Yellow-rumped.

Summer

In the thickets, the summertime birds include Wood Thrush and Veery. Soon, these birds will move into their respective breeding sites. Red-eyed Vireo and Warbling Vireo have returned by now. The Red-eyed Vireo is an abundant nester, and is found higher than twenty feet where it gleans leaves for insects. Within that same zone, expect Scarlet Tanagers and Baltimore Orioles. With all birds present and accounted for, the woods now ring with song. Wood Thrush are a favorite at dusk, with their flute-like notes beckoning the birder to venture deeper and linger a bit longer into the advancing dusk.

Even in late June, the Wood Thrush and Veery are still singing loudly. By now, late arrivals such as Rose-breasted Grosbeak, Grey Catbirds, Black-billed Cuckoo, and Willow Flycatcher have arrived. Breeding warblers include Black-throated Blue, Blue-winged, Yellow, Chestnut-sided, and Black-and-white Warblers. It should be noted that the Prairie Warbler has been found breeding here now for several years. Some interesting species lurk in the thickets -- Indigo Buntings, Common Yellowthroat, Blue-gray Gnatcatcher, House Wren.

In late June and early July, these meadowlands are carpeted in wildflowers. Sweet fragrances drift in the breeze, bringing the delightful aromas of wild thyme and succulent pasture grasses. In these fields, you will find the Bobolink and Eastern Meadowlark. The Bobolink is a long-distance migrant. Each spring it appears about May 7th after traveling thousands of miles from South America. Drastically reduced in numbers because of habitat loss, the Bobolink can now be found in only a few choice places where there are open hay meadows.

At one time, New England was 75% open land, and the Bobolink prevailed. Decades later, agricultural lands were abandoned, the forests grew back, and today New England is 75% wooded. The result has been the return of creatures such as bears and white-tailed deer. Woodland birds, such as Black-capped Chickadees and Blue Jays, are now more abundant. The breeding success of Bobolinks today has also been limited by the mowing of hay fields prior to the completion of nesting. Naturalists have learned that their numbers can be elevated by convincing farmers to postpone mowing by just a few days.

Fall

Late in the summer, the majestic monarch butterfly is seen in the fields that are now colored orange with the bloom of goldenrod. Things quiet down at this time of year before the frost. When the goldenrod and other weedy flowers go to seed after the first frost, fall migrants begin to appear. The weedy fields and woodland edges are great places to find sparrows. Careful observation and good identification skills will reveal Field and Tree Sparrows. Also during migration keep an eye out for the nomadic Vesper Sparrow. Occasionally, a Savannah Sparrow will be seen. Chipping and White-throated Sparrows are common.

25   Blueberry Hill

Closest Town: West Granville

Best Time To Visit: September, October, early November, April, May.

Methods Of Birding: Walking Trails.

Birds Of Special Interest: *Hawks* - American Kestrel (fall);
Warblers (May, August), Indigo Bunting (spring to summer).

Advice/Rules: A four-wheel drive vehicle will get you to the top and keep you
warm for hawk watching. Be sure to walk the interpretive trail with children.
No camp fires allowed. No motorized vehicles allowed on the walking trail.

A modest hilltop rises over a rural landscape in West Granville. Hawks work
their way over the summit, catching the uplifting thermals from the undulating
countryside. This is the setting of a very special forest managed by the New
England Forestry Foundation (NEFF). The Holden Rice Memorial Forest was
given to NEFF by Mr. Douglas Rice in 1973. He had bought the forest just
years earlier from a family by the name of Holden. Mr. Rice was a railroad
worker who traveled the Connecticut Valley from Springfield, Massachusetts,
to White River Junction, Vermont.

Later, more land was added to the old Holden Forest. Mr. Russell Phelon gave
1,000 acres abutting the Holden Rice Memorial Forest. Phelon was an inventor
who generated many patents. In 1944, he formed an engine ignition parts
company centered in West Springfield, Massachusetts. Together, the two pieces
of land created a haven for wildlife known by birders as Blueberry Hill. As is
standard practice with NEFF, the acreage has remained productive, fulfilling
Phelon's wishes for the land to be continually worked. Today his blueberry crop
is still maintained, and the forest receives managed cutting.

Getting There

From the center of West Granville, travel west 4.2 miles on Route 57. After
passing a campground, look for North Lane on the right. Travel 1.5 miles on
North Lane to the entrance on your right.

Blueberry Hill

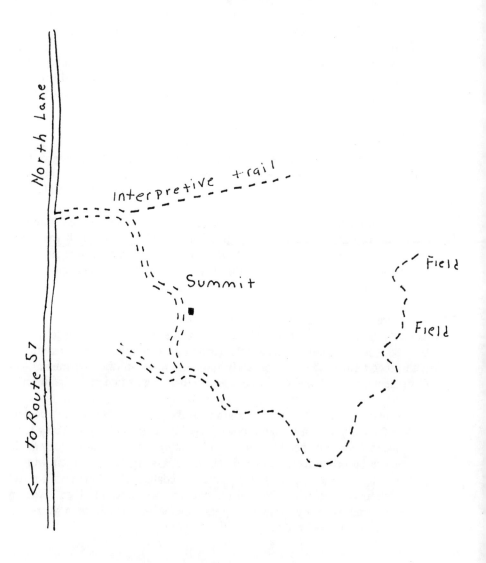

N

Road
Dirt Road
Trail
Structure
Field

Mile

0   0.5

North Lane

to Route 57

Interpretive trail

Summit

Field

Field

209

Birding Blueberry Hill

Fall and spring are the best times to visit this site. Although best known for hawk watching, the summit and surrounding forests are also good for observing migrating woodland species. In addition to acres of blueberry bushes, the site has a great deal of densely concentrated young trees growing in a succession from pasture. White birch is predominating along what is an excellent "edge" circumventing the open, blueberry-covered summit. This open view provides a distant glimpse of Mount Monadnock and the Greylock peak.

From the entrance off North Lane, there is an old dirt road in poor condition. It is possible to drive this to the summit of Blueberry Hill with a four-wheel drive vehicle that has good ground clearance. It is easy enough to walk, as the summit is only 0.3 of a mile from the parking area off of North Lane. However, hawk watching, by its very nature, can consume a whole morning, and a heated vehicle is often appreciated on cold fall days. At the summit, you will find an outhouse, as well as a precariously balanced giant boulder which provides one of many rocky seats for viewing.

Your arrival to this very convenient hawk-watching site will be filled with surprise as you begin to appreciate the vast 360-degree view. It will seem as if you have climbed several hundred feet; but, in fact, you have only ascended about one hundred. Most of the elevation was attained en-route to North Lane.

There are no major villages or developments that can be appreciated from this view, only countless miles of rolling green mountains and valleys. If you're the least bit astute, you will have arrived early, and although the forest is quiet, you will know that the summer birds that filled this land with their song just a month ago are still present in the fall, feeding quietly.

There are more kestrels seen here than at any other popular hawk watching summits. In 1999, more than 600 were seen. Kestrels are a challenge to find because they are smaller; but for this reason they cannot be so easily confused with other hawks. They are an early migrant, which further separates them from the majority of hawks, who concentrate their flights into mid-September.

The American Kestrel was once known as the Sparrow Hawk, admired by birders for its agility in bringing down larger birds in mid-flight. Many texts continue to refer to its perching method of hunting insects. Kestrels are widely believed to be primarily insectivores, but countless sightings of their winged pursuits suggest the might of this fearless predator. The American Kestrel migration may linger into November. Numerous reports of these birds in December and February strongly suggest that it be considered a year-long resident, with a minority of the population staying behind.

Blueberry Hill is also a good place to scope out migrating Bald Eagles and Ospreys. One reason is its proximity to the clean waters of Cobble Mountain Reservoir. Another factor could be the nearby Connecticut River Valley.

Rarely, there are reports of Golden Eagles here. The Golden Eagle nests just a few hundred miles north in Quebec. Primarily a western eagle, the Golden Eagle maintains a small eastern population in Quebec and in some of the Maritime Canadian Provinces. The Golden Eagle was once considered a rare but permanent resident of Massachusetts. By the second decade of the 20th century, they had become extirpated, seen only occasionally during the migration. October and November are the best months to witness their majestic flight.

September brings with it a better representation of the hawk family, and conditions are very exciting from about the 10th to the 20th. Broad-winged Hawks (*illustration* next page) are the main attraction, as is so often the case throughout New England, where birders have a near-obsession for this species. Broad-winged Hawks are large, strong, flyers that are seen almost entirely in the fall, and less often in the spring migration.

Because other hawks use the same weather patterns and thermals as the Broad-winged Hawks, they often get mistaken for similar species. They are ghosts during the breeding season, but in the fall they are suddenly revealed, often in the thousands, which may explain the excitement they generate. At Blueberry Hill, an impressive 11,000 birds were counted during the 1987 season. In 2000, there were 4,800 birds for the migration total.

While Blueberry Hill may not boast the numbers of hawks that other sites have, it is convenient, allowing for a more sustained presence of observers. For this reason, there are better counts from here than from Mount Tom. For many years, the local counting of hawks took place on Mount Tekoa in Westfield, Massachusetts. Tekoa is steeper and requires more time and effort to ascend. Hawk-watching sites are under an almost perpetual vigil, and Blueberry Hill is no exception. Few birds are missed!

Among the birds seen here by observers are Northern Harrier, Sharp-shinned, Cooper's, Northern Goshawk, Red-shouldered, and Red-tailed Hawks. A Merlin may sometimes be sighted, or even a Peregrine Falcon, but do not expect them. The Swainson's Hawk has never been confirmed. The Sharp-shinned Hawk and the Red-tailed Hawk are very common in migration. The Turkey vulture is also prevalent.

Because hawks are generally grounded by mid-afternoon, birders visiting the hill are often lured off of the peak and into the old Holden Forest, where they inevitably spend the remainder of the day in search of wood warblers and migrating or lingering songbirds.

Broad-winged Hawk

In order to do this, follow the trail (it has no name) from the boulder across the blueberry field, past the old house and barn, and down the other side of the cleared summit. Do not turn right -- even though the trail is more established in that direction -- but rather turn left and travel along the "edge" before entering the forest. Spend plenty of time in the "edge" among the new succession. If it is fall, expect to find Yellow-rumped and many other Warblers. Also, check for migrating Swainson's, Wood, and Hermit Thrush. American Robins will frequent the "edge" until the hard frost settles in for the season. Numerous reports of Eastern Bluebird are generated from the summit during migration. In winter, this is a fairly good site for Snow Buntings and other open-space-loving birds such as Horned Lark. A remote chance exists for Short-eared Owls and Snowy Owls.

Spring migration may include uncommon sparrows, and will definitely include a few species of warbler. Mid-May is best for the warblers. Later, the Eastern Towhee (Rufous-sided Towhee) returns and builds its nest in the thickets. These black and white birds are flanked with orange and a rufous (reddish) streak down the sides. They are more often heard than seen, but are not difficult to observe if you are the slightest bit persistent. Listen for their "drink your tea" call, and in the summer, a shorter call sounding like "drrrink or dreat."

If you continue down this trail, you will soon leave the field "edge" and enter some older growth, but then re-enter the edge again. The trees are a little bit older, but form a dense wall of birch . Soon, however, a small opening appears on the left, where blueberries grow. This is where you can usually find several Eastern Towhees. Yellow Warblers prefer this clearing and nest nearby.

Indigo Buntings are also present, and like the Eastern Towhee, more often heard than seen. Their song, unlike the towhee's, is easy to miss; and they keep to the treetops along the "edge," which makes them easy to overlook. They are reasonably common along fields, but are assumed to be rare by less experienced birders who fail to pick out their song or notice their small silhouette. The sight of this brilliantly colored bird is a moment not soon forgotten. Their indigo feathers capture the light and shine iridescence for all to see. Within the woods ahead, check for Great-Horned Owls and an occasional Eastern Screech Owl. In winter, Black-capped Chickadees and Tufted Titmice are common. Other winter residents include Hairy Woodpeckers and Dark-eyed Juncos.

After checking for birds in the small clearing, continue along the trail. There will be dense growths of shrubs and saplings on either side of you -- strong evidence of the farm that was once here. Eventually, this new growth begins to mature, and the trees get taller. The trail is narrow and looks like it was once used for ATVs. Presently, the walk is very peaceful, and only the songs of the Wood Thrush can be heard.

After walking for about a half hour, the trail becomes slightly wet, and it is often flooded with puddles in springtime. Do not let this discourage you because it twists through a grove of laurel and then emerges at the threshold of a forgotten pasture. It is definitely worth the effort. There are a few grassland species here in the spring and fall. Look for Bobolink, Field Sparrows, Savannah Sparrows, and American Kestrels. Eastern coyotes are numerous and add excitement to the walk when seen. The trail soon enters private property, and you will have to back-track from this point.

Interpretive Trail

The interpretive trail has a mix of tree species and therefore offers good birding. It starts at the parking space off of North Lane. A nice population of eastern hemlock provides cover for Barred and Great Horned Owls. In the spring, there are usually a few Black-throated Green Warblers found on the higher branches. They are suspected nesters and can be heard singing each spring.

Although the Phelon Memorial Forest is noted for its great hawk-watching, the 1,040-acre parcel has much to offer birders in search of woodland species. Frequent logging and adjacent open fields will leave this site an interesting place to bird amongst a heavily wooded landscape for generations to come.

26   More Great Birding Sites in the Berkshires

Monroe State Forest

Habitat

Forest: Northern hardwood, an old growth forest.
River: Clean Stream

Seasons/Birds

Fall : Neotropical migrants
Winter : Owls
Spring : Neotropical migrants
Summer: Thrush, warblers, woodland hawks.

Description

This is a large State Forest located in a quiet corner of Massachusetts. You will find the Bear Swamp Visitor Center and the Dunbar Brook Trail. Massive old-growth trees are found along the Dunbar Brook Trail. One tree (black birch) is 300 years old.

Getting There

Travel west on Route 2 through Charlemont, then take a right turn onto Zoar Road, and follow Zoar Road along the Deerfield River. When a fork with Rowe Road appears, bear left to stay on Zoar until it changes its name to River Road. Travel River Road 7.0 miles to Bear Swamp Visitor Center. The Dunbar Brook Trail is one mile beyond on the left.

Birding Specifics:

The Monroe State Forest is the best place to see Swainson's Thrush. Hermit Thrush and Veery are also numerous. There are Great Crested Flycatchers and some Alder Flycatchers. You will have a good chance of hearing the Winter Wren.

Northern Raven

Wild Acres

Habitat

Wetland: flooded marsh with dead standing trees.
Residential Street: side street off major route.

Seasons/Birds

Fall : Neotropical migrants
Winter : Quiet
Spring : Neotropical migrants (flycatchers), waterfowl, herons.
Summer: Songbirds, herons, flycatchers.

Description:

This is a convenient place (a short walk from your car) to find nesting Great
Blue Herons in a small, 8-to-13 nest rookery.

Getting There

On Route 7/20 heading north away from Lenox and toward downtown
Pittsfield, travel past the sign for Pleasant Valley Sanctuary and look for South
Mountain Road at the second blinking light from the golf course (after passing
restaurants and shops). From Route 7, turn left onto South Mountain Road,
pass under a powerline, around a corner, and arrive at the stone pillars for the
entrance to Wild Acres.

From the parking area, look for the pines and small building on the left near a
hillside. Find the path to the pond there, and keep to the right of the pond,
walking around the right side, along the shoreline, to a sign that says "trail."
Take this up a small hill to a second pond. You can view the pond and rookery
from a tall steel observation tower.

Birding Specifics:

There may be a variety of birds living among the marsh but the rookery is the
main attraction.

Hiram H. Fox
Wildlife Management Area

Habitat

Wetland: seeps, vernal pools, headwaters of Moss Meadow Brook.
River : Little River (technically a large stream)
Forest: northern hardwood forest with hemlock component.

Seasons/Birds

Fall : Neotropical migrants
Winter : Nuthatches, jays, owls, grouse, finches.
Spring : Neotropical migrants (flycatchers), owls, waterfowl.
Summer: Warblers, songbirds, owls.

Description:

This is a well-managed forest where wildlife abounds. There are a few controlled burn areas and log-cut sites which increase the diversity. The vast majority of the acreage is northern hardwood. Hemlocks hug the banks of ravines and streams. There are some interesting rocky outcrops, which serve as hunting sites for bobcats. Black bears are numerous here all year long.

Getting There

From Route 112 in Worthington and Worthington Four Corners, travel about 4.0 miles out of the center of Worthington to Goss Hill Road on the right. Follow Goss Hill Road for 1.0 mile to the parking area on the right.

Birding Specifics:

The site provides another opportunity to find the Morning Warbler. Look for them along the edges of cleared and logged land. They will be found nesting within the regenerating vegetation. The American Redstart and the Black-throated Green Warbler can also be found nesting here. Listen for the Winter Wren along the open areas and hemlock hillsides. Hermit Thrush and a few Swainson's Thrush are present during the breeding season. In the evening, the Barred Owl breaks the silence with its familiar call of "who cooks for you, who cook for you all."

Field Farm

Habitat

Fields: fields, pastures.
Forest: mixed woodlot.

Seasons/Birds

Fall : sparrows, buntings, nuthatches, hawks, owls, thrush (bluebird)
Winter : owls, buntings, sparrows, pheasant, wintering species (bluebird)
Spring : owls. Pheasant, grouse, sparrows, buntings, thrush (bluebird)
Summer: owls, pheasant, grouse, thrush (bluebird), sparrows.

Description

Field Farm is aptly named for the wide, open pastures and meadow-like fields that fill the vast majority of its 294 acres. Managed by the Trustees of Reservations, the site protects crucial open habitat among the largely forested Berkshires. Wetlands are mixed with some brushy places, and these help to create a diverse meadow habitat for the less common species that favor grasses.

Getting There

From Routes 7/43 in Williamstown, take Route 43 west. Turn right on Sloan Road and follow it for 1.0 mile to an entrance road on the right.

Birding Specifics:

Birds that love the open edge habitat are numerous here, as you might expect. Many of these species are rather rare in western Massachusetts, especially in the Berkshires. This makes the site an important one for seeing new birds. There have been over 111 different species recorded here. Those of most interest to life listers and birders seeking the open field experience are the Horned Lark, Eastern Meadow Lark, Snow Bunting, American Kestrel, and Eastern Bluebird. The Eastern Bluebirds are the most likely to be seen, except perhaps in the winter. They prefer the area around the old abandoned orchard.

The woodlot is home to Wild Turkey and sometimes Ruffed Grouse. Along the edges look for Chestnut-sided and Yellow Warblers in spring and summer. The American Tree Sparrow is noted by a black dot on its off-white breast (winter). American Goldfinch frequent the branches along the edge of the field. This is also a good place to see the Northern Flicker in the summer and rarely in the winter. In the wetlands and along the small pond, look for herons, which are sometimes seen with Blue-winged Teal. Tree Swallows nest in boxes strategically placed for them. American Woodcock exist here and have been seen in courtship flight. The handsome Cedar Waxwing can be found throughout the acreage feeding on the wild fruit provided by the numerous invasive shrubs taking hold in the open field.

Bird Identification Helper

For birders, identification is essential. The term "birder" is not the same as the term "birdwatcher," who is someone who watches birds without concern for identifying them. Since this guide has been written for birders (particularly those who are at all levels of experience), it is necessary to include a chapter on bird identification.

While most of us are able to discern differences among the common species, there are numerous, more uncommon species that provide real challenges to even the most experienced birder. For instance, there are difficulties for identification that arise when birds are observed at a distance or in poor lighting. Presented in this section are suggestions and guidelines that will allow you to make definitive and confident identifications in all kinds of unfavorable settings. However, before you proceed with this section, be sure you know how to identify the common yard and garden birds with confidence. This will help you establish a base that you can apply automatically to other birds within the same groups which are less common.

Helpful Tips for Identification

Size -- Become familiar with the sizes of common, everyday birds so that you can compare their sizes with things like an oak leaf or a pine cone (taking into consideration the range of variance in their sizes). Another way to do this is to note that a robin is larger than a sparrow, and a crow is bigger than both.

Shape -- Different species of birds have different shapes. Chickadees have large heads and thin tails. Owls have little or no neck and are full-bodied with short tails and large feet. Great Blue Herons have the long neck and long legs, which are visible when they fly. Knowing the shape or silhouette of a bird will speed identification and help in conditions of poor lighting or observation during sunrise and sunset.

Bill Shape -- When doubt arises, immediately check the shape and color of the bill. Insect eaters have thin or slightly curved bills, while seed eaters, such as finches, have thick bills. Many have combinations or medium-built bills, including Blue Jays.

Wings -- What is the shape of the wings while the bird is in flight? Are they angled, or wide and straight? A seagull's wings are angled, while a crow is an example of a straight-winged bird.

Tails -- The shape of the tail can help to classify the bird into a smaller sub-group, whereby you can arrive at a conclusion through a process of elimination.

Color Markings -- Where are the major color patterns? Are they on the breast in the form of streaks or on the head around the eye? What are the three major colors?

Eye Stripes -- Eye stripes can help set apart similar species. Be sure to notice where the eye stripe is. Is it through the eye or above it? Are there other stripes on the crown? How many stripes are there, and what color?

Eye Rings -- Eye rings can help to identify similar birds such as the thrushes. Some have them, and some do not.

Patches -- Some birds have large color patches. An example is the Northern Mocking-bird. It has a wing patch as well as patches on the tail. Many warblers have patches, some on the rump.

Wing Bars -- Knowing whether you saw wing bars can help you distinguish vireos, warblers, finches and flycatchers. How many wing bars does the bird have?

Voice -- Listen for the voice during flight or feeding. Does it have a guttural squawk, or a high pitched click?

Behavior -- Nuthatches climb along the trunks of trees, while flycatchers fly off from a perch, catch a fly and then return to the perch. Warblers are somewhat acrobatic in their movements, as are orioles. Some of the typically shy birds can be briefly curious. They may appear from the cover to investigate you, and then retire again. Does the bird hop or walk along the lawn? Take note of such less conspicuous behaviors.

Setting -- Be sure to notice the habitat that you are observing the bird to be in. Where is the bird in relation to its larger environment? Is it perched on a wire or feeding on the ground?

Feeding -- Birds can be considered seed-, fruit- or insect-eaters. Some eat small terrestrial animals or fish. See if you can determine what the bird is eating, as each bird has a specific preference beyond these general classifications. Both the Red-bellied Woodpecker and Northern Flicker are woodpeckers of similar size and appearance, but the Red-bellied likes acorns; the flicker prefers ants.

Flight Pattern -- If you cannot identify a bird while it is perched or on the ground, be sure to wait until it flies away. Birds have specific flight patterns that often give away their identity. For instance, the American Goldfinch have an undulating flight that is completely different from that of other small meadow birds, while the Northern Pintail can be distinguished from other ducks by its zig-zag flight. Sometimes birds are vocal when flushed or in flight, which can further identify them.

Advanced Strategies

Song

When observing birds, be sure to associate the song with the species and then listen for the song while in your house or while outside in the yard. Good birders are always tuned into the sound of nature as they live their daily lives. For some, this awareness may suddenly advance to another plane of consciousness. One of the joys of birding is the degree with which it increases awareness and observation skills. With the help of audiotapes and videos that are now available, anyone can achieve the ability to "bird by ear." (For audio- and video-tapes, see *Resources* listed at the end of this guide.)

Close Scrutinizing

Check every part of the bird's body. Notice the color of the legs and the eyes. Be sensitive to shades or hints of colors, especially in the breast feathers and the throat. Check the breast for stripes or spots. If the bird is above you, look under the tail. The undersides of the wings are also relevant. Gather as much information about the bird and its markings as you can, as quickly as you can.

Deformities

Good birders know that no two species of the same kind look exactly alike. Birds rarely fit the ideal image presented in the field guides. As with all other creatures, there are circumstances that affect their appearance. Unfortunately, sometimes these are deformities of the bill or legs. Do not let these anomalies throw you off.

Molts

Birds must constantly replace their feathers. They do this in stages, one section of the body at a time. The fall is when their appearance is most unrecognizable and when the identification of certain groups of birds, such as warblers, becomes very difficult. Through experience and the use of good field guides, birders will be able to pick out species even during a molt. To help this process, be sure to utilize the other methods listed here, such as observing shape and behavior.

Hybrids

Hybrids are rare, but they do occur. They usually take on the appearance of both parents. Birders are inclined to react to these birds by making them out to be a non-hybrid of a rare species. Some hybrids are seen among the warblers (Blue-winged X Golden -winged) and in the thrush family (bluebirds).

Exotics

These birds are either introduced from other lands/continents or escaped from pet shops or zoos. The Ring-necked pheasant is actually an exotic, as are the problematic House Sparrow and European Starling. There are many others, however, that we hardly ever see or hear about, such as the Muscovy and the Chuckar.

Birds That Are Difficult to Identify

Warblers

Somehow, the idea that wood warblers are the most difficult birds to identify has become widely accepted. It may be due to the *Roger Tory Peterson Guides*, which for years have labeled fall warblers as confusing. However, since warblers are often approachable and have nondescript markings that can be learned, the "confusion" must be due to other challenges.

Contrary to popular belief, warblers do not migrate through our region with a fall molt. Rather, their plumage is fresh. They have finished molting, having begun it after the breeding season, and simply lack those brighter colors seen in the spring. Another false notion is that warblers actually migrate in the fall. Instead, these birds have already passed through in late July and August. They breed, raise young, and then molt before heading south and into a long migration. Juveniles, on the other hand, do lag behind, and they are the cause of the fall warbler anxiety. Those that create the most confusion are probably the Pine Warbler, Blackpoll, Black-and-white, Bay-breasted, Northern and Louisiana Waterthrush, Yellow-rumped, and Magnolia Warbler.

The Pine Warbler can often be confused with the Blackpoll and the Bay-breasted. This does not apply to the mature males in spring plumage but to the immatures in the fall migration. Among the three, it is the Blackpoll and Bay-breasted females and immatures that are the most difficult to tell apart. But female Pines have a more uniform coloration and lack distinct wing bars. Picking out this feature can narrow down the difference between the two difficult species, which through years of close study by ornithologists are now believed to be best separated by their feet and breasts. The Bay-breasted has dark legs and feet, while the Blackpoll has lighter toes. In addition, the breast of the Blackpoll often has faint streaks and the Bay-breasted Warbler does not. Because birders are often looking up through the leaves and branches at birds, it may be worthwhile to note the differences between these birds' tails. Primarily, the Pine has more white on the underside of the tail than the other two. Remember to look at the shape of these birds and you'll see that the Blackpoll is smaller (thinner in appearance) than the other two.

Blackpoll and Black-and-white Warblers are also likely to be mixed up and difficult to identify in the field. In this case, it is the face that birders should focus on. The Black-and-white Warbler has two streaks or stripes, one above the eye and one much below it. The Blackpoll has an empty white area below the eye. To further distinguish these little birds, watch their behavior. The Black-and-white Warbler creeps on tree trunks in a manner similar to the nuthatches.

The waterthrushes are very similar (both prefer streams and shorelines), but the Northern lives along slow-moving water and streams, while the Louisiana thrives along the fast-flowing streams. However, they do overlap in some situations where the streams change course quickly. In such cases, look for a few tell-tale markings. Birders look first at the eyebrow stripe; it is white in the Louisiana and yellowish in the Northern Waterthrush. Be sure to check the bill, because the Louisiana has a bigger bill; and the Louisiana usually has a more clean-cut facial pattern with no yellow and little or no spots on the throat.

Mourning Warbler

Kentucky Warbler

At first glance, the Magnolia and Yellow-rumped Warblers look identical. Out in the field you may only get a fleeting glimpse, and it may be impossible to tell which bird you saw. Fortunately, these birds are often seen close-up as they flit about branches on cool spring mornings. Although constantly moving, they usually keep to one shrub or tree for some time, providing birders with much time for mental note-taking and recognition. You will want to look first at the wings -- the Magnolia has large white patches, and the Yellow-rumped has two thin wing bars. The Yellow-rumped can also be recognized by its large yellow crown. The Yellow-rumped also sends forth a loud check alarm call. If ever in doubt, do not sweat this one, as the Yellow-rumped is far more common.

Ducks

The problem with ducks is not that they are similar in appearance -- identifying them is simply a matter of proximity and overcoming the visual limitation imposed upon birders by these birds. They frequent ponds, rivers, and lakes, where their presence is always a distance from our observation point on solid ground. Therefore, the following provides information beyond the color marking of each species. Birders can look for such things as flock formation, voice, feeding habits, and take-off styles. The general shape of the bird is worth noting also.

Dabblers and Divers -- They rarely frequent each other's habitats. As mentioned in the habitat chapter, dabblers prefer the shallow waters and the large lakes and reservoirs. Thus, in most cases, you need not consider diving species if you are trying to name a duck seen in a small pond. Learn the process of elimination -- it is what makes for good birders afield.

Mallard -- The Mallard is extremely common and the most abundant duck in the state of Massachusetts. It takes off vertically and quickly. The voice of the Mallard is that of a classic duck quack. It is often seen at parks and feeding on lawns or corn fields.

Black Duck -- A common duck, the Black Duck is seen among Mallards and often mistaken for female Mallards. Black Ducks are the first to flee and are considered extremely wary. They share the same voice of the Mallard and have a similar take-off. They will flock and fly in V-formation. Look for a swift flight.

American Wigeon -- These birds are not common, but are not considered rare. They are very shy and will alarm easily. Look for the white wing patch and white belly in flight. Their confusing behavior of frequenting flocks of diving ducks makes them an exception to the aforementioned rule and can cause birders to miss them. The drakes have a whistle, while the hens have a loud moan.

Gadwall -- These are very rare and unlikely to be seen in this region. Look for the white wing patch. They fly in tight formation and in a straight line. The drake whistles.

Northern Shoveler -- This duck may be confused with the teals in flight because they twist and turn like the teals do when alarmed. Notice the long beak and short, low-toned calls.

Blue-winged Teal -- The Blue-winged is a small duck that has a distinct blue forewing patch that may look white from afar. It flies low over water and makes a loud peep call.

Green-winged Teal -- This small duck can tolerate cold weather and may stay well into winter. It flies in a swift but erratic pattern, often in large flocks of its kind. The drakes whistle, and the hens quack.

Northern Pintail -- Look for the white on the neck snaking up on back of this duck's head. Take-off is vertical and swift. It displays eloquent swimming on the water and moves gracefully whether on land, water, or in the air. A zig-zag flight pattern is a habit of this species when frightened. It feeds on corn in the fall. This bird has been heard both whistling and quacking.

Wood Duck -- The Wood Duck is unmistakable when seen perched in a tree or feeding on the forest floor away from water. A cavity nester along private shorelines, it prefers secretive ponds, marshes, and lakes with plenty of cover and standing dead timber. This bird is often spotted by accident, slowly moving at the back of a pond; but it can be identified by its alarm call when escaping through the woodland. This call sounds like a creaking rusty hinge.

Greater Scaup -- It is possible to see this bird during migration on large lakes and reservoirs, but it is not expected. It moves rapidly in flocks and can be identified by its white stripe along the edge of wing and by a swishing sound created by the wings in flight. It is often seen floating far out on the water during the day. The call is a hoarse "scaupp" sound.

Ring-necked Duck -- Birders report confusing this species with the Redhead. The Ring-necked has a blackish tip on its bill. The take-off is horizontal and gradual. Its call sounds like a trill.

Ruddy Duck -- The drake can be identified by its dark cap on the crown and white cheeks. It is an excellent diver and seldom chooses to fly away. These ducks are very silent, but its habit of raising tail feathers while floating is conspicuous for birders to notice.

Common Merganser -- The Common Merganser likes to winter-over when there is no ice. It is found on rivers and usually in small groups. This is a very large duck with a long white body and dark upper parts. The female has a brownish head that is not always seen in the field at a distance. Birders often know this bird by its habit of moving down stream and from the long white body that usually shows up from any distance. Mergansers fly in single file over the water. They are not afraid of swift-moving streams and are often seen sitting on rocks surrounded by strong currents.

Hooded Merganser -- These ducks are found in pairs and are distinguished from the Common Merganser by a white hood. They also take off differently -- avoiding a run along the surface with a vertical ascent. The call is a low grunt.

Sparrows

Experienced birders know that in order to identify sparrows, they must develop and rely on alternative methods. Sparrows are cover-loving species that do not tolerate human presence very well. The White-throated and the Chipping Sparrow are the exception, but even these birds are quick to flee when approached. To tag a sparrow for the life list you should employ several methods at once. When the sparrow flushes, look first at its shape. Is it medium or small? Does it have a square tail or rounded? Next observe its behavior and see if it is scratching the ground or if its moving from one hidden perch to another. Then take into account the habitat. Finally, you should be simultaneously checking for the bird's markings.

Of the eleven sparrows typically found in this region, many can be grouped in order to help narrow down the selection process after a sighting occurs. There are the brown-capped, streaked, crown-striped, and chest-spotted sparrows. The most difficult are the brown-capped; these include the Chipping, Field, Swamp and Tree Sparrows.

The Chipping is most familiar to the birder because of its preference for suburban lawns with wooded edges and evergreens. Knowing this bird will make identifying the others easier. Chipping Sparrows are smallish in build and are usually making "chipping" call notes. The Chipping is most similar to the Swamp Sparrow, which does not share the same habitat. Of the four, the Tree Sparrow is the only one with the dark breast spot. Field Sparrows have a rusty cap like the Chipping Sparrow, but do not have a dark eye stripe and have more prominent wing bars.

Of the three streak-breasted sparrows seen in the Western Massachusetts area, only the Fox Sparrow has a bright, rusty, red fox-like plumage. The Fox Sparrow is also larger than the others and is unmistakable when seen with its dark breast spot in combination with other field marks. Fox Sparrows are scratch feeders on the forest floor in brushy areas.

The Song Sparrow sings its familiar tune from an exposed perch near water, and this is when its dark breast spot is conspicuous. In contrast, the Vesper Sparrow has no breast spot and prefers habitat more closely associated with agriculture or grasslands. Finally, the Swamp Sparrow is a secretive denizen of the brushy edges along ponds and swamps. It is darker and has little streaking.

Both the White-throated and White-crowned have dark brownish-black cap stripes contrasted with white, but only the White-throated has yellow tinges and yellow patches below the beak. The White-throated is said to be more brown, but few birders will ever get the opportunity to compare, since the White-crowned is infrequently seen.

Vireos

The Red-eyed and the Philadelphia are sometimes mistaken for each other simply because of the location of these birds when encountered. Red-eyes are high up in the upper canopy of the forest and seldom provide birders a view close enough to witness the red eye. Likewise, they are often mistaken for the Tennessee Warbler, which also has an eye stripe and olive-colored wings and back.

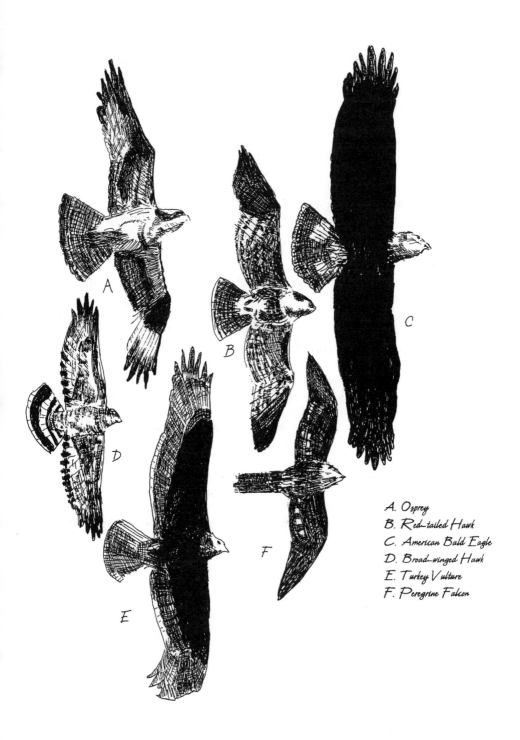

A. Osprey
B. Red-tailed Hawk
C. American Bald Eagle
D. Broad-winged Hawk
E. Turkey Vulture
F. Peregrine Falcon

Hawks

Hawks present a challenge to identification because of the distance from which they are often observed. Although they are sometimes encountered perched on a limb or silently floating above a wooded trail, their wary nature never allows us more than a moment's worth of observation. So, whether it be the factor of time or distance, hawks rarely give us any margin for error. Instead, birders must be prepared before they venture afield. Knowing and committing to memory the significant differences between the buteos, accipiters, falcons, vultures and eagles will make those quick glimpses revealing enough to know what bird you are experiencing. In time, sightings that may have been otherwise frustrating will become rewarding.

Of the group known as the buteos, it is the Broad-winged Hawk that is most often talked about. This is the hawk that so many claim to see during those fall hawk watches from lofty peaks and precarious ridges. They can be distinguished from the other hawks by their short wings and fanned tails. The Broad-winged is a short, stocky bird in comparison to other hawks. In the forest, when seen perched or swooping past, be sure to look for the large banding on the tail.

In contrast to the stocky build of the Broad-winged is the large, lanky Rough-legged Hawk. While birders are not likely to encounter these birds in the same habitat, they can be seen together during migration. The length of the wings is usually all that is needed to separate the two from each other. Broad-wings have much shorter wings than the Rough-legged. The dark, contrasting plumage of the Rough-legged is also notable from the ground at great distances.

Red-tailed Hawks often confuse birders who are expecting the bird to have a bright red tail. The red tail is usually visible, but more likely to appear rufous. Much of the time this hawk is identified by its dull-colored body and large size. Red-taileds have a habit of hunting somewhat like the American Kestrel, and they are known to "hang" in the air for many moments. The Red-shouldered can be distinguished by its behavior, which is much more hyperactive than the other buteos. During hawk watches, the Red-shouldered is picked out from the others by its crescent patch on the end of the wing.

In Western Massachusetts, there are three accipiters that you will encounter often. Two are nearly indistinguishable, the Cooper's and Sharp-shinned -- unless you are aware of the minor differences between them. The Cooper's is larger, about the size of a crow, and it has a lanky look to its wings, which are longer than the Sharp-shinned. The head of the Cooper's is also larger and the tail is rounded at the end. The Sharp-shinned Hawk is pigeon size, has a long narrow tail, and a small body. Some birders may mistake it for an American Kestrel, which is also small and long-tailed. However, the American Kestrel is really a falcon, and its angular wings make for a distinct flight pattern.

The third accipiter often found in the region is the Northern Goshawk. It does not share an identical plumage as the Sharp-shinned and Cooper's Hawk. Rather, the Northern Goshawk has a wide tail covered with contrasting heavy banding. It has a great deal of streaking on the breast and a faster wing beat than the Cooper's.

Merlins and American Kestrels are another source of confusion. They are both small falcons that inhabit open or "edge" habitat. To identify either of these birds is to achieve a recognition similar to that of a mother with twins. Once a birder has the opportunity to observe either falcon, they can know it from the other instantly. What do they recognize as the key differences? Experienced birders know the Merlin is a more robust and aggressive bird. They know the distinct checkered underparts of the Merlin from the finely streaked bellies of the American Kestrel. They know the kestrel has rufous and blue hints in its plumage. Merlins, on the other hand, appear dark and show fewer colors. While the Merlin has an indistinct mustache mark, the Kestrel's is dark and visible. Merlins have a direct flight from one perch to another. The American Kestrel flies as if it may be distracted or unsure of its destination.

Osprey, eagles, and vultures are frequently mistaken for each other. All are large birds with long wings, and from a distance birders are inclined to call them all eagles. Perhaps this is because so many people *want* to see eagles, but most of the time a large bird soaring high above usually turns out to be a Turkey Vulture. Turkey Vultures are fairly common and frequent the same places as humans. They can be identified instantly by their long "fingers" or slotted wing tips. The "tipsy" flight of the vulture is also a great way to distinguish it from an eagle. But the best way is to check the head size -- eagles have large heads and vultures have small ones.

Occasionally an Osprey may be mistaken for an immature eagle. Again, look at the head -- the Bald Eagle has a much larger head than the Osprey. Adult Osprey have a black headband, and Bald Eagles have an all white head and tail. Adult Bald Eagles have solid-colored, dark brownish-black wings, but the Osprey has a patch of darker colored feathers on the underside of the wings.

Sea gulls and Osprey are also sometimes wrongly identified. The Black-backed Gull can be especially similar-looking to an adult Osprey. But sea gulls have curved wings and seem to fly effortlessly, while Osprey have a labored look to their flight. The sea gulls also have neatly tapered wing tips.

Birding Terminology

Abundant - A species that is seen almost everywhere that suitable habitat for it can be found. A bird that is found in high numbers.

Accidental - A species that is seen outside of its normal range, as (for example) after a storm. May also refer to a species that is almost never seen and is unexpected or unusual.

Aerial Flyers - Birds that spend most of the day in flight, usually feeding on the wing.

Audubon Bird Call - A device made of wood which is held in the hand and twisted to produce bird-like sounds in order to lure or reveal birds.

Banding - The technique of capturing and attaching a band to a bird in order to record its movement, habits, distribution, cause of death, or other information.

Berry Eater - A species that feeds on fruit.

Bird Blind -A structure to conceal a human being in order to provide close, sustained observation of a bird.

Boreal - Birds that prefer the conifer lands of the north or similar habitat. Refers to the biome or boreal habitat found at high altitude or latitude.

Check List - A list of birds that are recorded in a particular region.

Common - A species that is easily found in its suitable habitat and season.

Conifers -Trees that produce cones, such as spruce and pine.

Dabbling Ducks - Ducks that feed in shallow water by tipping under the surface, but not habitually submerging (as distinct from diving ducks).

Deciduous - Trees of the broad leaf families that shed leaves.

Diving Ducks - These are species that dive and chase after prey beneath the surface of lakes and rivers.

Emergent Growth - Plants that emerge from the water with roots growing beneath the surface.

Exotic - A species that is non-native.

Far North - Regions over four hundred miles north of the Pioneer Valley.

Feeder Bird - A bird that can be associated with suburban bird feeders.

Flight Year - A winter in which there are repeated flocks or high numbers of winter finches coming down from the north, often during a seed cone shortage in boreal locations.

Flitting - The behavior of warblers and sometimes other species, characterized by short flights between branches and combined with acrobatics.

Frequent - A bird seen frequently, but is not common.

Hardwood - A tree that sheds leaves.

Irregular - A bird that is seen in its suitable habitat at an unpredictable rate.

Irruptive Species - This is a species that arrives in a flock from a distant region during the winter in response to food shortages and is unpredictable.

Kettle - The group of hawks that are together riding a thermal.

Life Bird - A bird never seen before by the observer.

Life List - An ongoing list that birders keep of the birds that they have seen throughout their lives.

Lifer - A species that has just been added to a life list and never seen before.

Local - A bird seen in one area and not others.

Migrant - Any species that travels in response to the breeding season or winter weather.

Neotropical - Referring to the tropics of the New World.

Nester - A bird that nests in a particular location.

Northerner - A species whose breeding range is to our north, but can be seen in specific places or at specific times of the year.

Occasional - A bird that appears infrequently, is seen from time to time, and occurs in low numbers.

Passerine - perching bird

Pish Call -The sound a birder makes that sounds like *Pissssh* and is used to lure birds in for observation.

Rare - A species that exists in low numbers and is not usually found.

Raptor - Birds of prey such as hawks, eagles and owls.

Regular - A bird that can be almost guaranteed to be seen at a site -- very consistent in its habitat

Resident - A bird that lives in a particular place and may also indicate a year-round existence in that location.

Seed Eater - A species that eats primarily seeds and has a suitable bill or beak for its diet.

Southerner - A species that spends most of the year in the South or that originally was confined to the South.

Specialty - A bird that is unique at a particular site. This is usually a rare bird that is difficult to find but may be common locally at a specific site.

Subtropical - The region above or below the tropics, or a region with some tropical characteristics.

Shorebirds - Birds that typically appear on the shorelines, especially on mud flats, and that frequent fields.

Thermal - A column of warm air that is rising.

Uncommon - A species that is not well represented, but might be encountered; has a modest population, but is seen only by searching.

Vagrant - A bird that appears unexpectedly from another region and may linger.

Very Rare - A species that is few in numbers and not easy to find (*not likely to see*)

Waders - A family of birds that feed by standing in the water.

Winter Finch - The group of finches from the North that appear erratically during the winter.

Winter Visitor - Any bird that is inclined to show up during the winter -- usually during severe weather or food shortages.

Resources

Recommended Reading

William Clark, Brian Wheeler.
Peterson Field Guides: Hawks of North America. 1987

Ken Kaufman. *Peterson Field Guides: Advanced Birding.* 1990

David Allen Sibley. *Sibley Guide to Birds.* 2000

American Bird Conservancy. *All the Birds of America.* 1997

Donald and Lillian Stokes. *Stokes Field Guide to Birds: Eastern Region.* 1996

James Rising. *Sparrows of the United States and Canada.* 1996

Peter Westover, ed.
Birding Western Massachusetts: The Central Connecticut River Valley. 1996

Journals of Principal Organizations

The Auk (quarterly)
>   Published by American Ornithologists Union
>   Museum of Natural History, Smithsonian Institution
>   Washington D.C. 20560

Birding
>   Published by the American Birding Association
>   P.O. Box 6599, Colorado Springs, CO 80934

The Living Bird (annual)
>   Published by Laboratory of Ornithology at Cornell University
>   159 Sapsucker Woods Road, Ithaca, New York 14850
>>   A clearinghouse for bird study, birding supplies, texts, audio tapes.

The Wilson Bulletin (quarterly)
>   Published by Wilson Ornithological Society
>   Division of Birds, Museum of Zoology, University of Michigan
>   Ann Arbor, Michigan 48104
>>   Dedicated to the advancement of ornithology and birding.

Local Magazines

Bird Observer
> Published by Bird Observer Inc.
> 462 Trapelo Road
> Belmont, MA 02478
>> Bi-monthly journal to enhance understanding and observation.

Bird News of Western Massachusetts
> Published by Allen Bird Club
> Editor Seth Kellogg
> 377 Loomis Street, Southwick, MA 01007
>> Seasonal booklet of local sightings and activities of Allen Bird Club

Sanctuary Magazine
> Published by Massachusetts Audubon Society
> Lincoln, MA 01773
>> An informative magazine on local wildlife and MAS news.

National Magazines

Bird Watchers Digest
> Pardson Corp, P. O. Box 110 Marietta, OH 45750
>> Sections include travel, how-to, backyard feeding.

Birders World
> Kalmbach Publishing Co
> P.O. Box 1612, Crossroads Circle, Waukesha, WI 53187
>> Gives colorful tips on backyard birding.

Web Sites

www.virtualbirder.com

www.wpi.edu/~rsquimby/birds

www.birdingpal.com/ma.htm

www.massaudubon.com

www.birding.about.com/cs/placesmass

www.massbird.org

www.birdingamerica.com/massachusetts

Phone Numbers for Birding Sites

1	The Meadows	860-537-9597	
2	Robinson State Park	413-786-2877	
3	Mount Tom Reservation	413-534-1186	
4	Ashley Ponds	413-525-6742	
5	Greater Springfield Area	860-537-9597	
6	Arcadia Wildlife Sanctuary	413-584-3009	
7	Northampton's East Meadow	413-562-3976	
8, 9	Wildwood/Orchard Hill, Amherst	860-537-9597	
10-12	Quabbin Reservoir	413-323-7221	
13	Highland Park	413-772-1548	
14	Griswold Conservation Area	413-772-1548	
15	Greater Greenfield area	Barton Cove	413-659-3714
		Greenfield Comm. College	413-772-1548
16	Notchview Reservation	413-684-0148	
17	Moran Wildlife Management Area	413-447-9789	
18	Dorothy F. Rice Wildlife Sanctuary	978-448-8380	
19	Mount Greylock Reservation	Bascom Lodge	413-743-1591
		Headquarters	413-499-4263
		Visitor Center	413-499-4262
20	Berkshire Lakes	413-442-6662	
21	Pleasant Valley Wildlife Sanctuary	413-637-0320	
22	Canoe Meadows Wildlife Sanctuary	413-637-0320	
23	Bartholomew's Cobble	413-229-8600	
24	Tyringham Cobble	413-298-3239	
25	Blueberry Hill	978-448-8380	
26	Greater Berkshire area	508-792-7270	

Useful Phone Numbers and Hot Lines

Voice of Audubon		1-888-224-6444
Western Massachusetts Hotline		413-523-2218
Berkshire Bird Hotline		413-523-2218
Environmental Police		1-800-632-8075
Massachusetts Audubon Society		617-259-9500
Trustees Of Reservations		413-298-3239
State Police	Northampton	413-584-3000
	Russell	413-862-3312

State and Federal Agencies

Massachusetts Department of Environmental Management
Division of Forest Parks
        100 Cambridge Street   19th Floor
        Boston, MA 02202 10800-831-0569

Department of Environmental Management
Pittsfield Office
        740 South Street
        Pittsfield, MA 01201

Division of Fish and Wildlife
Pittsfield Regional Office
        400 Hubbard Avenue
        Pittsfield, MA 01201   413-447-9789

International Association for Fish and Wildlife
        449 North Capitol Street   Suite 544
        Washington, D.C. 2001

Metropolitan District Commission
        20 Somerset St.
        Boston MA 02108   617-727-7090

U.S. Fish and Wildlife Service
Northeast Region
        300 West Gate Center
        Hadley, MA 01035   413-252-8200

Stewart B. McKinney National Wildlife Refuge
U.S. Fish and Wildlife Service
        Box 1030
        Westbrook, CT 06498

Birding Clubs

Allen Bird Club
P.O. Box 1084
Springfield , MA 01101
www.massbird.org/allen

Athol Bird and Nature Club
1978 Chestnut Hill Ave.
Athol, MA 01331
(978) 248-9491   *www.mrec-athol.org*

Hampshire Bird Club
c/o Hitchcock Center
525 South Pleasant Street
Amherst, MA 01002

Hoffman Bird Club
c/o Pleasant Valley Sanctuary
427 West Mountain Road
Lenox, MA 01240

Northampton Birding Club
P.O. Box 76
Northampton, MA 01061

Non-Profit Clubs and Organizations

Appalachian Mountain Club
5 Joy Street
Boston, MA 02108   617 523 0636

Appalachian Trail Conference
P. O. Box 807
Harper's Ferry, West Virginia 25425

Massachusetts Audubon Society
South Great Road
Lincoln, MA 01773   617 259 9500

Massachusetts Audubon Berkshire Counties
472 West Mountain Road
Lenox, MA 01240

Trustees Of Reservations
> 527 Essex St
> Beverly, MA 01915

> Berkshire Office
> P.O. Box 792
> Stockbridge, MA 01260

Defenders Of Wildlife
1244 Nineteenth St.
N.W. Washington, DC 20036   202-659-9510

Belchertown Conservation Commission
> Town Hall
> Belchertown, MA 01007

Amherst Conservation Services
> Town Hall
> Amherst, MA 01002

Friends of Quabbin Incorporated
> Quabbin Visitor's Center
> P.O. Box 1001
> Belchertown, MA 01007

Springfield Naturalist Club
> 27 Donomore Lane
> East Long Meadow, MA 01028

The Kestrel Trust
> P.O. Box 1016
> Amherst, MA 01004

Valley Land Fund Incorporated
> P.O. Box 522
> Hadley, MA 01035

New England Forestry Foundation
> 283 Old Dunstable Road   P.O. Box 1099
> Groton, MA 01450

Quick Locator Reference

The following is a complete list of the birds of Massachusetts; it is also a general checklist of birds found in southern New England. The list follows the nomenclature and taxonomy established by the American Ornithologists' Union (1998) and used by the Massachusetts Division of Fisheries and Wildlife. Next to the species listing are the numbers of the 26 sites included in this guide. The marked boxes show which species have some kind of status at the numbered site locations.

The Locator is intended to assist birders by showing which sites may reveal a certain species. The marked boxes indicate the species that (1) are mentioned in the text of the numbered site, or (2) have a significant presence at that site, or (3) are so abundant (such as American Robin) that their presence is assumed rather than discussed within the site text. Occasionally, certain species may be mentioned in the text description of a site, but do not appear often enough at that site to be included in this locator.

There are two ways to use the Locator. You can select a bird you wish to see and then look for the marked boxes indicating that bird's presence at one or more numbered sites. Then turn to the Table of Contents and find the page for the corresponding, numbered site description(s) to obtain more information about that particular bird's status and the best times for finding it there. Alternatively, you may look down the column of a numbered site and find marked boxes indicating which species may be found there.

	1 The Meadows	2 Robinson st.Pk.	3 Mount Tom	4 Ashley Ponds	5 More Springfield	6 Arcadia	7 East Meadow	8 Wildwood, Orchill	9 More Amherst	10 Quabbin Park	11 Quabbin Gate 40	12 More Quabbin	13 Highland Park	14 Griswold Cons.	15 More Greenfield	16 Notchview Res	17 Eugene D.Moran	18 Dorothy F Rice	19 Mt. Greylock	20 Berkshire Lakes	21 Pleasant Valley	22 Canoe Meadows	23 Bartholomew's	24 Tyringham	25 Blueberry Hill	26 More Berkshires
Loons - Grebes																										
Red-throated Loon				●																●						
Common Loon										●	●									●	●					
Pied-billed Grebe	●			●							●	●										●	●			
Red-necked Grebe									●	●																

	1	2	3	4	5	6	7	8	9	10	11	12	13	14	15	16	17	18	19	20	21	22	23	24	25	26
Shearwaters - Storm-Petrels																										
Northern Fulmar																										
Cory's Shearwater																										
Greater Shearwater																										
Sooty Shearwater																										
Manx Shearwater																										
Wilson's Storm-Petrel																										
Leach's Storm-Petrel																										
Gannets - Cormorants																										
Northern Gannet																										
Great Cormorant																										
Double-crested Cormorant	●																									
Bitterns - Herons - Ibises																										
American Bittern	●								●											●						
Least Bittern	●	●		●	●	●																				
Great Blue Heron	●	●	●	●	●			●		●		●		●		●	●	●		●	●	●				
Great Egret	●				●	●																				
Snowy Egret	●																									
Little Blue Heron																										
Tricolored Heron																										
Cattle Egret																										
Green Heron	●	●			●	●			●											●						
Black-crowned Night-Heron	●	●			●	●															●	●				
Yellow-crowned Night-Heron					●	●																				
Glossy Ibis						●																				
Vultures																										
Black Vulture																										
Turkey Vulture																										
Geese - Swans - Ducks																										
Fulvous Whistling-Duck																										
Snow Goose	●	●	●	●	●	●		●	●	●	●											●	●			
Canada Goose	●	●	●	●	●	●	●		●	●	●			●		●				●	●	●				
Brant																		●	●							
Mute Swan	●	●	●																							
Wood Duck	●	●	●		●		●				●				●				●	●	●					
Gadwall	●																		●							

Species	1	2	3	4	5	6	7	8	9	10	11	12	13	14	15	16	17	18	19	20	21	22	23	24	25	26
Eurasian Wigeon	●	●																								
American Wigeon	●	●	●	●	●	●			●	●	●	●														
American Black Duck	●	●	●	●	●	●	●	●	●	●	●							●	●	●	●	●	●			
Mallard	●	●	●	●	●	●	●	●										●	●	●		●	●			
Blue-winged Teal	●	●				●													●							
Northern Shoveler								●	●					●					●							
Northern Pintail	●	●				●	●		●		●				●				●			●				
Green-winged Teal	●					●		●											●							
Canvasback			●																							
Redhead	●	●	●							●	●								●							
Ring-necked Duck			●									●														
Tufted Duck				●																						
Greater Scaup																										
Lesser Scaup																										
King Eider																										
Common Eider																										
Harlequin Duck									●																	
Surf Scoter			●	●																						
White-winged Scoter			●	●																						
Black Scoter			●	●																						
Oldsquaw																			●	●						
Bufflehead			●	●			●	●	●	●	●	●						●	●							
Common Goldeneye	●	●	●				●		●	●	●	●							●							
Hooded Merganser	●	●					●	●	●	●	●								●							
Common Merganser										●																
Red-breasted Merganser			●																●							
Ruddy Duck																										
Kites - Eagles - Hawks																										
Osprey	●	●	●								●										●			●		
Mississippi Kite																										
Bald Eagle	●	●	●			●					●											●	●	●		
Northern Harrier														●	●					●	●		●	●		
Sharp-shinned Hawk			●						●				●	●		●	●	●				●	●	●	●	
Cooper's Hawk	●	●	●										●			●	●	●	●			●	●	●	●	
Northern Goshawk	●	●	●						●	●					●								●	●	●	
Red-shouldered Hawk	●		●			●				●	●												●			

	1	2	3	4	5	6	7	8	9	10	11	12	13	14	15	16	17	18	19	20	21	22	23	24	25	26
Broad-winged Hawk	●	●							●							●	●	●	●			●	●	●	●	●
Swainson's Hawk			●																						●	
Red-tailed Hawk	●	●	●	●		●			●			●				●	●			●	●	●				
Rough-legged Hawk															●	●										
Golden Eagle					●			●														●				
Falcons																										
American Kestrel		●	●			●	●		●			●		●			●	●				●	●	●	●	
Merlin		●	●				●										●						●	●		
Gyrfalcon																										
Peregrine Falcon	●		●						●															●		
Pheasants, Turkeys & Quail																										
Ring-necked Pheasant	●	●						●	●	●	●		●	●		●	●	●	●	●		●				
Ruffed Grouse	●	●						●	●	●	●		●	●		●	●	●								
Wild Turkey	●	●											●	●		●	●	●								
Northern Bobwhite																										
Rails - Cranes																										
Clapper Rail																										
King Rail																										
Virginia Rail	●							●		●																
Sora	●	●	●																							
Common Moorhen		●																								
American Coot		●		●																						
Plovers - Oystercatchers																										
Black-bellied Plover	●						●															●	●			
American Golden-Plover	●						●															●				
Semipalmated Plover							●															●				
Piping Plover							●															●				
Killdeer																										
American Oystercatcher																										
Sandpipers																										
Greater Yellowlegs	●																					●				
Lesser Yellowlegs		●	●																							
Solitary Sandpiper			●				●															●				
Willet	●					●																				
Spotted Sandpiper																						●		●		
Upland Sandpiper																	●									

Species	1	2	3	4	5	6	7	8	9	10	11	12	13	14	15	16	17	18	19	20	21	22	23	24	25	26
Whimbrel	●																									
Eurasian Curlew																										
Long-billed Curlew																										
Hudsonian Godwit																										
Bar-tailed Godwit																										
Marbled Godwit	●																									
Ruddy Turnstone							●																			
Red Knot																										
Sanderling																					●	●	●			
Semipalmated Sandpiper									●													●	●			
Western Sandpiper									●													●	●			
Least Sandpiper						●	●																			
White-rumped Sandpiper	●					●	●																			
Baird's Sandpiper	●	●																								
Pectoral Sandpiper	●	●					●																			
Sharp-tailed Sandpiper																										
Dunlin																						●				
Curlew Sandpiper																										
Stilt Sandpiper	●						●																			
Buff-breasted Sandpiper	●																									
Ruff																										
Short-billed Dowitcher																										
Long-billed Dowitcher	●	●				●		●								●	●									
Common Snipe	●	●				●																				
American Woodcock								●																		
Wilson's Phalarope																						●	●			
Red-necked Phalarope																										
Red Phalarope																										
Jaegers - Gulls - Terns - Auks																										
Pomarine Jaeger																										
Parasitic Jaeger																										
Laughing Gull																										
Little Gull																										
Black-headed Gull			●																							
Bonaparte's Gull	●	●	●																							
Ring-billed Gull	●						●			●									●							

	1	2	3	4	5	6	7	8	9	10	11	12	13	14	15	16	17	18	19	20	21	22	23	24	25	26
Herring Gull	●	●		●			●			●																
Iceland Gull																			●							
Lesser Black-backed Gull				●			●											●								
Glaucus Gull																										
Great Black-backed Gull				●			●												●							
Black-legged Kittiwake																										
Caspian Tern																										
Royal Tern																										
Sandwich Tern																										
Roseate Tern																										
Common Tern																										
Arctic Tern																										
Forster's Tern																										
Least Tern																										
Bridled Tern																										
Black Tern	●																									
Black Skimmer																										
Dovekie																										
Thick-billed Murre																										
Razorbill																										
Doves - Cuckoos - Owls																										
Rock Dove	●			●	●	●	●	●	●					●			●					●	●			
Mourning Dove	●	●																				●	●			
Black-Billed Cuckoo																										
Yellow-Billed Cuckoo																										
Barn Owl											●															
Eastern Screech Owl	●	●		●		●		●	●		●	●	●	●		●	●	●				●				
Great Horned Owl	●	●				●		●	●		●	●	●			●	●	●						●	●	
Snowy Owl	●		●						●						●			●		●	●			●	●	
Barred Owl	●		●												●	●	●	●	●	●	●	●				
Long-eared Owl	●			●			●										●					●		●		
Short-eared Owl																			●							
Northern Saw-whet Owl											●					●										
Goatsuckers - Swifts																										
Common Nighthawk	●	●				●			●															●		
Whip-poor-will																										

	1	2	3	4	5	6	7	8	9	10	11	12	13	14	15	16	17	18	19	20	21	22	23	24	25	26
Chimney Swift	•								•							•										
Hummingbirds - Kingfishers																										
Ruby-throated Hummingbird		•	•			•	•	•	•									•			•					
Belted Kingfisher	•	•	•		•	•	•		•								•				•					
Woodpeckers																										
Red-bellied Woodpecker	•	•	•			•		•	•									•				•		•		
Yellow-bellied Sapsucker	•	•	•	•	•	•	•	•	•	•	•		•	•				•	•	•	•	•		•	•	
Downy Woodpecker	•	•	•		•		•	•	•	•	•		•	•				•	•	•	•	•	•	•	•	
Hairy Woodpecker	•	•																•	•							
Three-toed Woodpecker										•																
Black-backed Woodpecker	•	•	•			•	•		•	•										•		•				
Northern Flicker	•	•	•			•	•			•				•				•		•		•	•			
Pileated Woodpecker	•	•							•						•											
Flycatchers																										
Olive-sided Flycatcher	•	•						•	•									•	•	•			•			
Eastern Wood-Pewee	•	•						•	•		•						•	•	•	•						
Yellow-bellied Flycatcher								•	•																	
Acadian Flycatcher			•							•						•		•		•	•					
Alder Flycatcher	•							•								•										
Willow Flycatcher			•	•					•		•		•			•		•	•	•						
Least Flycatcher	•	•	•	•					•		•		•	•		•		•		•	•	•				
Eastern Phoebe	•	•				•									•											
Say's Phoebe		•	•			•		•	•	•	•		•			•		•	•	•	•	•				
Great Crested Flycatcher	•	•							•	•										•						
Western Kingbird		•				•							•										•			
Eastern Kingbird																				•			•			
Shrikes																										
Loggerhead Shrike										•						•	•									
Northern Shrike										•							•									
Vireos																										
White-eyed Vireo																			•			•				
Yellow-throated Vireo		•		•	•															•	•					
Blue-headed Vireo																						•				
Warbling Vireo	•	•																	•							
Philadelphia Vireo		•																•								
Red-eyed Vireo	•	•	•		•	•			•	•	•		•	•	•	•	•	•	•	•	•	•	•	•	•	

	1	2	3	4	5	6	7	8	9	10	11	12	13	14	15	16	17	18	19	20	21	22	23	24	25	26
Jays - Crows																										
Blue Jay	●	●	●	●	●	●	●	●	●	●	●	●	●	●	●	●	●	●	●	●	●	●	●	●	●	
American Crow	●	●	●	●	●	●	●	●	●	●	●	●	●	●	●	●	●	●	●	●	●	●	●	●	●	
Fish Crow	●		●		●	●	●																			
Common Raven								●	●	●		●		●	●											
Larks - Swallows																										
Horned Lark	●													●										●		
Purple Martin						●											●									
Tree Swallow	●	●		●		●		●		●					●		●		●		●	●	●			
N. Rough-winged Swallow	●																				●	●				
Bank Swallow	●																									
Cliff Swallow	●																									
Barn Swallow	●																		●			●				
Titmice																										
Black-capped Chicadee	●		●	●	●	●	●		●	●	●		●	●		●	●	●	●	●		●		●		
Boreal Chicadee	●															●	●									
Tufted Titmouse	●		●		●	●		●					●				●	●			●	●				
Nuthatches - Creepers																										
Red-breasted Nuthatch	●		●	●		●			●			●	●				●	●			●					
White-breasted Nuthatch	●		●	●		●		●	●	●	●	●	●		●	●	●	●	●	●	●					
Brown Creeper	●																									
Wrens																										
Carolina Wren	●	●				●									●					●						
House Wren	●	●							●							●					●	●				
Winter Wren	●	●															●									
Sedge Wren				●									●		●		●	●					●			
Marsh Wren										●																
Kinglets - Gnatcatchers																										
Golden-crowned Kinglet	●								●				●			●	●	●						●		
Ruby-crowned Kinglet																	●									
Blue-Gray Gnatcatcher	●					●												●				●		●		
Bluebirds - Thrushes																										
Eastern Bluebird	●	●								●					●	●		●	●	●				●		
Veery	●	●				●										●	●	●	●	●	●					
Gray-cheeked Thrush			●												●	●	●	●		●	●			●	●	
Swainson's Thrush				●																					●	

Species	1	2	3	4	5	6	7	8	9	10	11	12	13	14	15	16	17	18	19	20	21	22	23	24	25	26
Hermit Thrush	●	●	●		●	●	●		●				●	●	●	●	●	●	●	●	●	●	●	●	●	
Wood Thrush	●	●	●		●	●	●		●				●	●	●	●	●	●	●	●	●	●	●	●	●	
American Robin	●	●	●	●	●	●	●	●					●	●	●	●	●	●	●	●	●	●	●	●		
Gray Catbird	●	●	●	●	●	●		●						●				●								
Northern Mockingbird	●	●																								
Brown Thrasher	●					●		●														●				
Starlings - Pipits - Waxwings -																										
European Starling	●	●				●	●		●					●						●						
American Pipit												●								●						
Cedar Waxwing	●	●						●			●			●				●		●			●			
Wood Warblers																										
Blue-winged Warbler			●			●	●	●				●	●	●					●			●				
Golden-winged Warbler						●		●														●					
Tennessee Warbler	●		●																			●				
Orange-crowned Warbler											●															
Nashville Warbler	●													●		●	●									
Northern Parula		●														●								●		
Yellow Warbler	●	●	●	●	●	●	●		●	●	●	●	●	●				●	●	●	●	●				
Chestnut-sided Warbler	●	●	●	●	●	●	●	●	●	●	●		●	●				●	●	●	●	●				
Magnolia Warbler																●	●	●	●	●	●	●				
Cape May Warbler								●	●	●	●					●	●	●	●	●						
Black-throated Blue Warbler	●	●	●	●		●	●	●	●	●	●	●	●	●		●	●	●	●	●				●		
Yellow-rumped Warbler	●	●	●	●				●	●	●	●	●	●	●		●	●	●	●	●				●	●	
Black-throated Green Warbler	●	●	●				●	●	●	●	●	●	●					●	●	●						
Blackburnian Warbler	●		●											●					●	●		●		●		
Pine Warbler	●	●	●	●		●	●					●														
Prairie Warbler	●			●		●																●	●	●		
Palm Warbler	●	●						●													●	●				
Bay-breasted Warbler													●													
Blackpoll Warbler									●	●		●	●			●		●	●	●						
Cerulean Warbler								●		●	●			●												
Black-and-white Warbler	●	●					●	●	●	●	●	●	●					●	●	●	●	●		●		
American Redstart	●	●	●				●	●	●	●	●	●									●	●				
Worm-eating Warbler		●			●																					
Ovenbird						●			●	●				●			●	●			●	●	●			
Northern Waterthrush	●																●			●		●	●			

	1	2	3	4	5	6	7	8	9	10	11	12	13	14	15	16	17	18	19	20	21	22	23	24	25	26
Louisiana Waterthrush	●	●	●																			●				
Kentucky Warbler				●				●													●					
Connecticut Warbler																										
Mourning Warbler	●																	●	●			●				
Common Yellowthroat					●							●						●	●			●	●			
Hooded Warbler		●						●															●			
Wilson's Warbler		●												●				●		●		●				
Canada Warbler		●												●						●						
Yellow-breasted Chat																		●		●		●				
Tanagers																										
Scarlet Tanager	●	●	●	●					●									●			●					
Sparrows																										
Eastern Towhee	●	●			●	●	●		●	●	●	●					●	●				●	●	●		
American Tree Sparrow	●	●		●	●	●	●		●	●	●	●			●	●	●		●			●	●	●		
Chipping Sparrow	●	●		●	●	●	●															●	●			
Field Sparrow	●			●	●	●	●															●				
Vesper Sparrow						●	●	●	●	●					●	●		●		●		●	●	●		
Lark Sparrow	●																									
Savannah Sparrow						●		●				●		●	●	●		●				●				
Grasshopper Sparrow																										
Henslow's Sparrow																										
Nelson's Sharp-tailed Sparrow					●																					
Seaside Sparrow																										
Fox Sparrow	●	●					●						●								●			●		
Song Sparrow	●	●			●	●		●				●				●	●					●				
Lincoln's Sparrow			●					●													●					
Swamp Sparrow	●	●	●	●		●					●						●		●	●		●				
White-throated Sparrow	●	●	●				●		●			●				●	●	●		●		●	●	●		
White-crowned Sparrow	●											●								●	●	●	●	●		
Dark-eyed Junco		●				●				●		●			●	●				●				●	●	
Lapland Longspur															●	●										
Snow Bunting										●					●									●		●

	1	2	3	4	5	6	7	8	9	10	11	12	13	14	15	16	17	18	19	20	21	22	23	24	25	26
Cardinals																										
Northern Cardinal	●	●	●	●	●	●	●	●	●	●	●	●	●	●	●		●	●		●	●	●	●			
Rose-breasted Grosbeak	●	●	●		●				●	●	●	●	●	●	●			●			●	●	●			
Blue Grosbeak	●						●	●												●		●		●		
Indigo Bunting						●	●	●									●									
Dickcissel																●						●				
Blackbirds - Orioles																										
Bobolink	●		●			●			●						●	●						●	●			
Red-winged Blackbird			●	●		●			●		●	●	●	●	●	●	●		●			●	●			
Eastern Meadowlark			●											●	●	●						●	●			
Rusty Blackbird	●																			●						
Common Grackle	●		●	●		●		●					●	●		●	●		●							
Brown-headed Cowbird	●			●									●	●								●				
Orchard Oriole	●		●			●		●		●	●											●	●			
Baltimore Oriole	●		●											●							●		●			
Finches																										
Pine Grosbeak			●													●		●					●			
Purple Finch	●			●						●		●		●				●			●		●			
House Finch	●			●	●			●																		
Red Crossbill															●	●	●	●	●							
White-winged Crossbill																●		●	●							
Common Redpoll	●					●										●		●	●	●						
Hoary Redpoll																										
Pine Siskin	●					●			●	●				●		●	●	●		●	●	●		●		
American Goldfinch																●	●	●	●	●	●	●				
Evening Grosbeak															●								●			
Old World Sparrows																										
House Sparrow	●																					●				

NOTES

Index to Illustrations

Also Available from
New England Cartographics

Maps

Holyoke Range State Park (Eastern Section)	$3.95
Holyoke Range/Skinner State Park (Western)	$3.95
Mt. Greylock Reservation Trail Map	$3.95
Mt. Toby Reservation Trail Map	$3.95
Mt. Tom Reservation Trail Map	$3.95
Mt. Wachusett and Leominster State Forest Trail Map	$3.95
Western Massachusetts Trail Map Pack (all 6 of the above)	$15.95
Quabbin Reservation Guide	$4.95
Quabbin Reservation Guide (waterproof version)	$5.95
Wapack Trail Map	$3.95
Connecticut River Recreation Map (in Massachusetts)	$5.95

Books

Guide to the Metacomet-Monadnock Trail	$10.95
Hiking the Pioneer Valley	$12.95
Skiing the Pioneer Valley	$10.95
Bicycling the Pioneer Valley	$10.95
Hiking the Monadnock Region	$10.95
High Peaks of the Northeast	$12.95
24 Great Rail Trails of New Jersey	$16.95
Golfing in New England	$16.95
Steep Creeks of New England	$14.95
Hiking Green Mountain National Forest (Southern Section)	$14.95
Birding Western Massachusetts	$16.95

Please include postage/handling:

$0.75 for the first single map and $0.25 for each additional map;
$1.50 for the Western Mass. Map Pack;
$2.00 for the first book and $1.00 for each additional book.

Postage/Handling _____

Total Enclosed _____

Order Form is on the next page.

*   Ask about our GEOLOPES -- stationery and envelopes made out of recycled USGS topographic maps. Free samples available upon request.

Order Form

To order, call or write:
New England Cartographics
P.O. Box 9369
North Amherst MA 01059
(413) - 549-4124
FAX orders: (413) - 549-3621
Toll-Free (888) 995-6277

Circle one: **Mastercard   Visa   Amex   Check**

Card Number_____

Expiration Date _____

Signature_____

Telephone (optional) _____

Please send my order to:

Name _____

Address _____

_____

Town/City _____

State _____ **Zip** _____